OUT OF LUCK

'This admirable book provides a clear and cogent narrative of the different forms and meanings of poverty in this country over the past two hundred years. With stringent economy Stephen Garton appraises the measures that have been employed to alleviate poverty and control the poor; with controlled passion he indicates the human consequences of these measures. I know of no better introduction to the subject.' Stuart Macintyre, author of *Winners and Losers*.

OUT OF LUCK

POOR AUSTRALIANS AND SOCIAL WELFARE 1788–1988

STEPHEN GARTON

ALLEN & UNWIN
Sydney   Wellington   London   Boston

© Stephen Garton 1990
This book is copyright under the Berne Convention. No reproduction without permission. All rights reserved.

First published in 1990
Allen & Unwin Australia Pty Ltd
An Unwin Hyman company
8 Napier St, North Sydney, NSW 2059, Australia

Allen & Unwin New Zealand Limited
75 Ghuznee Street, Wellington, New Zealand

Unwin Hyman Limited
15–17 Broadwick Street, London W1V 1FP England

Unwin Hyman Inc
8 Winchester Place, Winchester, Mass 01890 USA

National Library of Australia
Cataloguing-in-Publication entry:

Garton, Stephen.
 Out of luck: poor Australians and social welfare 1788–1988.

 Bibliography.
 Includes index.
 ISBN 0 04 442137 0.

 1. Public welfare—Australia—History. 2. Social service—Australia—History. 3. Poor—Services for—Australia—History. 4. Australia—Social conditions. I. Title. (Series: Australian experience).

362.50994

Set in Times by Graphicraft Typesetters Ltd, Hong Kong
Printed by South Wind Productions, Singapore

To my mother and her mother—their story lies here

Author's Note

This book preserves contemporary units of measurement. There are twelve pence to the shilling and twenty shillings to the pound. One pound is equal to two dollars and one guinea is equal to two dollars twenty.

A mile is equivalent to approximately 1.61 kilometres, and an acre to 0.405 hectares.

Contents

Illustrations viii

Abbreviations ix

Preface x

Introduction 1

1 A poor colony 6

2 Survival of the fittest 23

3 Colonial charity 43

4 Workers' welfare 62

5 Pensions and pills 84

6 One long Depression 108

7 A welfare state? 131

8 A banana republic? 151

Notes 172

Select bibliography 195

Index 201

Illustrations

Gray's Inn Lane   11
The Sydney Rum Hospital   18
The Parramatta Female Factory   26
A member of the nomad tribe of workers   35
Melbourne beggar   38
Discovering the urban poor   40
Feeding the poor   46
The Sydney Benevolent Asylum   49
The Parramatta Women's Asylum   55
A selector family near Katoomba   64
The sweated outworker   71
Ridiculing the struggle of the unemployed for assistance   73
Vicars Woollen Mills   78
The new Ministering Children's League Home   88
The new cottage home   93
The independent aged poor   97
Dulwich Asylum, Queensland   100
The introduction of new nerve cures   102
Chippendale slums   110
Aboriginal woman and child at Billila   117
A food distribution depot at Pyrmont, Sydney   120
Melbourne street children in the 1920s   122
The Labour movement's caustic comment that the nation would live within its income   125
Relief for the unemployed near Sydney   128
The emergence of the social worker   143
Poverty in the 'lucky country'   147
The aged were still a large proportion of the poor   153
Advertisement for the Smith Family in 1976   161
Drug company advertisement   166

Abbreviations

ACOSS	Australian Council of Social Service
ADB	*Australian Dictionary of Biography*
AONSW	Archives Office of New South Wales
BPP	*British Parliamentary Papers*
CPD	*Commonwealth of Australia Parliamentary Debates*
CPP	*Commonwealth of Australia Parliamentary Papers*
HRA	*Historical Records of Australia*
MJA	*Medical Journal of Australia*
NSWLAV&P	*New South Wales Legislative Assembly Votes and Proceedings*
NSWPP	*New South Wales Parliamentary Papers*
QLAV&P	*Queensland Legislative Assembly Votes and Proceedings*
QPP	*Queensland Parliamentary Papers*
SAPP	*South Australia Parliamentary Papers*
SMH	*Sydney Morning Herald*
VPP	*Victoria Parliamentary Papers*
VV&P	*Victoria Votes and Proceedings*
WAPP	*Western Australia Parliamentary Papers*

Preface

The Gospels declare that the poor are always with us. If that is so then many commentators on Australia have ignored their existence. Opinion makers as diverse as the novelist and essayist, Anthony Trollope, statistician and economic historian, Timothy Coghlan, and politician Harold Holt, have argued that poverty was negligible in Australia. Such men are part of a broad cultural stream which has perpetuated the image of Australia as a 'workingman's paradise'. But what of the man who could not find work? What of the woman whose work was remunerated at lower levels than men or not at all if she worked at home? What of those too old or too ill to work and families without breadwinners to support them? These Australians did not live in a worker's paradise and their lives are an integral part of the Australian experience.

The terms 'poverty' and 'the poor' are convenient ones. They help describe a disadvantaged group but they also obscure the fact that there are different poor populations, whose misfortunes have different origins. The plight of the deserted mother, for instance, is different from that of the infirm pensioner or the unemployed labourer. The common link between diverse cases of material poverty is their origin in the failure of social and economic systems to provide adequately for all. To compensate, many societies have developed methods to assist the poor. In the modern market economy, a complex array of organisations and measures have evolved to cope with the problem of poverty, ranging from private benevolence to cash payments from the welfare state. The nature and extent of these forms of assistance are an arena of contest, where competing ideas about the causes of poverty have produced different remedies for the problem. What have been the results of these historical contests? How have they affected the experiences of poor Australians?

Any work which attempts to answer some of these questions is particularly reliant on the labours of others. My indebtedness to other works will be apparent from the endnotes but I owe a special debt to those historians—Dickey, Roe, Macintyre, Mendelsohn,

PREFACE

Kewley, Jones, Castles, O'Brien and Kennedy, to name but a few—who have done much to advance the study of poverty and social policy in Australia. The influence of these works on my understanding of the problems discussed here is more than can be adequately acknowledged in reference notes.

The staff of a number of libraries and archives have helped in my researches; in particular those of the Mitchell Library, the John Oxley and Fryer Libraries, the La Trobe Library, the Archives Office of New South Wales, the Queensland State Archives, Fisher Library and the National Library of Australia. A number of authorities have granted permission to reproduce photographs; they are acknowledged in the text. Karen Yarrow, Joanna Martin, Joan Hitchen and Ruth Bennett typed drafts of this work with skill and patience. Hilary Weatherburn provided tremendous assistance with the hunt for illustrations. The Griffith University Division of Humanities Research Sub-Committee funded a number of visits to distant libraries. The University of Sydney History Department provided funds for research assistance and illustrations.

Heather Radi provided much needed criticism and spilled a great deal of ink on early drafts. Without the good-hearted but regular harassment of John Iremonger this work would have taken a lot longer to complete. The final manuscript benefited considerably from the editorial skills of Fiona Inglis and Michelle Wright. Judith Allen, Brian Dickey, Mark Finnane, Hilary Golder and David Walker made helpful suggestions at various stages. Colleagues at Griffith University allowed me to develop some of this work as course materials and their criticisms, particularly those of Geoff Dow and Ian Hunter, helped refine some of the arguments. Students at the University of Sydney discussed some of my ideas and forced me to clarify particular arguments. The efforts of Lesley and Gloria Garton to assist the struggles of the disadvantaged have been a constant inspiration. Marie Wilkinson spent many hours discussing 'the welfare' with me, prompting many fruitful inquiries. None of these people is responsible for the final product—the shortcomings of the account are mine alone. My father helped with repairs to my inner city hovel, leaving me with precious time to write. Without the constant encouragement and support of Lyn Garton and Pat White I would never have put pen to paper.

Introduction

In 1883 Richard Twopeny, son of an Anglican archdeacon and a prominent journalist, wrote of his tours round the Australian colonies: 'The distribution of wealth is far more equal. To begin with, there is no poor class in the colonies. Comfortable incomes are in the majority, millionaires few and far between'.[1] Twopeny was just one of many colonists and visitors who marvelled at the prosperity of Australia and the distribution of that prosperity to all its citizens. The colonies may have lacked the wealth and splendour of London but they also lacked the slums of a St Giles or Whitechapel. In Australia few were rich but all were comfortable. These views underpinned Australia's reputation as a 'workingman's paradise', an image of considerable longevity in Australian cultural commentary. Modern economic historians have echoed the views of Twopeny concerning colonial Australia. R.V. Jackson has argued: 'Australians were well fed, well clothed and well housed ... Australian cities were spacious, healthy, and free of large areas of extreme poverty'.[2] Similar statements were made about Australia during its second 'long boom', after 1945. In 1969, W.C. Wentworth, Minister for Social Services in the Gorton Coalition government, concluded that Australia was 'probably the country in the whole world where the impact of poverty is least'.[3] In the 1960s and 1970s many commentators were fond of calling Australia 'the lucky country', overlooking the irony in Donald Horne's original formulation, perpetuating the notion of Australia as a prosperous and egalitarian society.

Leopold Muller, who arrived in Sydney with his family in 1880, did not share Twopeny's view of Australia. He had been lured to the colony by 'the glowing accounts, promises and prospects held in the papers ... but upon arrival found myself deceived'. He had travelled throughout the colony in search of work but only found occasional employment. In a plaintive letter he wrote: 'I beg to show that tho a man is heartily willing to work he may nevertheless not be able to obtain it'.[4] Others agreed. In 1898, after the colonies had recovered from the depression of the early 1890s, charity workers found Mrs H, a widow with two young children, living in a 'state of destitution under very painful circumstances'. She occasionally earnt a few shillings washing and received some food each week from the Benevolent Society. But her rent was 4s a week and the youngest child was dying of measles. The family lived on bread and water and only survived because a sympathetic landlady didn't feel able to collect their rent.[5]

In the 1960s Mrs Hall, wife of a builder's labourer and mother of twelve, was just one who did not share the view that Australia was a 'lucky country'. The Halls lived in a Housing Commission home in Melbourne, but even with cheap rent the family faced 'just a bare existence'. For Mrs Hall 'it was a constant struggle ... after groceries there's nothing left'. The strain proved too much and she suffered a nervous collapse.[6] Another who struggled was Mavis, a 25-year-old deserted mother with two children and pregnant with a third. In 1969 her husband left after an argument and she survived in a small rented room for a few weeks, quickly running out of money after failing to find a job. In desperation she applied to the Brotherhood of St Laurence for emergency assistance. For more permanent help she was advised to take out a maintenance order on her husband in order to qualify for the government's family assistance program. But she did not want to pursue this course of action for fear that her husband would never return.[7]

The evidence of these Australians was generally ignored by the purveyors of the 'workingman's paradise' and 'lucky country' images. Only in times of serious economic depression, in the 1890s or 1930s, did images of poverty become part of the national consciousness; but these were quickly forgotten, except by those who lived through them, when prosperity returned. In the 1970s and 1980s Australia's worsening economic climate and declining standards of living again challenged the widespread belief that Australians lived in an egalitarian and prosperous society. Prime Minister Bob Hawke and Treasurer Paul Keating enjoined all Australians to 'tighten their belts'. But for over 12 per cent of the population, belt-tightening was near impossible. This was the group defined as living on or below the 'poverty line'. Bald statistics miss the human dimension of the problem; two million people were in this situation.[8] Even in the more prosperous 1960s, research suggested that 7 per cent, or over half a million people, lived on or below an austerely defined 'poverty line'—and many more struggled to make ends meet.[9] If this was the situation at a high point of prosperity, when a large social security system was in place for the maintenance of the poor, what are we to make of statements concerning the absence of extreme poverty in the colonial period?

Unfortunately, it is difficult to estimate the extent of poverty in Australia's past. Australian historians do not have the benefit of Mayhew's study of London's poor in the 1840s, Charles Booth's investigations into the extent of poverty in London in the 1890s nor Seebohm Rowntree's 1901 survey of poverty in York. It was not until the 1966 Melbourne University Institute of Applied Economic Research survey of poverty in Melbourne that we began to get reliable estimates of the extent of poverty in Australia. But such complaints obscure more fundamental problems in defining and measuring poverty. Poverty is not a clear and obvious object that can be easily grasped. In some developing nations, notably Sudan in the 1980s, widespread starvation is perceived as an unproblematic case of absolute poverty. But in developed western nations poverty is a concept usually defined in a relative way: a situation worse than some other, more acceptable, situation. Differing views of what is an acceptable standard of living will markedly affect perceptions of the character and dimension of poverty in any society. Equally there are different types of poverty. Some people live in chronic or permanent poverty but others may suffer only temporary poverty due to unemployment or ill-health (crisis poverty) or due to declining fortunes in old age (life-cycle poverty). In this way many more people experience poverty at some point in their life than conventional poverty-line measurements indicate.

Despite the difficulties in defining and measuring poverty some Australian historians have attempted to estimate its dimensions. Jill Roe has persuasively argued that 10 per cent of the population lived in permanent poverty, and a similar proportion in temporary poverty (except during serious recessions), throughout the 19th and early 20th centuries.[10] This is less than Charles Booth's finding that 30 per cent of Londoners in the 1880s and 1890s were poor.[11] Australia might have had less poverty, but a figure between 10 and 20 per cent is sufficiently large to undermine confident claims that Australia was immune to its effects. That there were fewer of them would have been of little comfort to those Australians who lived in impoverished circumstances. Although attempts to estimate the extent of poverty may be fraught with problems of definition and measurement, social, labour, urban, welfare and women's historians have uncovered abundant evidence of poverty in Australia.[12] They have charted the existence of urban slums and the plight of struggling farmers, unemployed labourers, the aged, and deserted and widowed mothers. These studies have provided a stock of information and methods to help identify the social groups vulnerable to poverty in Australia's past. Although the actual experience of the poor may be elusive, the conditions in which they have lived and their responses to the world they inhabited are vital elements of Australia's history.

Poverty is generated within specific social and economic structures. In the modern capitalist economies, these structures include the relations between workers and employers, the dynamics of international trade, finance and politics, and the 'sexual economics' of relations between men and women.[13] It is these structures which have been largely responsible for the unequal distribution of goods and power. They have also provided the arena in which people have perceived their world and acted in it. Within the limits set by these larger forces, misfortune and bad luck have also contributed to that calamitous slip from the struggling working class to the dependent poor. Sudden illness, accident, infirmity and the death or desertion of a breadwinner had serious effects on many families. These misfortunes are a key element of the experience of poverty.

What have Australians done to alleviate the plight of the poor? Part of the answer to this question lies in the Christian heritage of the Anglo-Saxon culture that has dominated Australia since the late 18th century. St Paul deemed charity to be one of the three Christian virtues. If poverty was a constant, then benevolent alms-giving was the perpetual Christian duty. But what is laid down in scripture is subject to interpretation. The word 'poverty' has had a troubled history. In the middle ages, the vow of poverty was undertaken by monks believing that it would bring them closer to the path pursued by Christ. Nevertheless, those religious orders, notably the Franciscans, which embraced the vow of poverty found themselves in conflict with a Vatican hierarchy concerned with accumulating ever greater wealth and power.[14] In the 18th century the evangelical revival in the Protestant churches challenged the notion of poverty as an inevitable or sanctified state. Some saw it as a personal corruption capable of being eradicated by moral reform. Evangelicals received support from a secular quarter. Some political economists, utilitarians and liberals believed that the market, and later the state, could contribute to the gradual disappearance of poverty.[15] Poverty was no longer a state to respect but a blight on society to be cured or eradicated.

The European colonisation of Australia occurred at the height of these new ideas about poverty. In Britain they led to a questioning of the traditional right of the poor to receive parish assistance. In Australia they inspired a struggle to prevent the introduction of a Poor Law system into the colonies, Instead the colonial poor had to rely on the uncertain benefits of private benevolence and government charity. The uniqueness of colonial systems of poor relief continued into the 20th century with the emergence of a welfare state. At the turn of the century Australians were not afraid to forge new social policies for the fledgling nation and many believed that Australia had become the 'social laboratory of the world'. The consequence was a system of social security benefits financed from general revenue at a time when the rest of the western world was moving towards insurance schemes for the alleviation of poverty. What were the historical contours of these peculiar systems of assistance? What were the consequences for the poor? How did the poor respond to these forms of assistance? These questions highlight the fact that charity and welfare have been important parts of the historical experience of poverty.

1 A poor colony

Aboriginal culture before European colonisation adapted to both times of plenty and times of hardship, but the effects of material hardship were relatively evenly distributed. In contrast, 18th century English society was marked by extremes of wealth and poverty. Moreover it was a society that had been undergoing a significant historical transformation, responsible for new forms of poverty and new understandings of what poverty meant. The roots of this transformation go back a number of centuries. How far is in dispute. But most historians agree that the gradual commercialisation of agriculture from the 14th century contributed significantly to the erosion of a 'feudal' society based on reciprocal duties and obligations, and the emergence of a new capitalist society based on wage labour, production and profit. Land became a commodity that could be bought and sold, and to accumulate wealth it was profitable to take uneconomical strip farms and create large fields geared to producing crops for sale and enclose village commons and turn the land into extensive pastures for sheep and cattle.

Properties geared to producing for larger markets needed a sizeable casual workforce and the villagers displaced by enclosures, land sales and the pursuit of profit became a landless labouring class, moving from property to property following seasonal labouring or going to towns in search of work in trades, manufactories and other employments associated with Britain's growing mercantile economy. Labourers who left the old village communities were divorced from family and parish systems of support and were prey to the vagaries of the market, and seasonal or more permanent forms of unemployment. These were symptoms of the larger structures shaping 18th century British society and the consequences were vast wealth for the few, prosperity for the new middle classes and artisans, but material uncertainty for many. The convicts transported to Australia in the late 18th and early 19th centuries were largely drawn from those groups set adrift by the emergent forces of the market economy.

Poverty in Britain

In 1700 London was a city of half a million people, swollen each year by 8000 people emigrating from the countryside. In the next century the pace of social change quickened, hastened by enclosures. Between 1761 and 1780 the British Parliament passed 4039 Enclosure Acts, facilitating the accumulation of property and the dispossession of villagers and small landholding families. Rural dislocation was rapid and momentous. By 1800 London's population had increased to a million, twice the size of Paris, and there were fourteen other towns and cities with more than 20 000 inhabitants.[1]

Those who went to the towns and cities were often disappointed. Many only found poorly paid and intermittent work as labourers, carters and domestic servants. Others found their skills, previously valued, undermined by the new factory system. They faced the choice of starvation or joining the ranks of the labouring classes. It is impossible to know the full extent of poverty. Some contemporaries stressed the plight of individual groups. In 1800 Patrick Colquhoun, police magistrate and pamphleteer, declared that there were 10 000 unemployed domestic servants in London.[2] But it is difficult to sift fact from fancy in the evidence of men like Colquhoun, who hoped to dramatise social evils to push the cause of improved police forces. Some recent estimates, however, suggest that as many as three-quarters of London's population in 1800 were poor.[3] This is probably an upper limit but one indicative of the dimensions of the social crisis confronting British authorities.

The victims of rural dislocation did not always submit meekly to their fate. Riots against rising bread prices were a frequent occurrence in villages and towns. Labouring families protested at the manipulation of the market by entrepreneurs, merchants and shopkeepers and asserted a 'moral economy' of fairness and the right of the people to food in opposition to market forces and the new ethics of profit. There may also have been a 'political' component to some rural crimes. People who burnt barns and haystacks on the properties of large landowners, or poachers who killed game on landed estates but left the evidence behind, gained nothing from their acts but signalled their anger over the enclosure of village commons.[4] Against this evidence must be placed the high rates of crimes against fellow workers. Many did not pick wealthy targets but instead seized the opportunity to steal from neighbours and other inhabitants of the poorer areas of villages, towns and cities.

Rural unrest caused considerable anxiety amongst the propertied classes but conditions in the cities and towns also provoked concern amongst the magistrates, clergy and reformers who investigated the rookeries and lanes of the poorer districts. It was not just poverty that caused alarm. The 'morals' and habits of the urban poor were of even greater concern. Henry Fielding, novelist and magistrate, observed in the London poor of the 1750s: 'the destruction of all morality, decency and modesty; the swearing, whoredom and drunkenness which is eternally carrying on in these houses ... and the excess of poverty and misery of most of the inhabitants'.[5] These were widespread sentiments among the 'better-off' classes influenced by the puritan, dissenting and evangelical currents in 18th century intellectual life. The culture of drinking, fighting, prostitution, stealing and begging which seemed the lifeblood of the urban poor was both offensive to these observers and the cause of deepening poverty.

Alarm at the life of the poor was not only a result of worsening conditions in 18th century London but also of sharper divisions in the city space.[6] In 1700 London was the largest city in Europe. It was a city of narrow streets and lanes, gin palaces, tenements and lodging houses. Violence was common, drink an accepted part of social activity and gambling and thievery were rife. Smallpox, tuberculosis, typhoid and dysentery were epidemic. In the early 18th century, however, drinking, gambling and violence were just as much the habits of the aristocracy as they were of the poor. The rich could retire to their estates but in the city there was considerable social intercourse between the different social groups. Within the space of half a century this began to change. There was a growing geographical isolation between the classes. Two Londons were created; the better-off in the West and the poor in East London.

The emerging middle classes were powerful instruments of change. Horrified at the habits of aristocrat and labourer alike and concerned about the ravages of epidemic diseases, they sought greater regulation of the urban space. The Paving and Improvement Acts facilitated improved drainage, paving and lighting of the streets. Some parishes organised local police forces and magistrates to enforce good order on the streets. Parts of the city were cleaned up, both physically and 'morally', and became the preferred addresses of the respectable classes. As a result the poor were confined to parts of the city untouched by urban reforms—Chick Lane, St Giles, Saffron Hill, Covent Garden, Cow Cross and Grays Inn Lane and other parts of East London. Cheap rents attracted immigrant workers and areas like St Giles became ghettos for Irish labourers and domestics. Public and private greed exacerbated the differences between East and West London. A window tax encouraged landlords to brick-up or blacken the windows of the East London tenements. The poor were increasingly isolated both geographically and culturally. It was their growing 'otherness' which made them the brunt of popular fears and convinced many of the need to develop new methods to contain the threat of poverty.

There were two traditional systems of poor relief.[7] One was charity. Churches and private organisations fulfilled their Christian duty to give alms to the poor by providing food and shelter to the destitute. From the 14th century charities and churches were also involved in the provision of hospitals, lunatic asylums and homes for the aged. During the 18th century evidence of increasing vagrancy and urban squalor led to greater charitable efforts. Old hospitals were extended, new hospitals and asylums built, foundling hospitals and orphanages opened for the care of children, the new dispensary movement distributed cheap medicine for the poor, and many new societies, such as the Society for Bettering the Condition of the Poor, were established to distribute food and religious guidance to the poor.

The second system of relief was a unique system of parish assistance known as the Poor Law. At its inception in the 14th century it had been designed to prevent labourers from leaving villages in search of work elsewhere and thus driving up wages in parishes where there was a shortage of labour, while reducing them where there were too many workers. It was a measure to regulate the labour market as much as a system to assist the poor. By 1790 the Poor Law was a complex system of laws and regulations governing the provision of poor relief to the impotent, able-bodied and criminal poor. Each parish (there were 15 000) in England and Wales had Poor Law overseers who levied rates on local property owners to provide a permanent fund for poor relief. Under the Act of Settlement (1662) the poor could only receive help in their designated parish of settlement, usually their birthplace, and Poor Law overseers could refuse assistance to people from other parishes, exacerbating the plight of those travelling in search of work.

There were different systems of relief under the Poor Law. Although practices varied from parish to parish, it was common for overseers to provide pensions and allowances, usually money but sometimes food, for the impotent poor—the aged, widowed and deserted families, and the sick. If incapable of looking after themselves, or homeless, the impotent poor were sheltered in parish workhouses. The able-bodied poor, however, were required to work in order to receive parish relief. This was sometimes work for local landowners or employment on projects of parish improvement: building roads and bridges. If there was no work the able-bodied had to agree to go to the parish workhouse where they were required to perform tasks such as breaking stones, or carrying out repairs to the building. This was known as the work or workhouse test. Able-bodied unemployed men had to demonstrate to overseers that they were genuinely unemployed by agreeing to work for the parish or be admitted to a workhouse in return for doles or food for themselves and their family. The test was intended as a deterrent to pauperism, the belief being that only those who were really in need would agree to dole work or workhouse incarceration.

The Poor Law established assistance as a right for all those who could not provide for themselves. Settlement provisions and workhouse tests were measures to prevent those who could work from seeking relief rather than employment, but by the early 1790s a combination of poor harvests and the return of men after the wars with France created acute rural unemployment and led to measures which undermined the workhouse system. In 1795 a number of Poor Law overseers and officials gathered in Speenhamland and drafted new regulations waiving the workhouse test for the unemployed and authorising the payment of doles to the unemployed and allowances to the employed whose wages were too low to allow them to support their families. These officials accepted that unemployment and starvation wages were not the fault of individuals, and that the poor had a legitimate claim on parish assistance.

In late 18th and early 19th century Britain few people found the Poor Laws satisfactory.[8] Thousands of pamphlets, political broadsheets, articles and books discussed the faults of the Poor Law and proposed remedies. On one side of the debate were political economists such as Adam Smith, Frederick Eden and Rev. T.R. Malthus, who believed that despite the workhouse the Poor Law perpetuated poverty by encouraging people to remain unemployed and supported by parishes rather than seeking work. They advocated the free market and argued that the market forces of supply and demand would ensure that everyone who wanted employment would find it. People had to be free to search for adequate employment, leaving districts with an oversupply of labour for those where there was a scarcity. Adam Smith confidently predicted that market forces would eventually lead to higher wages and the eradication of poverty. They identified the Speenhamland allowance system as a major cause of idleness and misery. By artificially propping up low wages, allowances encouraged dependency rather than self-reliance.

On the other side of the debate were men like Samuel Taylor Coleridge, poet and conservative philosopher, who feared that the new forces of wage labour and industrialisation were undermining the traditions of English society which were the safeguard of peace and stability. Coleridge considered the Poor Law a means of pre-

A POOR COLONY

Gray's Inn Lane from Mayhew's *London Labour and London Poor*. Images of an idle, drunken and immoral poor were common throughout the nineteenth century.

serving the village society and the habits of deference and paternalism which characterised relations between labourer and master.

Underpinning these debates were differences over the nature of poverty. For conservatives the poor were a part of the natural order of society and a reminder of one's Christian duty to give alms. By some estimates they were a significant proportion of the population. In 1780 Arthur Young, prominent landowner, commentator and traveller, declared that out of a population of nine million in England, eight million could be categorised as poor.[9] This estimate reflected beliefs that the poor were all those who lived in conditions worse than those of a skilled craftsman. The poor thus included the labouring poor (those working but receiving a small income) and paupers (those receiving charity or Poor Law assistance). Critics of the Poor Law, however, believed that allowances and pensions encouraged the labouring poor to become paupers. Poverty, in their eyes, was a choice and unemployment a sign of a preference for indolence. By the early 19th century these ideas contributed to an emerging language of class; the labouring poor were reclassified as the working classes and the term 'poor' came to signify a smaller group living on the margins of society.[10]

Advocates of the free market believed the solution to poverty and unnecessary pauperism lay in the abolition of assistance to the able-bodied or, at the very least, stricter enforcement of the workhouse test. These Poor Law critics supported the principle of 'less eligibility'; conditions in the workhouse and any assistance provided had to be lower than anything attainable by a worker in the lowest paid employment to ensure that people sought any work in preference to dependency. George Nicholls, critic and later Poor Law Commissioner, wrote: 'I wish to see the Poor House looked to with dread by our labouring class, and the reproach for being an inmate of it extend downwards from Father to Son ... for without this where is the needful stimulus to industry?'[11] The workhouse was seen as an important weapon against idleness and in the late 18th and early 19th century considerable efforts were made to increase the size and number of parish workhouses.

Evangelicals were also prominent critics of the Poor Law. They believed that pauperism was a sign of moral weakness. They helped forge a division between workers and the poor that allowed for a 'moralisation of poverty'. In their view there were two types of pauper: the deserving, whose condition was no fault of their own and the undeserving and indolent, who sought to exploit the generosity of charities and Poor Law overseers. The deserving poor were the aged, the ill and widowed and deserted families. The undeserving were the 'idle, indolent and immoral' able-bodied poor. Evangelicals supported campaigns to force the undeserving back into the labour market. The poor were immoral because they lacked the habits of industry, thrift, abstemiousness and self-help. The children of the poor also lacked these habits, condemning them to further poverty. Education, industrial training and religious instruction were the means to moral reform, best achieved in the enclosed environment of an institution. There adults and children could be isolated from the urban squalor that bred indolence and placed under influences for moral improvement. Evangelicals criticised traditional workhouses and asylums because they provided shelter but paid little attention to the moral well-being of the inmates. The new ideal institutions were industrial schools and reformatories for wayward and neglected children, inebriate asylums for drunkards and lunatic asylums for the insane, where 'moral therapy' would make the idle industrious.[12]

Under the Poor Law of the 17th century criminality was a type of poverty and parishes were required to provide houses of correction for criminals. Few parishes had the means to provide such houses and by the 18th century the aim of law enforcement and punishment was to deter the poor from committing crimes. Deterrence involved the selection of only a few law-breakers and their subjection to public punishment. The focus of punishment was the criminal's body. Whippings, brandings and hangings were the public spectacles calculated to instil horror, fear and presumably obedience in the general populace (the population of potential criminals). In this framework there was little need for a police force and fears that such a force might turn against the propertied classes reinforced the deterrence principle of law enforcement. But growing fears about urban unrest and increasing crime led to calls for improved police forces, the protection of property and harsher penalties for offenders.[13]

During the 18th century the number of capital offences rose from 50 to over 200. This dramatic escalation in the severity of criminal jurisdiction was known as the 'Bloody Code'. The enforcement of the code, however, suggests a more complex picture than one of ruthless repression. More people were executed in the 17th than the 18th century and by the early 19th century, although convictions for capital offences rose, executions continued to decline.[14] Despite the increasing severity of the code its enforcement seemed to be more lenient. Some magistrates were inclined to show mercy and deliver a stern moral lecture rather than pass sentence. Others convicted offenders on lesser charges or commuted the capital sentence to one of transportation. The number of people subject to the rule of law was small.

The absence of systematic statistical collections hampers investigation of crime rates, but in the early 19th century the first comprehensive figures on commitments to trial for indictable offences demonstrate that a rapid escalation in the crime rate only began in the early 19th century. In 1805 there were 4605 committals to trial and by 1845 this figure had risen to 24 303, a small figure by today's standards. Contemporaries feared they were in the midst of a crime wave but recent investigations have suggested that these increases reflect the rationalisation of criminal law to reduce the number of capital offences, greater concern on the part of magistrates to implement the law, the emergence of centralised police forces and the escalation in private prosecutions. It was not until the early 19th century that the focus of criminal jurisdiction shifted from deterrence to the regular policing and prosecution of criminals and the construction of a rising crime rate fanned official and popular fears about a dangerous criminal class.[15]

The deterrence model of punishment also began to be challenged in the second half of the 18th century. A leading critic was the utilitarian philosopher Jeremy Bentham. He believed that the legal code needed to be reformed to ensure that a graduated scale of sentences tailored punishment to fit the seriousness of the crime. In tandem with this proposal was one for a new system of punishment. Its focus was not the body but the mind of the offender. Bentham's scheme, the Panopticon, involved confinement in a new type of prison where the inmates would receive religious and moral instruction, isolated from their fellows and observed by warders for signs of moral improvement. Similar ideas were advocated by evangelical reformer John Howard whose 1777 work, *The State of the Prisons*, was an indictment of the state of gaols and a plea for a new reformative regime of discipline, labour and instruction. The evangelical and utilitarian schemes focused on criminality as a state of moral corruption, similar to other types of moral infirmity, and amenable to reform within the new institutional environment of the penitentiary.[16]

Conflict between the advocates of deterrence and the supporters of the penitentiary heightened with the revolt in the American colonies in 1776. The colonies refused to accept transported convicts. Accommodation in the hulks was seen as a temporary measure and new schemes for dealing with convicts were canvassed. It was in this context that Bentham developed his scheme for the Panopticon. This is a well-known story. The advocates of transportation and deterrence held sway and the colony of New South Wales was established. The critics of transportation, however, had an important and far-reaching influence in constructing new understandings of crime. These new meanings paralleled those given to poverty. Increasingly the able-bodied urban poor, the inhabitants of the city rookeries and criminals merged into a single category—the dangerous class—bred in an environment of moral corruption. The poor were no longer a natural part of the social order but a group to be disciplined and reformed.[17]

The convicts transported to the Australian colonies between 1788 and 1868 have been seen as the victims of industrialisation, but for many contemporary middle-class commentators there was little doubt that the convicts were from the dregs of society. The comments of magistrate Patrick Colquhoun, in his 1795 pamphlet *Treatise on the Police of the Metropolis*, are typical: 'It is in these receptacles (public-houses) that Thieves and Robbers of every description hold their orgies and concert and mature their plans of depredation of the peaceful subject'.[18]

The important investigations of Clark, Robson and Shaw have revealed that the majority of convicts were sentenced at urban courts, were usually single, aged between 20 and 45, commonly convicted of theft and the majority were convicted more than once. On this evidence they concluded that the convicts were professional criminals of the type described by Colquhoun. More recent studies, however, have complicated this picture. Although many of the early convicts were serious offenders, the majority transported to Australia came after 1820 and of these half were first offenders, and on average they were more literate and healthy than the general British working class. Moreover many were skilled workers. Far from being the dregs of society, the convicts may have been more skilled and better educated than the average British working-class person. Although they were usually convicted of larcency this was more often a casual workplace theft than a premeditated act of a desperate 'Fagin' surviving in the twilight world of drunkards, thieves and prostitutes. These historians question the existence of a professional criminal class, except in the minds of anxious reformers, magistrates and historians. By their account convicts were workers who stole.[19]

The problem in all these accounts is the attempt to classify the convicts as a single group. The convicts who arrived before 1820 were more likely to be serious offenders than the majority that came later, but even accounting for these differences there were clearly many convicts who by desire or force of circumstance made a living from thieving and prostitution. Equally there were many others who in hard times turned to theft to supplement inadequate or intermittent wages. These distinctions, however, were lost on contemporaries, who viewed the convicts through the moral lens of middle-class opinion. Nonetheless, their views shaped the experiences of the convicts in the colonies and the provisions made for the colonial poor.

A colony's survival

A thousand people arrived on the First Fleet, bringing with them a culture attuned to producing and controlling poverty. By 1800 the colony's European population was 5000, located in Sydney, Rouse Hill and Norfolk Island. By 1810 there were 10 454 Europeans on the mainland and 1321 in Van Diemen's Land. Only a third were convicts. Around Sydney there were 95 637 acres under cultivation to feed this population.[20] Settlement was sparse, scattered and agriculturally based. The British government and their representatives, the colonial governors, did not recognise any Aboriginal entitlement to the land. In British eyes the continent was *terra nullius* (no person's land), paving the way for unrestricted occupation and exploitation of resources.[21]

The first five years of European occupation have been called 'the hungry years'.[22] The story is a familiar one. Crops failed, seeds rotted in the ground or were destroyed by weevil, and the drought in late 1790 and early 1791 made conditions worse. Provisions were rationed but supply ships failed to arrive and the colonists, ignorant of the bountiful natural resources available, barely survived. Scurvy and other dietary diseases were chronic. The convicts were caught in a 'vicious cycle'. There was not enough food and, as a consequence, they were too weak to work to produce enough food. Some convicts robbed their fellows to obtain sustenance. Governor Phillip's response to this crisis was to disperse the burden. In 1790 the already reduced ration was cut again and officials were forced to accept the ration received by convict men, while women and children received only two thirds of the male allowance. This did not please officers who believed they were entitled to better rations than convicts, but Phillip realised that reducing food for convicts even further to accommodate the officers' complaints ran the risk of starving the only labour force.

After the departure of Governor Phillip there was a shift towards private agriculture. Convicts were assigned to landowners who were required to maintain them. This was one means of reducing the call on government stores, a policy encouraged by the British government, concerned at the rising cost of administration. Another means was to grant land to emancipist convicts to encourage independence and self-sufficiency.[23] By 1810 only a third of Sydney's population were still clothed and fed at the crown's expense.[24] But the increasing number of emancipists and free immigrants not supported by the government were dependent on the seasons and their own skills to survive and prosper. Not all were successful.

By 1800 the economy of the colony was on a firmer footing. Productive farms were established near the Parramatta and Hawkesbury Rivers. Natural disasters, however, still undermined the colonial economy. Severe droughts in 1803 and 1809 reduced crop yields and threatened the livelihood of farmers. From 1813 to 1815 another drought reduced the wheat yield by two-thirds.[25] Other hazards were common. In 1806 crops in some districts were destroyed by 'flymoth, blight, smut and rust'.[26] Early governors attempted to ease the burden of farmers and encourage agriculture by controlling the market. Damaged and weevilled crops were bought by the government stores which paid adequate prices to maintain farmers and stimulate production.

Governor King identified small landholders as a group facing particular economic problems, some of their own making. He found most of the recently arrived free immigrants 'useless to themselves and a burden to the public.' They lacked capital and usually brought only their 'large' families. Their failure to make the land productive meant they needed assistance from the public stores. Small landholders, emancipist and free alike, with little capital, did not have the resources to ride out poor harvests and droughts. They lacked the money and supplies to encourage assigned convicts to perform necessary tasks in their free time. King believed that the rum trade was an additional enemy. In 1802, 47 landholders were forced to assign their farms to creditors after getting into debt. They had sent their produce to 'monopolising traders', instead of the Commissariat, in return for rum and left their families destitute, forced to 'live in wretched hovels'.[27]

Some turned to theft as a way of making a living. Crime was reported frequently in the early colonial press. John Smith bashed and robbed a woman, taking her watch, earrings and money.[28] Henry Stanley, a labourer, broke into the house of a settler in Seven Hills and stole four bushels of wheat.[29] Some escaped conviction. In 1805 a woman with a babe in arms was let go by a shopkeeper after he caught her stealing calico.[30] Criminal statistics suggest that crime was not nearly as prevalent as contemporaries feared might be the case in a convict colony. Rates of arrest paralleled those in Britian and between 1800 and 1806 a third of those brought before the Sydney criminal court were acquitted.[31] Nonetheless crime was the resort of some and they did not always restrict their activities to thefts from shops and prosperous colonists. In 1805 a woman living in the Rocks was visited by her neighbours. She went out on an errand and returned to find half her stores gone.[32]

The early governors, from Phillip to Macquarie, had a high degree of control over the lives of the colonists. They were responsible for organising convict labour and maintaining those in their charge with food and clothing from the government store. They had other responsibilities towards the convicts and colonists who could not support themselves. Health was one. A tent hospital was established in 1788 for the immediate needs of the colonists. In 1792 a brick hospital of two wards was built at Parramatta. The Rum Hospital in Sydney was opened in 1811. In the colony of Van Diemen's Land small wooden huts were opened as hospitals in Hobart in 1804 and Launceston in 1808. The growth in the emancipist and free populations placed new pressures on the governors to provide services for colonists suffering particular misfortunes. By the early 19th century lunacy was a problem that could no longer be dealt with as a crime or a breach of convict discipline. In 1811 the first colonial lunatic asylum was opened at Castle Hill. Old age was also a problem. During Macquarie's term of office a small hut on the outskirts of Sydney town was used to accommodate 40 aged people who had no one to support them.[33]

The Sydney Rum Hospital built during Macquarie's term as governor. The provision of facilities for the ill was a high priority amongst colonial authorities. (Photo courtesy Mitchell Library)

Modern perceptions of the convicts have been influenced by the opinions of contemporary commentators. Most agreed with David Collins, lieutenant to Governor Phillip, that the convicts were 'rogues and villains'.[34] This was the oft-repeated conclusion of officials, military officers, surgeons and visitors to the colony. Some, including Watkin Tench, found the convicts 'behaved better than expected',[35] and emancipists such as D.D. Mann had an obvious motive in arguing that the colony was 'not nearly as debauched as the tongue of prejudice has too frequently asserted'.[36] But most officials and free colonists viewed the convicts with suspicion. This attitude reflected the growing separation between the poor and the better-off strata in 18th and early 19th century British society. Transportation brought the two together. Officials and officers were in daily contact with the inhabitants of the urban rookeries, rural labourers and vagabonds in their charge. The social tension in this contact underpinned the vehemence of prevailing attitudes towards the convicts. Many believed authority and force were the weapons to control the behaviour of convicts. Those more favourably impressed by the convicts held hopes for the future of the colony and sought the means to ensure that convicts and their children became useful citizens.

The plight of orphaned girls concerned some colonists. Richard Johnson, the first Anglican chaplain to the colony, Samuel Marsden, Governor King and his wife Anna King, campaigned to rescue orphan girls from a life on the streets. King was shocked to see 'so many girls between the ages of eight and twelve, verging on the brink of ruin and prostitution'.[37] Marsden hoped to 'root out the vile depravities bequeath'd by their vicious progenitors'. These colonists feared that orphaned girls turning to prostitution would undermine colonial morality and poison the character of the next generation. Critics claimed that many street girls were not orphans but neglected, arguing that government assistance would encourage more parents to abandon their children. Undeterred by these claims Governor King opened the Female Orphans Asylum in Sydney in 1801. There orphaned and neglected girls were given a basic education, religious instruction and training in domestic arts such as needlework and spinning. The asylum had accommodation for 50 girls, at a time when there were only 500 children of convicts in the colony. Opinion was divided as to the effectiveness of the asylum. The emancipist D.D. Mann claimed 'it laid the foundation for ... a life of virtue and industry',[38] but Rev. W.P. Crook believed the girls had not been improved. Governor Macquarie, however, supported the asylum and sought to provide a similar institution for boys. In 1819 he stated that there were many male orphans in the colony 'left entirely destitute of support and consequently living in a miserable state of poverty and nakedness'.[39] In 1819 Macquarie opened the Male Orphans Asylum.

Aborigines were forced off their land and the crippling effects of smallpox epidemics, which cut the Aboriginal population from about 750 000 to 300 000 by the 1820s,[40] undermined their opposition to occupation. Frontier tensions frequently erupted into violence, as settlers pushed further into Aboriginal lands. Europeans held little regard for Aborigines or their culture. The 'noble savage' ideal that had influenced men like James Cook was quickly replaced by arguments that Aborigines were savages, on the lowest rung of the 'great chain of being'. This was the view of most colonists but one opposed by a small group of evangelical missionaries and officials. They believed the Aborigines were part of the family of man and capable of moral improvement. They believed that Aboriginal culture was 'primitive' but the 'child-like' Aborigines were capable of becoming Christians.

These ideas influenced Macquarie. In 1814 he established an

'institution for the civilisation and education of the natives'. This was a humanitarian endeavour but one that had no understanding and little sympathy for Aboriginal culture. In 1817 the *Sydney Gazette* reported on the efforts of the 'native school':

> the chiefs were then again called together to observe the examination of children ... several of the little ones read; and it was grateful to the bosom of sensibility to trace the degrees of pleasure which the chiefs manifested on this occasion ... In a few years this benevolent institution will amply reward the hopes and expectations of its liberal patrons and supporters, and answer the grand object intended, by providing a seminary for the helpless offspring of the natives of this country, and opening the path to their future civilization and improvement.[41]

Similar ideas motivated missionaries and protectors in the 1820s and 1830s. Rev. L.E. Threlkeld at Lake Macquarie and George Augustus Robinson at Flinders Island sought to provide a sanctuary for Aborigines and schools to facilitate their 'civilisation'. Their success was mixed. Some Aborigines professed to be Christians but others resisted or assimilated Christian ideas into traditional practices, undermining confidence in the 'civilising' mission. Many took it as evidence of the irredeemable 'barbarism' of the natives. Tragically Robinson's efforts at Christian protection led to a rapid decline in the Aboriginal population in his charge. Within a decade, 150 of the 200 Aborigines on the island had died.[42]

Hospitals for the care of the sick and insane and asylums for the education of orphans and Aborigines represented the inital efforts of governors to assist those who could not provide for themselves or had no families or friends to support them. But as the colonies grew and the proportion of colonists not maintained on government stores increased, the broader issue of poor relief became relevant. What was the best means of organising assistance for unfortunates and reform for the morally dissolute? This was the question that confronted early colonial administrators and the debates around this question reflected broader debates in Britain. Was a system modelled on the English Poor Law the answer? Or should colonists heed the warning of critics of the Poor Law, such as Sir Frederick Eden who, in his 1797 pamphlet *The State of the Poor*, accused the Poor Law of promoting 'vagrancy, dependency and dissoluteness'? Was private benevolence the answer to this dilemma? Each of these solutions was canvassed as colonists confronted the limitations of colonial society in their struggle to plant the familiar institutions of home in alien soil.

There were few colonists with the financial resources or interest to engage in private benevolence. Nonetheless some clergy, officials and wives of officials attempted to replicate the activities of their counterparts in Britain. Their success, however, depended on government support. The Female Orphans Asylum was a government institution with a committee of private citizens overseeing its operation. Other initiatives were undertaken during Macquarie's term of office. In 1813 the New South Wales Society for Promoting Christian Knowledge and Benevolence was founded by seven evangelical Christian colonists. They hoped to pursue missonary work but with financial assistance from Governor Macquarie devoted much of their time to distributing food to the poor in Sydney. They helped 618 people in the first five years of their operation. In 1818 this society was renamed the Benevolent Society of New South Wales, its declared aim to relieve 'the poor, the distressed, the aged and the infirm ... and to encourage industrious habits amongst the poor'.[43] It sought public subscriptions but most of its funds came from the Governor. A second important charity was the Bible Society, establised in 1817 'to promote the interests of religion and morals amongst the lower classes of the inhabitants'.[44] The evangelical mission of benevolence through moral reform exerted a powerful influence over early charitable endeavours in New South Wales.

The early governors, notably King and Macquarie, subsidised private benevolence but they also explored the possibility of giving charity committees independent financial resources. A parish-based system of poor relief was clearly impractical but Macquarie attempted to organise a modified poor law system. He granted land to committees of clergy and landholders in Richmond, Windsor and Parramatta 'for the purpose of forming a permanent and increasing fund for the relief of the distressed and indigent poor'. Applicants for relief had to have resided in the district for at least a year to qualify for assistance. Commissioner Bigge concluded that Macquarie's efforts had aimed to establish a poor relief system 'on the same principles upon which the poor laws in England are maintained'.[45]

The efforts of Macquarie, Governor and Mrs King, and those involved in the Benevolent and Bible Societies signalled important changes in colonial society. New South Wales and Van Diemen's Land had been founded as convict colonies and officials and colonists alike feared the existence of a society of 'rogues and villains' drawn from Britain's increasingly despised poor. In the first 30 years of European settlement the colonies were sufficiently small to allow the development of a highly centralised system of power and authority for the disposal and control of convict labour. By the time of Macquarie, however, there were signs that colonial society was no longer simply a dumping ground for convicts. The emancipation of convicts, the arrival of a small group of free settlers, extensive land grants and the growth of trade and agriculture created a society where good fortune, good harvests, adequate capital and individual effort could ensure prosperity. Those no longer entitled to be fed from government stores, however, had to rely on selling their skills in the marketplace. Not everyone prospered and in the absence of village and family support, parish provisions or widespread private benevolence, the governors assumed the prime responsibility for organising and financing assistance for the aged, orphaned, sick and destitute.

2 Survival of the fittest

In 1827 Peter Cunningham, a naval surgeon with long experience working on convict transports, published his recollections of life in New South Wales. He had been favourably impressed by the colony but in the Rocks in Sydney he found an area that reminded him of St Giles in London, where the inhabitants spoke the 'St Giles Greek' dialect.[1] Like many commentators of the time, Cunningham believed the Rocks signified that transportation had failed to improve the character of London's criminal class. But there are other ways of reading Cunningham's commentary. It is evidence that some colonists could only afford the cheap lodging house and hotel accommodation of the poorer districts of Sydney. Despite claims that the colonies afforded an opportunity for prosperity some found their circumstances little changed from those they had left in England. This remained a feature of colonial life. At the 1828 muster there were 54 726 inhabitants of European descent in the small convict settlements clustered round the coast and rivers of New South Wales and Tasmania. By 1861 there were over a million colonists living in six largely self-governing colonies. A year earlier, however, Henry Graham, Sydney Health Officer, reported to a Select Committee that the condition of the working classes in some areas of the city was 'worse than in any part of the world'.[2] This was disturbing news to colonists who had comforted themselves with the belief that Australia was now a 'workingman's paradise' free of the dilemmas of the old world.

Three migrations were responsible for the large increase in the colonial population. Convicts were the first, and three fifths of the 160 000 convicts transported to Australia arrived after 1820. Overtaking transportation as a source of white population was free immigration. Between 1820 and 1850, 195 000 free immigrants arrived in the colonies, many enticed by assisted passage and the offer of employment. This was only a small proportion of the two million who emigrated from Britain in this period but Australia's distance from Europe made North America a more attractive destination.

The discovery of gold in the 1850s overcame the problem of distance. In that decade over half a million immigrants arrived in Australia, most without assisted passage.[3]

The influx of free immigrants undermined the convict character of the colonies. The British government, under pressure from colonists, began to wind down the transportation system. In 1840 transportation to New South Wales ceased. In 1853 Tasmania followed and only Western Australia continued to receive convicts until 1868. The cessation of transportation also meant the withdrawal of direct British government finance and the end of the government Commissariat as a stabilising influence on the colonial economy. Landowners, farmers and traders were more vulnerable to the variable winds of market forces. Workers and their families were likewise more vulnerable to fluctuations in the market for their skills and the cycles of boom and bust in the economy. This was a context in which fortunes could be made but there were also fewer safeguards against destitution.

Land and labour

The convicts were the bulk of the early labour force and although most were guaranteed food, clothing and shelter, the conditions for their labour were sometimes harsh and protests severely punished. In 1820 convicts were 40 per cent of the population of New South Wales and 50 per cent of the population of Van Diemen's Land. Few free colonists held hopes for them being useful workers. John Oxley, a prominent landowner, complained that convict settlers were frequently drunk and licentious. The Rev. William Cowper had little sympathy for the convicts, even after the expiry of their sentence. He felt that most were immoral and believed that out of 4376 emancipists only 369 were of good character. This was a common view and one perpetuated by visitors such as Peter Cunningham and exclusivist settlers such as James Macarthur and James Mudie.[4] These views influenced the treatment of convict workers. Prominent landowner Alexander Berry came to believe that strict discipline and the lash were the means to ensure that 'profligate' assigned convict servants worked.

Some governors attempted to limit the power of masters over assigned convicts by making ill-treatment illegal and requiring masters to obtain a magistrate's order before they could flog refractory convicts, but isolation, and magistrates who ignored infractions of these rules, afforded landowners the opportunity to abuse convict servants. James Brine, assigned to a landowner in the Hunter Valley in 1834, was denied clothing and bedding and forced to spend long periods in a creek washing sheep. His pleas for a blanket to protect him from the cold while working were ignored. Georgina Baxter was denied food by her master in an effort to force her to work harder. Angry and resentful convicts responded to ill-treatment by working slowly, breaking tools or absconding. In 1834 two convict women went further and killed their master.[5]

Not all masters supported the idea of punishment as the means to discipline convict labourers. James Atkinson, in his 1826 treatise on farming, advised masters to treat the convicts with fairness rather than a flogging. Disputes about the best treatment for convicts arose out of the problem of labour discipline. What was the best way to make convicts work hard? While men like Berry thought the threat of punishment useful, many masters and officials in charge of government gangs found the task work system more effective. Convict workers were given specific jobs or tasks and once these were completed they were free for the rest of the day or week. After their tasks were finished many worked extra hours for their master in return for indulgences of food and clothing. Convicts on government gangs could finish work at 3 p.m. and spend the rest of the day working for wages. Masters found that task work and the provision of adequate food, clothing and accommodation were measures rewarded with hard work and loyalty. Edward John Eyre, landowner, explorer and later Governor of the West Indies, found his assigned servants hardworking and well-behaved. Although convict labour was forced labour, convicts had a measure of control over their work and conditions.[6]

Despite the image of the colonies as slave societies, two-thirds of the convicts received only one or no floggings.[7] Harsh punishments were reserved for the minority of convicts who refused to submit to the labour discipline of gangs or assignment. Officials in Britain and the colonies, however, believed that transportation needed to be a deterrent to crime and harsh penalties were essential to achieve this end. After the report of Commissioner Bigge in 1822 new measures were introduced to further discipline refractory convicts and strengthen transportation as a form of deterrence. Places of secondary punishment were established at such sites as Port Macquarie, Port Arthur, Moreton Bay and Norfolk Island and there refractory convicts confronted harsh conditions and brutal overseers. In 1836 Major Joseph Anderson, in charge of Norfolk Island, ordered 100 lashes for William Riley because he smiled while on the chain gang and a further 100 lashes for singing a song. Two convicts received 300 lashes each for failing to sow corn properly. Officials like Anderson and Captain Patrick Logan (the Beast of Brisbane)

The Parramatta Female Factory in the 1830s. Colonists could rest content knowing that troublesome convicts were incarcerated in forbidding penal institutions. (Photo courtesy National Library of Australia, Rex Nan Kivell Collection)

earned reputations as sadistic and cruel superintendents. But few convicts spent time at these places of secondary punishment. Port Arthur, the largest establishment, received only 12 700 convicts in 40 years.[8]

Women convicts faced particular difficulties. Only 25 000 women, a seventh of the total number of convicts, were transported, creating a marked sex imbalance in the population. By 1820 there were nine white men in New South Wales, and ten men in Van Diemen's Land, for every white woman.[9] Historians have argued that this imbalance was responsible for a high incidence of male sexual violence towards women in the colony. The policing of this violence was hampered by the prevalent view that women convicts were drunken 'whores', of worse character than the male convicts. Commissioner Bigge found the women 'disordered, unruly and licentious'.[10]

In the 1820s female factories were established to house women convicts before assignment and incarcerate those who committed further crimes or refused to work. These were overcrowded and filthy institutions. In 1826 Mary Hamilton died at the Parramatta Factory from the effects of starvation.[11] Some women protested at conditions in the factories. In the 1830s the notorious Mrs Ajax organised women at the Parramatta Factory to riot after they were placed on starvation rations. Women at the Hobart Factory disrupted the pious lectures of local clergy with peals of laughter. Such behaviour confirmed the worst impressions of officials.[12] But convict men could be equally denigrating. A rich vernacular—bat, crack, bunter and mutton—signified women as the objects of male contempt and desire.[13]

The problems of women convicts ran deeper than a double standard which led many to view the actions of women in a harsher light. Governors were anxious to 'promote the interests of virtue ... by the encouragement of lawful marriage'. For convict women marriage afforded an opportunity to leave the Factories or an unsatisfactory servant position. But they had fewer options than women who remained in Britain. At the 1828 Muster 58 per cent of adult women employees were classified as domestic servants, 15 per cent as housekeepers, 4 per cent as special servants and 6 per cent as laundresses. These were usually poorly paid positions involving long hours and laborious tasks, often under the supervision of oppressive and unsympathetic masters and mistresses. Sexual harassment was a further problem. These conditions made marriage an attractive alternative. By the 1840s the marriage rate for women in the colonies was nearly 10 per cent higher than that in Britain.[14] Australia was being seen as a land rich in resources to fuel Britain's economic expansion and investors aimed to exploit these resources, providing employment for men but few jobs for women, other than domestic service.

Land was the major source of profit for colonists. Agriculture was essential to feed the increasing colonial population but the primary source of wealth became wool. Between 1820 and 1850 exports increased from two million pounds of wool to over 40 million pounds. By 1850 Australia was supplying half of all the wool consumed by British mills. The increasing demand of British manufacturers for wool pressured the British government to explore measures to foster colonial pastoralism. Governors made more land grants. Between 1821 and 1828 one and a half million acres were granted, three times the acreage of all grants before 1821. Men of capital were most able to profit by the expansion of settlement. In 1822 Alexander Berry established a property of 10 000 acres near the Shoalhaven River. British investors also saw scope for profit and a few private companies, notably the Australian Agricultural Company, established in 1824, purchased the farms of small landholders to create large pastoral properties. Some, frustrated at government limits on the extent of settlement, squatted on large areas of land beyond the prescribed areas. There they established large pastoral enterprises and consolidated their claims over the next 50 years. British government concern at the rising costs of colonial administration led to the 1831 Ripon Regulations. Henceforth crown land was to be sold not granted. By 1840 annual sales had reached 200 000 acres, mainly in New South Wales and Van Diemen's Land.[15]

The land grabs of the 1820s and 1830s made land more difficult to acquire for those who did not have substantial reserves of capital. After the abolition of grants in 1831 it became harder for emancipists and poorer free immigrants to acquire large properties. They were more often small farmers rather than pastoralists, making them more vulnerable to seasonal fluctuations in agricultural fortunes. Droughts and poor harvests were regular problems. In 1827 a late harvest in Van Diemen's Land caused a fall in prices and forced some farmers to borrow money 'on very disadvantageous terms'. Some became so indebted that they had to forfeit their farms while others continued on 'in very embarrassed circumstances'.

In 1828 a severe drought on the mainland crippled those settlers who could not make any provision for a lean season. The crops in many districts 'almost entirely failed'. Once down many farmers struggled to regain their former condition. In 1831 Governor Darling reported that the recent unfavourable seasons meant that 'most of them are in a lamentable condition':

> Many of those who supplied themselves on credit two or three years ago, when cattle and stock ... sold at an extravagant rate have been completely ruined. Their lands have passed into the hands of Mr Terry and people of that Class, who lend money at an exorbitant interest and soon obtain possession of the Estates of their Debtors.[16]

Those with little capital were least able to ride out poor seasons and bad harvests.

Planners of the new colony of South Australia hoped to avoid the problems of agricultural settlement that afflicted the other colonies. They adopted the ideas of Edwin Gibbon Wakefield, dissenter and radical, who believed that land had to be sold at a sufficient price to guarantee that settlers had the right character and enough capital to overcome the tribulations of farming. A sufficient price would encourage workers to pursue thrift and industry in order to save enough to afford a property. South Australia was to be a colony of sturdy yeomen rather than a convict settlement. In the 1860s South Australia's agricultural settlement expanded rapidly and the colony became the granary for Victoria and New South Wales. By the

SURVIVAL OF THE FITTEST

1880s, however, it was obvious that settlement, boosted by abnormally good seasons, had gone too far. Those farms beyond the Goyder Line became dust bowls and the settlers bankrupt.[17]

Life on farms was arduous. This was particularly so for women, who combined the tasks of mother, wife and extra farm hand. This situation was worse if the farm was failing and husbands had to pick up labouring, shearing or fencing work to pay off debts or tide the farm over a poor season. Wives left behind to maintain the family and farm worked long hours feeding animals, milking, making clothes and preparing food. Even those women whose husbands were still at home had to work hard to keep the family farm afloat. In the 1840s Annie Baxter, the wife of an army officer turned farmer, struggled to keep her husband's Macleay River property profitable. She spent her days cooking, cleaning, churning butter, minding the poultry yard and tending the other animals; chores that left her 'so fagged that I don't know what to do with myself'. At times she felt weak and depressed and prey to frequent illnesses.[18]

Men whose farms were failing and those forced to sell went labouring or returned to towns in search of work. Their fortunes depended on their skill and market conditions. In the 1830s skilled tradesmen could command good wages of 7s to 10s a day, while labourers, shepherds, fencers and shearers prepared to work in the country could earn 6s a day plus board and accommodation. The shortage of pastoral workers kept wages high. But wage rates are deceptive guides to affluence. They have to be placed in a broader context. Much rural work was seasonal, leaving workers without income on the days spent travelling from one job to the next and during the off season. Employers also had the means to recoup some of the money they paid as wages. Pastoral workers on distant properties purchased food and other essential items from employers who charged high prices. The truck system, as it was known, yielded high profits for employers and considerably reduced the earnings of workers.[19]

In the 1830s and 1840s attempts were made to encourage immigration to the Australian colonies. The motives of supporters of these schemes differed. Employers, squatters, and landowners hoped to increase the supply of labour to force down wages. Others worried about the character of the colonial population. Rev. J.D. Lang, concerned at the high proportion of unskilled Irish Catholic emancipists and settlers, assisted the immigration of skilled Protestant tradesmen. The sex imbalance in the population was also a concern. In the 1830s 3000 single women were given assisted passages to the colonies. Supporters of this scheme hoped that greater numbers of women would foster marriage and family life.[20]

A few, however, were worried about the suitability of the female immigrants. Governor Bourke believed many of them were of 'low character'.

Other schemes provoked concern. The British Colonial Office believed that immigration would empty Britain's crowded cities and workhouses of paupers. The Land and Emigration Commission provided assisted passages for pauper immigrants. In 1832 the *Sydney Morning Herald* angrily condemned this as a scheme to burden the colony 'with a class of dependents'.[21] Governor Bourke agreed that most arrivals under this scheme were 'unfit as immigrants'. They were generally unable to find work and soon became a drain on government and charitable funds. Some colonists favoured schemes for family immigration in the belief that this would ensure social stability. In the 1840s Caroline Chisholm, through the Family Loan Colonization Society, facilitated the arrival of 5000 mechanics and their families.[22]

Immigrants were attracted to Australia by reports of plentiful jobs and good wages. But there were hidden costs. Those who stayed in the major port towns found the cost of food, clothing and rent high. In Sydney rent for a two-room worker's cottage was 10s a week and for a three-bedroom house, 14s to 25s a week. Rent could consume 50 per cent of a family's income. Workers in Van Diemen's Land were worse off. In Hobart in the 1830s wages were lower but the price of food and housing higher than in Sydney.[23]

In the 1830s the economy may have been buoyant and wage rates high but some workers still found unemployment and underemployment a problem. Many newly arrived workers found little demand for their skills. In 1836 a group of emigrant mechanics petitioned Governor Bourke complaining that conditions in New South Wales did not correspond to the claims of emigration agents in London. Many of their number faced 'disappointment, misery and perhaps ultimate ruin' because in many trades there was no work or too many tradesmen. They listed such employments as collarmakers, confectioners, coachmakers, coppersmiths, farriers, carvers and plumbers as those worst affected. They had little or no employment and could not afford Sydney's high rents.[24]

The relative prosperity of the employed classes in the colonies was shaken by the collapse of the economy in 1841. A slump in the price of wool and the withdrawal of British capital revealed the vulnerability of the dependent colonial economies. Wages were forced down. By 1843 skilled tradesmen were earning only 4s a day and some only 2s 6d. Worse, many could only get a few days work a week. These men, however, were better off than the unemployed. Officials recognised that distress amongst the families of the unemployed was widespread but their primary concern was to diminish what George Grey, Governor of South Australia, termed the evil of the 'pauper population'.[25] The unemployed lived in a hostile environment. Attempts by the Melbourne unemployed to petition the Governor for assistance in 1842 were dismissed by the *Port Phillip Gazette*. It declared that 'only two out of ten were genuine cases'.[26] In this climate the unemployed only received help if they were prepared to work on government gangs. Governments provided food or meagre wages for labourers prepared to work building roads, bridges, jetties, clearing land or, if there was no useful work available, breaking stones.

Despite the depression immigrants continued to arrive in the colonies, exacerbating unemployment and stretching government relief services. In 1841 tents were erected in Sydney's Domain to house 2000 immigrant families and 172 single women. The men received a family food ration in return for two days work on a government gang. Some pressed the Governor to extend this system to other workers. In 1843 a register of unemployed men willing to work on government gangs was opened at the Immigration Office in Sydney. In ten days 700 men had registered, many more than could be employed. The government provided work for only 332 men at daily wages of 3s for mechanics and 2s for labourers. Governor Gipps reported that there were 'at least as many more still wanting employment'. Later enquiries revealed 1243 unemployed with 2505 dependants in a population of 29 973. The majority of the unemployed were labourers and mechanics and at the 1841 census there were 4178 such men living in Sydney. Even accounting for the drift of unemployed to the city it is possible that a fifth to a quarter of Sydney's labouring population were unemployed.[27] In the early 1840s the South Australian Emigration Agent provided work for 300 to 400 unemployed men and food for nearly 2000 infirm aged, women with dependent children and orphans each week: almost an eighth of Adelaide's population.[28]

Men and women tackled the dispiriting task of hunting for work. One labourer lamented: 'I have been round to every shop until I am tired; the people make a laugh at us, and say it is no use for us to call'.[29] Contemporary observers remarked on the sight of many walking the streets 'with wretchedness seated on their countenances, and abject poverty exhibited on their persons'.[30] The evident distress of many prompted official action to assist the unemployed, but there were sharp divisions in the colony over the extent and form of this assistance. Governors and officials accepted that the unemployed had a right to relief in times of serious economic crisis but the principle of less eligibility underpinned their efforts. Wages on government relief work gangs were set well below market rates to ensure that only the needy applied. A form of workhouse test operated. Men were denied assistance if they refused offers of private employment or failed to turn up for work on government gangs. In South Australia the Emigration Agent made families receiving assistance live in huts in Emigration Square in the hope that the shame of public scrutiny would deter people from seeking relief.

The meagre wages and punitive conditions attached to these relief schemes led to protests and strikes by the unemployed who claimed a right to more generous assistance based on the old Poor Law system of allowances. These claims were rejected by colonial authorities. The *Port Phillip Gazette* declared the strikes by relief workers to be foolish and dangerous and Governor La Trobe used these protests to cut relief wages even further. Some prominent citizens, alarmed by these mass demonstrations and strikes, sought to defuse conflict by supporting schemes to send the unemployed to country districts to find work.[31]

Some merchants, professionals and businessmen also felt the effects of the 1840s depression. The collapse of the wool export market ruined many speculators. In 1841 a Bankruptcy Act was passed to facilitate the liquidation of many companies. In 1842, 600 bankruptcies were finalised. The following year charges of fraud against a bank in Sydney led to a loss of confidence and a run on bank funds. Within two days, savers and investors had withdrawn £20 000 from the colony's banks. Many small investors lost their life savings and prominent colonists were ruined. Richard Jones, merchant, pastoralist, magistrate, member of the Chamber of Commerce, Member of the Legislative Council and President of the Bank of New South Wales was one of the largest landowners in the country and owner of a number of whaling ships. In 1843 he was declared insolvent and all his ships and estates were sold. By the late 1840s he had managed to recover his situation sufficiently to buy some property in Queensland but he never regained his former wealth or prominence. He died a few years later.[32]

The depression was most acute between 1841 and 1843 but some colonies recovered more slowly than others. By 1843 South Australia and the Port Phillip district were showing signs of recovery. Trade was improving and the number of people registering for relief was declining. In 1844 the opening of the Kapunda copper mine in South Australia was a significant boost to the colony's economy. By 1846 there were only 107 people employed on government gangs in Port Phillip but there were still 1580 people receiving relief in Sydney. Recovery was slowest in Tasmania. By 1844 there were still 2600 emancipists, free labourers and convict pass-holders employed on government gangs. Wages for free labourers there were lower than in any other colony and by 1848 there were still 200 unemployed free labourers in Hobart in receipt of government assistance. By the late 1840s the colonial economies, with the exception of Tasmania, had recovered from the depression but wages for many mechanics and labourers had failed to return to levels attainable in the late 1830s.[33]

The discovery of gold in the 1850s was a significant boost to the colonial economy and population. In that decade the European population of Australia more than doubled. Boats leaving Britain were crammed with people seeking fortunes in the colonies. Many also came from Europe, America, and 50 000 from China. Most went to Victoria. In the 1850s Victoria's population increased fivefold and by 1861 the colony had 46 per cent of Australia's population. There was also a large internal migration. Men left South Australia, New South Wales, Western Australia and Tasmania in great numbers to travel to the gold fields of Victoria. Shortages of labour in these colonies meant wage rises for those labourers and mechanics who remained behind. Families left behind by men going to the gold fields, however, faced great difficulties if the breadwinner failed to earn a living or send money back. In 1852 the Directors of the South Australian Destitute Board remarked on the 'cases of great distress occasioned by heads of families leaving for the gold fields'.[34]

Life on the gold fields was difficult. Men worked long hours for uncertain rewards. Local suppliers were able to make considerable profits selling equipment and food at inflated prices. Frustrations simmered over government regulation of the fields and competition from Chinese labourers. They flared at Eureka over the imposition of licence fees on miners. Despite the lure of gold very few made their fortune. Geoffrey Serle estimates that only 100 men made fortunes on the Victorian fields. Only two out of every ten miners made more than the wages they might have expected as skilled workers and two in every three miners made no profits at all.[35] Most had to return to the workforce.

The 1850s was a decade of significant economic growth. The value of Australia's exports increased tenfold in this decade, and gold was the major export earner. There were other benefits. The dramatic increase in the colonial population created greater domestic demand for produce, boosting agricultural and manufacturing production. In the second half of the 19th century high export prices, a rapidly expanding wool market and high levels of public and private investment boosted the colonial economy, but this economic growth was not distributed evenly between the colonies.

Victoria was the greatest beneficiary. By the 1860s it was the most populous and prosperous colony. In contrast Western Australia was still a small colony, with a fragile economy, and labour shortages led colonial authorities to continue transporting convicts there until 1868, fuelling economic expansion while keeping down wages. Economic growth also failed to arrest more long-term problems in Tasmania. In the 1840s Tasmania began to lose its mainland markets for agricultural produce to South Australia, and its prosperous whaling and sealing industry collapsed. The continued supply of convict labour in this decade undermined employment for free and emancipist labour. Their wages were lower than those for their mainland counterparts and many found it more difficult to find work. From 1847 to 1851, 24 280 people emigrated to other colonies. More left with the discovery of gold. By the 1860s Tasmania had a higher proportion of invalids, prisoners and paupers than other colonies—more than the total of South Australia and Queensland combined, even though these colonies had more than double the population of Tasmania.[36]

Despite sustained economic growth after 1850 the colonial economies were not immune from cycles of boom and bust. In these circumstances many workers were vulnerable to unemployment and poverty. In 1855 the combination of a recession and a sudden flood of migrants into South Australia created an acute unemployment crisis. The Destitute Board had 3027 paupers on its books, three times the number of the previous year.[37] Recessions in Melbourne in 1860, Sydney in 1866 and in Queensland between 1866 and 1872 increased levels of unemployment and many unemployed protested at their plight. In 1860 a crowd of unemployed marched on Parliament House in Melbourne and stoned it. A more serious incident occurred in Brisbane in 1866. A large crowd shouting 'Bread or Blood' marched through the streets until authorities dispersed them with gunfire. The government in New South Wales showed more restraint in their dealings with Sydney's unemployed. In 1866 a Select Committee was established to inquire into their problems. It concluded that distress amongst labourers, mechanics, artisans and their families was 'appalling'. The Report estimated that there were 3000 unemployed and with dependants perhaps as many as 10 000 people were affected. Ninian Melville, a cabinet maker and representative of the unemployed, complained that the men had been called 'loafers'. He denied the charge, claiming that 300 men had applied for 72 positions as stone-breakers at Picton. 'Stout-hearted' men had cried when they failed to get one of these jobs. Private registry offices were exploiting this situation by offering work at greatly reduced rates of pay. The Report sympathised with the men's situation but offered little help other than a recommendation that manufacturing be encouraged.[38]

A member of the nomad tribe of workers, western NSW around 1900.
(Photo courtesy NSW Government Printing Office)

The source of colonial wealth was also the basis of economic insecurity for many workers. Although daily wage rates in the 1860s and 1870s were high and unemployment low, rarely above 4 per cent, casual work was the lot of many unskilled workers. The pastoral and agricultural strength of the economy built seasonal rhythms into work routines. This affected labourers directly involved in primary production and also packers, carters, wharf labourers and seamen involved in the transport of produce. In rural areas labourers had to travel long distances, following the seasonal work and moving from job to job to stretch out their working year.

For this 'nomadic tribe' of workers there were days wasted travelling between jobs, periods when there was no work and a male culture which encouraged them to drink their earnings rather than save to tide them over periods of illness or to ensure a comfortable old age. For workers involved in the transport and shipment of produce there were periods of intense activity when a season was on and then days or weeks when they were idle. These patterns meant that many workers earnt good daily wages but did not work every day of the week or every month of the year. Unemployment may have been low in the boom years of the late 19th century but underemployment and casual work were significant features of the colonial labour market.[39]

Newly arrived immigrants, expecting a worker's paradise, were sometimes disappointed. In 1878 Charles Matthews, a tradesman who had been in Sydney for some weeks, had failed to find any employment and his savings had been spent. In the same year John Raymond, an ex-soldier, arrived in the colony with his wife and three children. He remained unemployed for three months and was 'reduced to the very lowest state of distress'. He pawned the family's possessions and after eviction from their rented house the family was forced to live in a small damp room with no furniture or bedding.[40] Althought the stories of destitute families did not find a place amongst images of colonial prosperity, a few observers charted a darker side to colonial life.

Colonial slums

Peter Cunningham's observations of life in the Rocks were repeated many times by other commentators. Most focused on the habits and morals of the slum dwellers in colonial cities. In 1834 the *Sydney Morning Herald* lamented the morals of a drunken populace where 'in their wretched habitations may be found cups and vessels reeking with the deadly poison'. In *Settlers and Convicts* Alexander Harris painted a colourful picture of the Rocks in the 1840s as a den of criminals, ruffians and diseased prostitutes where 'drunkenness, profanity and unchastity are the prevalent habits'. In 1859 Frank Fowler found Melbourne slums 'as bad in every vicious element' as St Giles and 'riot and debauchery ... as vile as Whitechapel'.[41] The novelty of Australia's convict colonies fascinated Britain's reading public and commentators fed that public stories of the fate of London's dangerous classes. Writers, Harris in particular, flavoured their observations of colonial life with liberal doses of pathos and melodrama that echoed the genre of slum literature popular in Britain. It is difficult to separate fact from literary convention and artistic flourish but slums did exist in the colonies. There the poorer classes found casual work and shelter.

The Rocks in Sydney and Little Bourke Street in Melbourne were centres of an informal economy where the unemployed, beggars, waifs and the destitute could make a living. In addition to theft and prostitution there was employment running errands for publicans and sly-grog sellers, rowing boats for others to rob ships moored in the harbour, gambling or minding contraband for local 'fences'. The young 'street Arabs' who sold matches or begged for food were common sights that alarmed clergy, philanthropists and reformers. There were other forms of casual work for the poor. Young Sydney boys collected oysters and sold them at a shilling a quart to wealthy colonists strolling along the harbour foreshores for picnics.[42] Not everyone thrived in this culture. Homeless men, known as Yarra-bankers in Melbourne and 'sundowners' in Sydney, were common sights in 19th century cities.

Another common sight were Aboriginal fringe dwellers. By the 1840s the Aborigines in south-east Australia had been dispossessed of their land. They had few options. Some went into the care of missionaries. Others came under the protection of government officials and survived by earning a living as casual labourers. Edward Curr, recalling his days in the Port Phillip District in the 1840s, saw many Aboriginal fringe dwellers living in camps on the edge of the city. They came into Melbourne to beg or pick up jobs chopping wood, carrying water and other tasks in return for tea and flour.[43] In this way they maintained a sense of independence. In Sydney there were Aboriginal camps in Circular Quay and other parts of the city until the 1870s, before pressure from citizens forced their removal to distant settlements at La Perouse and reserves near the Murray River.

Crime remained an important means of making a living or supplementing an inadequate wage. Isabella Dogherty, a domestic servant, stole four silver spoons from her master and tried to sell

Melbourne beggar. Despite the images of a workingman's paradise, there were also representations of an urban underclass in the colonial cities. (*Illustrated Sydney News*, 8 September 1872)

them. Patrick Cochrane and Hugh Riley were arrested after they rifled the pockets of a man named Butler. Some men formed criminal gangs.[44] In Sydney the 'Forties' was a feared mid-19th century criminal gang, a forerunner of the larrikin pushes that robbed and terrorised passers-by later in the century. Some turned to crime at an early age. In the 1860s William Johnson, aged eleven, stole 67 pounds of lead roofing. Alfred Hoare, aged thirteen, stole screws from a boat and Alfred McDonald, aged nine, stole a watch and pawned it. Bridget Larkins, a fourteen-year-old domestic servant, stole £6 from her mistress. An informal community existed amongst some of the young waifs and strays of the colony. Henry Burgess, aged eleven, slept out and survived for many months, assisted by boys who gave him bread and butter, before his discovery by philanthropists.[45]

By the mid-19th century, Australia was one of the most urbanised countries in the world. Sydney, Melbourne and Adelaide alone had 29 per cent of the mainland white population. Although Australia's colonial cities were extensive, with only 5 persons per acre, well below overseas rates, the population was not evenly distributed. The inner city areas had 60 to 70 persons per acre. Overcrowding owed much to the peculiar character of colonial cities. These were port cities.[46] They were the entry point for British imports and centres for the export of Australia's pastoral and agricultural produce. They were the first point of arrival for immigrant families, many of whom preferred to stay in the city rather than move to unfamiliar country districts in search of work.

The cities were also places where seasonal labourers went to spend their earnings. Workers in the transport industry, who brought goods to the city, usually stayed a few days before returning. Boarding houses, common lodging houses and hotels provided temporary or permanent lodgings for casual and itinerant labourers near the docks, while poor families rented accommodation in the inner city areas. In the 1850s the flood of new arrivals and the return of disappointed labourers from the diggings increased the demand for cheap accommodation, drove up rents and forced families to share lodgings. The construction of new housing failed to keep pace with demand and further exacerbated overcrowding in the colonial cities.

The 1859 inquiry into the condition of the working classes in Sydney found many families 'in distress, destitution and misery'. Unemployed labourers and mechanics with families to support and women with children deserted by husbands going to the gold diggings were the majority of people in distressed circumstances. Their living conditions were 'deplorable'. The committee found a row of

Discovering the urban poor—Clarence Street, Sydney, 1875. Reformers sought to use images such as these to push the cause of moral and urban reform. (Photo courtesy Mitchell Library)

25 hovels sheltering 100 people in rooms 'scarcely high enough for a man to stand in'. In one house of two rooms lived a husband and wife, five children and a lodger. Most houses had no ventilation or sanitation and some had floors lower than the surrounding street. Every time it rained the houses were flooded. Everywhere were 'green pools of mud and putrid water'. The streets were the domain of the 1000 destitute children police found in the city and back lanes of the Rocks and Woolloomooloo. Although the Committee recognised that high rents, unemployment and wife desertion were the causes of this 'misery', its preferred remedies were 'education, sanitation, recreation, active sympathy in the intercourse of the classes, control of intemperance ... and settlement of industrious families on public lands'.[47] These were humane sentiments but were of little practical benefit to the families living in these circumstances.

Boarding house accommodation flourished in the rapidly expanding cities of the mid-19th century. In 1859 investigators found six-room houses in Sydney accommodating 70 people. One large building, they claimed, housed 315 Chinese.[48] In 1860 there were 88 lodging houses in Melbourne's inner city around the west end of

Bourke and Collins Streets. Cheap lodgings stood side-by-side with pubs, brothels, clubs and gambling dens. New 'chums' were met at the wharves and railway stations by touters who directed them to particular houses. There they ran the risk of being robbed by the more experienced inhabitants. Some paid by the week or month, others just stayed for a night. In 1854 the Melbourne *Argus* claimed these houses were places of 'extortion, drunkenness, riot and robbers'. They were also some of the few places that casual labourers could afford to live.[49]

In 1875 concern about the moral tone of the inner-city lodging house culture in Sydney prompted more detailed investigations of the problem. The inquiry drew largely on the evidence of the police who patrolled these areas of the city. Sub-inspector Samuel Johnston knew of 35 common lodging houses on his beat around Hunter and Margaret Streets. Other police pointed to areas around Kent, Clarence and Sussex Streets as the worst in the city. There, in houses such as Niagara House, the Lancashire Lass, Glasgow Boarding House and the Sydney-Melbourne Lodging House, men could get a bed for a shilling or sleep on the floor for sixpence a night. A few houses in Macquarie Street catered for respectable women and there were temperance houses which hoped to shield sober labourers from the temptations of the city slums. The police considered that some houses, especially those owned by Chinese, were little more than brothels. At Cohen's Court couples could rent a bed for a few hours at the cost of a shilling. Most were filthy and overcrowded. A house owned by the Wards in Sussex Street was typical. It had five rooms containing 29 beds. The bedding, when it existed, was rarely changed and riddled with lice and bugs. The rooms were poorly ventilated and in summer the men slept naked. In winter the lack of bedding forced them to sleep fully clothed.[50]

In the 1870s doctors, health officers, politicians and philanthropists voiced serious concern about the colonial slums. Frequent outbreaks of typhoid, sometimes known as the colonial or pauperising fever, and cholera epidemics highlighted health problems associated with slum housing. Doctors noted that the majority of victims of these diseases lived in the poorer districts of the colonial cities, notably Petrie Terrace in Brisbane, Glebe, Darling Harbour and the Rocks in Sydney and South Melbourne, Fitzroy and Collingwood in Melbourne. Mortality from gastro-intestinal diseases in Sydney, Melbourne and Brisbane was twice the rate of London and Birmingham. Between the 1860s and the 1890s infant mortality rates in the colonial cities were twice that of the rural districts and as high as those in London.[51]

Evidence of high mortality rates in the colonial cities challenged claims that Australia was free of the slum conditions of European cities. In the 1870s, when concern about epidemic diseases and mortality rates reached new heights, some blamed the slum inhabitants. Disease was seen to reflect the low moral character of the poor. But investigations, particularly the 1876 Sewerage and Health Board Inquiry into Sydney, added to the stock of evidence that the problem lay in overcrowding and inadequate sewage and waste disposal. This inquiry found a tenth of Sydney's homes unsatisfactory. Other problems were highlighted in this and similar inquiries into Melbourne's noxious trades in the 1880s. Suburbs in low lying and swampy areas had the highest incidence of disease. Sewage drained into the main streets of these suburbs. Waterways were particularly polluted. Abattoirs, tanneries, tallow works, oil and glue factories, soap and candle manufacturers and manure works added noxious wastes, blood and offal to the raw sewage in ponds, creeks, rivers and waterways around the inner city areas.

Attempts to combat these health hazards confronted serious obstacles. There was strong resistance in colonial parliaments to measures to regulate trade and manufacturing. The colonies lacked public health regulations to force firms to dispose of waste without polluting waterways, to facilitate garbage collection by local councils or to restrict overcrowding. In England this type of legislation had been introduced in the 1840s. When comparable colonial legislation was passed in the 1880s it was limited, poorly enforced and ineffectual. Effective solutions were further undermined by miasmic theories of disease. Until the 1880s and 1890s many doctors believed that offensive odours were the source of disease. Attempts to control sewage and waste products aimed to cover the smell rather than properly dispose of the problem. Even when more effective sewerage systems were developed in the late 19th century they were built first in the better-off areas, sometimes draining waste into poorer areas. The residents of poorer districts were the last the benefit from sewerage systems and stricter public health regulation.[52] As a consequence high mortality rates in the inner city areas continued into the early 20th century.

3 Colonial charity

In 1833 an 'emigrant' wrote to the *Sydney Morning Herald*, declaring that 'we should keep away so heavy a burden as the poor laws'.[1] This was an argument repeated throughout the 19th century. The Commissioners of the 1871 Victorian inquiry into charitable organisations saw charity as a means of preventing the introduction of 'the obnoxious poor law'.[2] The attempt by Governor Macquarie to establish self-sufficient local poor relief schemes came to nothing, defeated by the belief that private charity was the best means of assisting the poor. The Australian colonies did not follow the lead of Britain's American colonies, where a Poor Law system had been adopted with little question, in part because Australian colonisation occurred later and at a time of intense criticism of the British Poor Law. The long period of debate about the problems of the poor relief, which culminated in the 1834 New Poor Law and the virtual disappearance of assistance for able-bodied men, made many Australian colonists wary and contemptuous of relief systems resembling the Poor Law.

In the 1820s and 1830s British and colonial authorities recognised that Australia was becoming a place of permanent and profitable white occupation and not just a convict dumping ground. In establishing the institutions of civil society colonists sought to avoid the mistakes of Britain. A parish system of poor relief was impossible in the sparsely populated and scattered outposts of Australian colonisation but poor law principles of a right to assistance, pensions and allowances, and legislative support for poor relief were also rejected. Instead the basis of poor relief in 19th century Australia was private charity and colonial philanthropists applauded the fact that efforts to establish systematic government provision for the poor had been thwarted.

The reality, however, was more complex. Colonial charities survived because they were subsidised by governments. In some colonies, notably South Australia, governments were centrally involved in poor relief and for some groups, such as lunatics, governments provided direct assistance. Colonial philanthropists promoted the virtues or private benevolence but their efforts were underpinned by government initiatives.

Private benevolence

Why was private charity seen as a better means of poor relief than government assistance? One clue to this question lies in the threatened strike by the Committee of the New South Wales Benevolent Society. In 1828 Governor Darling sought a greater involvement in the administration of the Society's Asylum, built in 1821 at government expense. In a dispatch to Britain, Darling quoted the Committee's rebuff:

> should the Government interfere further than it does at present, then the Inhabitants could no longer take any interest in the Institution ... they not only would not subscribe at all, but ... would induce a greater number of the Poor to seek for support from the Asylum, instead of restraining them.[3]

The threat to no longer subscribe to the Benevolent Society was a hollow one. The government already provided almost three-quarters of the Society's annual revenue. The more direct warning was that government control would encourage the poor to seek more support. The philanthropists on the Committee argued that they were a check on the indolence of the poor. How?

Philanthropists established charitable societies on a subscription basis.[4] Anyone could purchase a society's subscriber ticket at a cost of one or two guineas, a price sufficiently high to ensure that only better-off colonists contributed. Subscribers could purchase any number of tickets. They were then entitled to vote in the elections for the organising committee of the society, which managed and distributed the available funds, and could authorise assistance (a recommendation) for a person for every ticket they held. This vested considerable power in members to determine who would receive relief. Subscribers were obliged to guard against the 'idle poor' by inquiring into the circumstances of each applicant to ensure that they deserved assistance. Admission to most charitable institutions, hospitals and homes, or out-door relief in the form of food or medicine was dependent on receiving a subscriber's recommendation.

A direct and personal relationship between philanthropist and applicant was the nub of the charity ideal. If this was established, then philanthropists could distinguish between the deserving and the undeserving. Philanthropists feared impostors. These were the undeserving poor who deceived philanthropists to obtain relief or who received help from more than one society (double-dippers). If philanthropists failed to check imposture then this would encourage pauperisation—people living off charitable assistance instead of working or seeking support from friends and relatives.

This was the central dilemma for philanthropists. How could they fulfil their Christian duty to assist the poor without encouraging imposture and pauperisation? Many placed a high priority on interviewing and investigating applicants for relief to uncover the undeserving. A further safeguard was to ensure that the assistance provided was meagre, just enough to prevent starvation, but insufficient to attract impostors. Philanthropists opposed direct government involvement in charity, such as that proposed by Darling, because they believed that government officers lacked the incentive to adequately investigate applicants. Only subscribers had the personal interest and moral rectitude to scrutinise the poor. This was the ideal, but what was the reality of colonial charity?

From the beginnings of white occupation the government played a dominant role in feeding and clothing colonists. Through the Commissariat, hospitals and asylums the governors had a large measure of influence over assistance for dependent colonists. In the early years of colonisation the circle of colonists wealthy enough to subscribe to private charities was small, leaving many societies dependent on government subsidy to continue their operations unless they could tap other sources of revenue. The New South Wales Bible Society received assistance from British missionary societies. The larger churches had independent means, but even they sometimes called on government assistance. In 1836 the Catholic Church petitioned Governor Bourke for funds to build an orphans asylum and were granted £600.[5]

Although the British government, represented by the Governor, provided the bulk of funds for many philanthropic enterprises, governors generally accepted that the administraton of institutions, asylums and poor relief funds was best left in the hands of clergy, philanthropists and prominent citizens. This was the model adopted by King and Macquarie for the Girls Orphans Asylum, the Natives Institution and the Boys Orphans Asylum. Subsequent governors continued this tradition. Governor Darling funded the Female School of Industry (1826) and many other institutions and charities. In Van Diemen's Land, Lieutenant-Governor Arthur financed the King's Orphans Schools (1828) and provided funds for the Benevolent and Stranger's Friend Society (1829), Maternal and Dorcas Society (1835) and the Hobart and Launceston Benevolent Societies (1835).

The gold rushes greatly increased the pool of subscribers for charities, propelling a significant expansion in colonial philanthropy

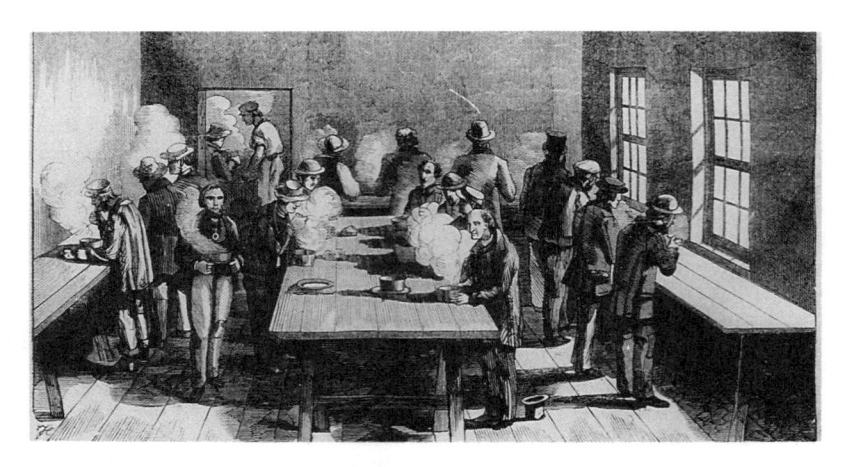

Feeding the poor—the Kent Street Soup Kitchen. (*Illustrated Sydney News*, 7 August 1868)

after 1850. In Victoria the number of charities increased nearly threefold, reaching 400 different societies by the 1870s.[6] In New South Wales the Benevolent Society expanded its operations and a number of other charities were established. Many of these were small local benevolent and district hospital societies which had few subscribers and little government subsidy. The larger hospital and benevolent societies, however, had as many as 500 subscribers and contributions totalling thousands of pounds a year. But this level of philanthropic activity still disappointed some.

In 1861 George Allen, Secretary of the New South Wales Benevolent Society, complained that the extent of charity work was 'disgraceful ... so few people are subscribers and the same people subscribe to them all'.[7] Allen was clearly frustrated at the lack of resources to achieve his goals. But his complaint also reflected the character of many of the colonists attracted to Australia by gold and land. They were more concerned to make their personal fortune than contribute to the 'moral and social well-being' of the colonies. The number of colonists with the wealth, sense of social obligation or evangelical commitment to devote time, money and energy to philanthropy remained small. The churches played a major role in poor relief but many of their activities were moved by sectarian concern. Churches replicated each other's efforts in building asylums and orphanages to ensure that their congregations did not have to seek assistance from the agencies of other denominations.

Even after the gold rushes, governments subsidised many charities. In the 1860s and 1870s they provided half to three-quarters of the funds for most charity hospitals and many of the large societies. This meant governments had considerable influence in determining who would be assisted. In return for subsidies, governors, and from the 1850s the colonial secretaries in each of the colonies, had the power to sign orders, similar to subscriber recommendations, authorising people to receive food or admission to an asylum or hospital. There were other important areas of government influence. In the absence of private efforts colonial governments were directly responsible for the maintenance of lunatics and, in South Australia, Queensland and New South Wales, for the care of the infirm aged.[8]

The nature of government involvement in the administration of charities varied from colony to colony. At one extreme was post-goldrush Victoria, where private charities flourished and there was little direct government influence over the daily running of most charity societies. At the other extreme was South Australia where the Emigration Agent and, after 1849, the Destitute Board was almost solely responsible for the 'relief of the destitute poor'. The Destitute Board was a government body of appointed clergy, philanthropists and concerned citizens directly responsible to the Colonial Secretary. The Board administered the distribution of food to the needy and after 1852, when an asylum was opened, provided care for the infirm aged. Private charities were few and mainly church organisations. In South Australia the direct government involvement in poor relief came closest to the Poor Law model.[9] Poor relief in New South Wales, however, was also centralised. The Benevolent Society was the dominant charity in the colony and although it was a private society it retained close links with the government.

The situation was different again in Western Australia in the 1850s and 1860s, where government provision for sick and infirm convicts existed alongside direct provision for impoverished emancipist and free immigrant families. In Queensland and Tasmania there were few charities and responsibility for the distribution of food and blankets to the poor, particularly in country areas, fell to the police.[10] Despite the high priority given to private benevolence as a safeguard against pauperisation, colonial governments played a large, and often direct, role in the distribution of poor relief.

Women played a prominent role in many charitable organisations. Men controlled the committees which administered the hospitals and large charitites but women were involved in auxiliary committees and as volunteer workers in a great range of charities, many of which were concerned with the problems of women and children— lying-in homes for pregnant women, maternal welfare societies, homes for neglected children, refuges for 'fallen women' and homes for single mothers and their children. Charity was seen as a legitimate avenue of public action for middle-class women.

Some historians have also argued that the evangelical emphasis on morality and social pity which underpinned much 19th century philanthropy held a particular appeal for women anxious to make a contribution to religious and social progress. Philanthropic work was an area of women's power, seen as an extension of their natural domestic role, in a society where public life was dominated by men.[11] Through the efforts of subscribers and volunteer workers, charities were able to provide a wide range of poor relief services.

Out-door relief

Australian philanthropists declared their concern to police imposture and these ideals permeated the activities of many colonial charities. In the 1820s the Benevolent Society stated that 'the great majority come to want and wretchedness through their immoralities' and for this reason 'idle and dissolute impostors ... should not be relieved'. Similar sentiments were expressed in the annual reports of many charitable societies. The competition for scarce philanthropic subscribers led some societies to criticise others for 'encouraging idleness'. 'Better to subscribe to the Benevolent Society' declared the Society's annual report of 1838 for this very reason.[12] Colonial philanthropists eschewed money allowances in favour of poor relief in the form of food, clothing and medicines, in the hope of discouraging 'idlers' who might try to spend money on drink or other 'luxuries'. The principle of 'less eligibility' operated. Food orders, drawn on local stores, or from a society's own stores, were given to successful applicants for out-door relief but these only provided the bare essentials.

By the late 1820s the numbers receiving out-door relief from charities was significant. The Benevolent Society provided food for 100 to 200 families each week. In addition, the Benevolent Asylum admitted 100 to 150 people each year and cared for 50 to 60 inmates each week. Checking impostors was relatively simple. Sydney society was sufficiently small for philanthropists to assert that they knew the 'idlers' in their midst. In 1828 the Benevolent Society identified men such as Hugh McMullen, John Brind and Samuel Haigh as applicants for relief who refused to undertake work tests, preferring a life as beggars to the discipline of the asylum.[13]

In the 1850s charities found a greatly increased demand for food, clothing and temporary accommodation. Few charities kept precise statistics but those that did recorded greater calls on their services, particularly from new arrivals and families deserted by men leaving

The Sydney Benevolent Asylum—an imposing charity edifice. The asylum had a lying-in hospital, and a stores department where the poor queued to receive out-door relief and until 1861 the asylum also housed the aged and infirm. (*Benevolent Society Annual Report*, 1900)

for the gold fields. The South Australian Destitute Board provided out-door relief for over 1000 people in December 1855, a tenfold increase on June 1854. This was a temporary increase but by 1860 numbers had stabilised to two or three times those helped in 1850. Similarly the Benevolent Society increased its out-door assistance threefold in the 1850s, reaching 3000 adults and children by 1860. Hospitals also recorded an increase in the number applying for medical help and medicines in outpatient departments. Melbourne Hospital outpatient numbers increased from 8000 to 11 000 patients between 1859 and 1861.[14]

The increases caused concern. In 1861 Sir James Palmer, Member of the Victorian Legislative Council, declared that the number of out-door cases in Melbourne had grown 'so much as to cause apprehension'.[15] The rate continued to grow despite the fact that the gold rushes were over. The lack of reliable statistics prevents any firm conclusion but the annual reports of many colonial charities in the 1860s reported increasing numbers of applicants. The 1873 New South Wales Public Charities Commission found it alarming that, in a country where the working classes 'were much better off', the proportion of paupers receiving out-door relief in New South

Wales was one in 176 while in England and Wales it was only one in 187 people.[16] Even if the Commission's figures were exaggerated, there were sufficient paupers to disturb philanthropists.

Philanthropists sought to assist the deserving poor and the people most commonly defined as deserving were deserted and widowed mothers and their children, newly arrived immigrant families, the aged, and families of sick, injured or gaoled men. Deserted and widowed families were a large proportion of the poor. By the 1860s they were reported to be half to three-quarters of all the recipients of food and clothing from large charities such as the New South Wales Benevolent Society and the Melbourne Ladies' Benevolent Society. The committees of charity hsopitals, such as Brisbane Hospital, also reported that deserted and widowed mothers were the majority of those seeking assistance in outpatient departments.[17] In the case of deserted wives and children charities had to act because legislation to allow deserted mothers to petition for maintenance was inadequate. A court summons cost a guinea, well beyond the means of impoverished mothers, and even if the court action was successful it was a responsibility easily evaded by husbands if they went to country districts or other colonies. The plight of these groups earned the sympathy of philanthropists.

In 1855 Mrs Hilda Roberts was deserted by her husband and left with five young children, one an infant, and no money or employment. The Melbourne Ladies Benevolent Society found her worthy of assistance and gave orders totalling 15s a week. She was a typical case. In the same year, Mrs Brown, a mother of eight children, the eldest thirteen years, was 'reduced to poverty by the misconduct of her husband' and was assisted by the Society. Mary Matthews struggled to support her four children after the death of her husband. She worked hard for meagre rewards and missed meals to make ends meet. Eventually she collapsed through 'over-exertion' and was supported at the rate of £1 a week until she recovered. The Society was anxious to encourage self-help and get people off the books. Anna Bright, a widow with eight children, was given rent money by the Ladies' Benevolent Society to enable her to save some money to purchase a mangle so that she could work from home as a laundress.[18]

Newly arrived immigrants with no employment, friends or relatives were particularly vulnerable to poverty if they had few savings. Some societies focused their attention on this group. In the 1840s and 1850s the Sydney Stranger's Friend Society and Melbourne Immigrants Aid Society were each helping over 500 families a year. In 1842 Michael Shaw arrived in Sydney with his wife and family of small children but could not find immediate employment. He spent all his savings on food and eventually his landlord sold his possessions for arrears in rent, leaving the family 'quite destitute'. The Stranger's Friend Society provided food and rent till he was able to gain employment.[19]

The neglected and ill appeared often in the records of assisted people. In 1855 the Melbourne Ladies' Benevolent Society found Simon Peters, aged twelve, diseased and entirely destitute in a 'miserable shed' in a back lane. They provided him with food and clothing until he could be admitted to an asylum. Stephen Jones, a young boy with an infected foot, was persuaded to go to the hospital to have it amputated. The Society paid for an artificial foot. In 1857 Brian Keith, 'a hardworking man' with a family to support, lost sight in both eyes after an accident in the quarry where he worked. The Society supported his family in the hope that an operation would restore his sight and allow him to work again.[20]

In Tasmania, where Police Magistrates had a significant role in the distribution of relief, there was a fixed rate of ration for mothers of 2s 6d for every dependent child up to a limit of 7s 6d. Magistrates, however, used discretion to provide extra help for those considered particularly needy or cut assistance to people thought less deserving. In 1871 a Tasmanian magistrate provided only 3s for Mary Hodson, whose husband was in gaol, to support her four children. Honora Cotton, a widow with four children, received the maximum rate of 7s 6d but Catherine Hitlands, deserted and supporting seven children, received 10s. The magistrates helped other people. William Evans, aged 80, was too old and decrepit to work but rather than send him to an asylum the magistrate authorised a 3s food ration each week.[21]

The recommendation system was designed to be the safeguard against imposture, but in the rapidly expanding cities of the 1850s and 1860s there were many who did not know a subscriber. Many charities and hospital committees established investigation and interview procedures. Applicants for relief without a recommendation had to present themselves to a committee to be interviewed about their circumstances. If the committee was satisfied that the applicant was deserving then relief was provided. D.J. Thomas, medical officer at Melbourne Hospital in 1862, confirmed that such tests were 'essential to preserve a spirit of independence among the labouring classes' particularly when philanthropists suspected that many applicants 'were not fit objects of charity'.[22] William Gillbee, a Board member and surgeon at Melbourne Hospital, prided himself on being able to make impostors 'break down when they are investigated'.[23] Other societies paraded their philanthropic vigilance by claiming that they sent visitors to recipients of relief to ensure that they were not lazy, dissolute, earning undeclared income or wasting their money on drink.

Some philanthropists laid great emphasis on charity as an instrument of moral reform. The city missionary societies sought to convert urban 'savages' to Christian habits before giving assistance. In 1858 a volunteer for the Ladies' Melbourne and Suburban City Mission, called to help a starving and sick woman, reported:

> I was called on to visit one of those abodes of wretchedness and infamy in—Lane. In this house, or hovel, lay one of those abandoned females suffering under the fearful consequences of her mode of life ... I tried to fasten on her mind the conviction that loathsome and polluted as was her poor sinking body, her soul was still more loathsome and polluted in the eyes of a just and holy God.[24]

It is not surprising that some communities bitterly resented the intrusion of philanthropists into their lives. Another worker for the City Mission complained that 'in—Street I could do little good. Met with many rebuffs and refusals'.[25] The evangelical fervour of many philanthropists was the hard public face of charity. The private face, however, was more complex.

Close examination of charity records suggests that much of the rhetoric about the evils of imposture and the need for investigation was not matched by action. Some did advertise their success. In 1866 Edward Griffith, a member of the Brisbane Hospital Committee, approved the application for outpatient treatment from a woman deserted by her husband. Twelve months later he refused another application from this same woman after discovering that she had a small infant, proof that she had since found a 'husband'.[26] In 1871 Charles Trevelein, Secretary of the Launceston Benevolent Society, stopped the food ration for Mrs Huskisson, a widow with three children, after hearing reports that she managed a 'disorderly house'.[27]

What is revealing is that philanthropists reported these successes so rarely. Other evidence points to failures. Committees often complained that they lacked sufficient volunteers to investigate applicants. But there were deeper problems. Charity was a gift relationship where the philanthropist hoped that assistance would oblige the poor to be good citizens. But equally, philanthropists needed the poor to demonstrate the moral worth of the giver and this tension was sometimes used by the poor to their own advantage. Trevelein warned that he would cut the rent allowance to Mrs Smith, a widow with four children, because she continued to live in a brothel and kept 'bad company'. Smith, however, threatened to abandon her children and when she received further assistance she took the money, packed up and left for the diggings.[28]

A few philanthropists acknowledged that they were powerless to prevent imposture. John Hudson, Chairman of the Launceston Benevolent Society, admitted there was no preventing imposture. In 1871 he concluded that: 'if we relieve only the deserving poor the task would be light. But the majority are the bad, improvident and the dissolute and their children'.[29] These views were echoed by other philanthropists. Sir James Palmer argued that 'out-door relief was administered in a liberal spirit' but it was not susceptible to checks for imposture.[30]

Some blamed abuse of the recommendation system for allowing imposture to flourish. In 1862 Edward Barker, a Melbourne physician, argued that subscribers to Melbourne Hospital did not have numbered tickets, making it impossible to check whether subscribers had signed more recommendations than they were entitled to. Some wrote recommendation tickets without checking the circumstances of the applicant. D.J. Thomas, a medical officer at Melbourne Hospital, claimed that the Hospital Committee accepted recommendations from people who were not even subscribers.[31]

The 1873 New South Wales Public Charities Commission accepted reports of some subscribers issuing 300 orders in a year, many more than their entitlement. The clergy were serious offenders. John Moon, a district surgeon, found that local clergy were recommending a hundred patients a year to the Sydney Infirmary 'irrespective of their character'. Other offenders were the officers of the Colonial Secretary's departments, who issued charity orders with little concern for the suitability of the applicant.[32]

Some charitable committees were complicit in practices to subvert the rigour of the recommendation system. In 1862 D.J. Thomas noted one such practice. Each morning a crowd of people without recommendations gathered in the forecourt of the hospital hoping to receive outpatient assistance. At a set time in the day a member of the medical staff would send them down to Rody Heffernan's office, a short distance from the hospital. Heffernan, a solicitor, respectable gentleman and subscriber to the hospital, waited in his office and filled out the papers of the morning crowd so that they could receive treatment. He gave scant attention to the applicants and recommended anyone who turned up at his office.[33]

These failures in the recommendation and investigation system point to tensions and conflicts amongst colonial philanthropists. Some placed great store on the evangelical concern with moral reform. Others, however, were prepared to overlook imposture to ensure that the needy received assistance. They drew their ideals from a longer Christian tradition of charity which gave priority to the act of giving. George Allen of the New South Wales Benevolent Society accepted that out-door relief was frequently imposed on, 'but we act upon the old proverb "it is better to let ninety-nine guilty persons escape than let one innocent suffer"'.[34] Samuel Mansfield, Master of the Sydney Benevolent Asylum, admitted that relief was given to the 'undeserving' to 'prevent cases of dire distress'.[35]

Underpinning the anxiety about imposture was the fear that many of the women, who were the majority of applicants, were being supported by men or were supplementing the assistance with earnings from prostitution. But for others this was not the most pressing problem. Many charities, particularly Ladies' Benevolent Societies, provided assistance for 'fallen women' and lying-in houses for unmarried mothers. They hoped that Christian kindness, especially for those women 'seduced and abandoned', would encourage reform. The more immediate problem, however, was to ensure that children, even of 'dissolute parents', were cared for. The 1871 Tasmanian inquiry into charity concluded that out-door relief for the undeserving was 'undesirable' but necessary 'for the sake of the children'.[36]

Asylums

Some of the poor were placed in asylums and hospitals. The infirm aged, blind and sick, incapable of looking after themselves, and the homeless, single mothers, neglected and delinquent children needed care and accommodation more than food relief or employment assistance. The range of charity institutions was enormous. They included hospitals for the sick, asylums for the infirm aged and incurably ill, lying-in hospitals for impoverished mothers, homes for the deaf and blind, inebriate asylums, temporary shelters for new immigrants and the homeless, homes for fallen women, and infants homes, ragged schools, orphanages and industrial schools for children. Some hospitals and shelters assisted people suffering temporary misfortune. But asylums for the blind, incurably ill and infirm aged were a product of the Christian tradition of providing permanent refuge for the unfortunate poor who had no friends or relatives to support them. Schools, orphanages and reformatories drew on a more recent evangelical and utilitarian concern with training and improving the individual. These diverse traditions were readily adopted in the colonies.

Care for the infirm aged was an important priority for govern-

The Parramatta Women's Asylum, 1900—one of the new and expanding government institutions for the aged. (Photo courtesy Mitchell Library)

ments and charities. The early emancipists and immigrants left families and friends behind, and while some established new networks, others had none to assist in times of need. By the 1860s governments and charities faced the problem of the ageing of the large numbers of convicts and settlers who had arrived in the 1820s and 1830s. Between 1841 and 1861 the proportion of the population aged over 60 years rose from 1.91 per cent to 3.05 per cent in New South Wales. This demographic pressure was worse in Tasmania. From the 1840s the exodus of young workers to the mainland, a depressed economy which attracted few immigrants and the ageing of the emancipist population left the colony with an aged population double the proportion of New South Wales, and a significant demand for asylum care. Many colonial asylums recorded increasing rates of admission in this period.

In 1843, 364 people were admitted to the Sydney Benevolent Asylum. By 1861 this figure had increased to 733. In the 1860s there were nearly 500 inmates in the major Melbourne benevolent asylums and a similar number in the Hobart Queen's Asylum. In

Sydney the accommodation pressures and revelations of inadequate resources led the government to assume control of the care of aged and infirm paupers in 1862. New government asylums were opened at Liverpool and Parramatta. By the 1880s they had over a thousand inmates. In the years from 1859 to 1885 the number of inmates in the Adelaide Destitute Asylum rose from 157 to 764.[37]

To be admitted to an asylum applicants had to receive a subscriber's recommendation or government order. Although there would have been little doubt that the infirm aged and incurably ill were deserving, charities retained the rituals of interview and recommendation. Philanthropists and government officials feared that the ready provision of asylum care might allow unscrupulous relatives to off-load their family responsibility. In 1884 R.J. Gray, Under-Secretary of the Queensland Colonial Secretary's Department, bemoaned the absence of measures to compel families to maintain aged, ill and infirm relatives. He cited the case of one woman at Dunwich Asylum whose three sons all had employment but refused to contribute to her maintenance. The superintendent of the Asylum believed that a third of the inmates had relatives and families to support them.[38] For these reasons many philanthropists supported measures to make admission a time-consuming and difficult process. This exacerbated the plight of the unfortunate.

In 1879 Catherine Cashmere, aged 72, was found by police, lying ill in a gutter. They believed she would be best placed in a Benevolnet Asylum but when they found a recommendation would take up to four days they took her to a hospital. There doctors diagnosed her as incurably ill and discharged her as suitable only for asylum care. Police had to place her in a lock-up until a government order could be obtained. Thomas James, a 49-year-old painter, went to police complaining of serious pain. The police tried a hospital but Thomas was refused admittance because there was no doctor or committee member available to sign a recommendation. Believing the case serious, the police tried a Benevolent Asylum but again, because it was late at night, there were no subscribers or government officials to sign an order. The police took Thomas back to a lock-up and went in search of a doctor or subscriber to arrange hospital admission. After considerable delay Thomas was admitted to a hospital but died a few hours later.[39]

The majority of aged and infirm asylum inmates were men. This reflected the sex imbalance in the population. In the 1850s, 70 per cent of those aged over 60 years in New South Wales and Victoria were men. They were 60 per cent in the 1880s. The evidence is partial and scattered but in the 1870s and 1880s there were more than twice as many male inmates as female at the Melbourne Benevolent Asylum, Dunwich Asylum in Moreton Bay and the Sydney Government Asylums. Philanthropists blamed drink and the roughness of rural life. In 1871 Ephraim Zox, prominent Melbourne philanthropist, found the inmates of the Melbourne Asylum to be men 'from the diggings' worn out by 'exposure and intemperance'.[40] Florence and Rosamund Hill, English philanthropists touring the colonies in the 1870s, found that many inmates of the Adelaide Asylum were bushworkers who had 'lost heart' and turned to drink.[41]

Many asylums, particularly those for the blind, aged and destitute, were prison-like. They were places of permanent confinement where warders policed daily routines, and strict rules governed the lives of the inmates. In 1867 the Committee of the Adelaide Destitute Asylum erected a wall round the institution to prevent inmates from going into town for a drink with friends. The 1868 Rules and Regulations of the Tasmanian Pauper Depot give a clearer indication of the extent of institutional regulation:

- Paupers must deliver up all moneys an admission.
- Paupers must provide their own firewood, clean the Depot and perform other light duties. Refusal will lead to reduced rations, confinement and separation from other inmates.
- Paupers who repeatedly refuse to work will be placed on a restricted diet.
- Paupers shall not leave the institution without permission
- Paupers will rise by 6 a.m. in summer and 7 a.m. in winter and will muster before dusk.
- Paupers will not smoke in the dormitories.
- After silence bell in the evenings pauper inmates are not to hold any conversation or be out of bed.[42]

Conditions in asylums such as these paralleled those in prisons and English workhouses. Through these strict measures philanthropists hoped to ensure the smooth running of the asylum and deter people from seeking admission except when all other options had failed.

Hospitals were administered by charities for the treatment of sick paupers. Many workers feared the stigma of this type of care and sought to insure themselves against the costs of sickness and injury by joining Friendly Societies. In return for weekly contributions of a few shillings these societies provided lodge doctors, allowances for time off work and sometimes funeral benefits. By 1880 there were 35 000 Friendly Society members in New South Wales alone. But these safeguards were not available to workers without regular employment to maintain their contributions or to families without a male breadwinner. These people had to seek treatment at hospitals staffed by honorary doctors. Less serious cases were treated in the outpatient and dispensary departments but more serious cases were admitted to in-patient departments for surgery and other treatments. Recommendations, interview or government order were still the main admission procedures but some hospital committees admitted paying patients, usually injured sailors paid for by ship owners, or Friendly Society patients, at a charge of up to 3s a day. Some district hospitals were small but the major charity hospitals in Sydney and Melbourne had over 300 in-patient beds each. An 1878 survey of colonial hospitals found 106 hospitals in Australia making a total of 3805 in-patient beds. Victoria was best served with one bed for every 395 persons, South Australia the worst with one for every 805 persons.[43]

Hospital and benevolent asylums provided an important service for the sick, injured and dying but conditions in these institutions were sometimes less than ideal. Time and again government inquiries found charity institutions overcrowded, dilapidated and filthy. The 1861 Inquiry into the Sydney Benevolent Asylum found that the wards were badly overcrowded and poorly ventilated. There were burial grounds at the back of the asylum and during heavy rains burial refuse drained into the wards.[44]

Conditions at Sydney Hospital were worse. In 1873 Public Charities commissioners found the buildings in a bad state of repair, the wards poorly ventilated and the water-closets broken and infrequently cleaned. Each day the water supply to the hospital was cut off between 3 and 6 p.m. Outpatients had to leave without getting blood washed off and instruments and bandages could not be cleaned. The food was poor. Meat was found boiled black, potatoes mouldy and tea 'sloppy'. The wards swarmed with cockroaches. They crawled over the walls and beds, over patients forced by overcrowding to sleep on mattresses on the floor. Some got into bandages. Patients frequently contracted skin diseases, eye infections, pneumonia and bronchitis after admission. Death was not the end of their woes. The mortuary was infested with rats which mutilated the bodies.[45]

Similar conditions existed in colonial lunatic asylums. In the 1860s the New South Wales Colonial Architect, James Barnet, often visited the Tarban Creek Asylum, near Gladesville, and found blocked water-closets, overflowing drains and rats crawling over the patients. At this time a small group of doctors, clergy and philanthropists pressed colonial government to improve lunatic asylums. Their aim was to turn them from places of confinement for the unmanageable into hospitals for treatment of the morally ill. They drew their ideas from the English 'moral therapy' movement, led by men like Samuel Tuke and John Conolly who argued that a combination of pleasant asylum surroundings, work, religious instruction and the moral authority of the medical superintendent would transform the lunatic into a placid and industrious person able to return to the wider world.

These ideas influenced Frederick Norton Manning, Australia's leading alienist (psychiatrist). In 1868 he reported to the New South Wales government on ways to improve the colony's asylums and focused on more humane architecture, landscaping, education and moral discipline as the keys to 'successful' treatment. Although it was a number of years before the improvements suggested by Manning were implemented, he ensured that moral therapy became an important ideal for the treatment of the insane.[46]

Philanthropists also believed that moral therapy was essential for the care of children. Education, religion and self-discipline were considered vital to transform children from the dangerous classes into useful citizens. This was an early priority of colonial authorities. In 1826 the British government advised Lieutenant-Governor Arthur to establish orphan schools in Tasmania: '[orphan schools] are no less essential as an object of charity than for the general interest of the community by bringing up to industrious habits a Class of Unfortunate Beings, who would otherwise be left without other means of support than what they might obtain by Acts of Violence and Dishonesty'.[47]

Through the use of orphanages, reformatories and schools, churches, philanthropists and moral reformers hoped to remove orphaned, neglected and delinquent children from the morally corrupt environment of the city slums and bring them under influences for improvement in institutions. They believed that children were less habituated to crime than adults, more pliant and more easily influenced by the humane moral force of teachers. In this way, by encouraging habits of self-reliance among children, philanthropists hoped to tackle the root of pauperism.

Philanthropists were anxious to encourage the admission of children to charity institutions. They often discovered neglected and orphaned children while inspecting the back streets and slums of colonial towns and cities. Some child savers worked hard to convince 'immoral' parents to admit their children to their care and resisted attempts by the parents to remove the children. Police cooperated with charities and referred orphaned and deserted children to charitable institutions. In 1828 two boys were brought by police to the King's Orphans School in Hobart after their mother had died and their father returned to England. In 1829 Edwin Brown, aged nine years, was found by police 'wandering about in a state of total destitution'. Both his parents had died and he had lived on his own in the bush near Hobart for a few years. Similarly, in 1836, two brothers aged eight and twelve, were found by police in a park in Hobart. Their mother had deserted them and their father was a drunkard. They were starving and lived on the streets. These were familiar problems even 30 years later. In 1870 police apprehended George Brown, aged ten, after he stole some fruit. His father was dead and his mother could not be found. He lived in some old abandoned boilers on a Hobart wharf, 'deserted, friendless and destitute'.[48]

The gold rush period was a time of heightened concern for the welfare of children. Philanthropists remarked on the great number of children wandering the streets begging. Children deserted by fathers going to the diggings often had to fend for themselves. New charities were established to deal with the problem. In 1852 a meeting of prominent Sydney citizens led to the establishment of the Society for the Relief of Destitute Children. The aims of the society were: 'to relieve them [destitute children] from their degraded, neglected state, to receive them into a place of protection, where they would be under influences for good ... and to train them in habits of honest industry'.[49]

A year later the Society opened the Randwick Destitute Children's Asylum, which, at the height of its significance in the 1870s, accommodated 700 children. Some philanthropists also sought to improve the morals of street children who remained with their parents. The Ragged School system of day classes for poor children, modelled on the British movement, was introduced to the colonies in the 1850s. These schools provided a rudimentary education for the children of poor families. But some schools found that many children did not attend or only attended irregularly because they disliked the routines, while some parents wanted their children to work. In 1870 the Hobart Ragged School Committee boasted that it had 400 children attending classes, but admitted that it had to distribute food and clothes to the pupils to encourage regular attendance.[50]

In the 1860s colonial governments, alarmed at reports of increasing numbers of neglected and delinquent children, assumed more direct control over their education. Through industrial school legislation police were given powers to place neglected and delinquent children in government reformatories. These government institutions provided religious and industrial education for children. The most famous were the nautical training ships—the *Vernon* and later the *Sobraon* in Sydney, *Nelson* in Melbourne and *Fitzjames* in Adelaide—where the addition of naval discipline was thought to encourage obedience and industriousness. Frederick William

Neitenstein, superintendent of the Nautical Training Ship *Vernon* (1878–95) was an impassioned advocate of the industrial school system. A large, Bismarckian character, with an impressive moustache and forbidding countenance, Neitenstein hoped to create a 'moral earthquake' in the boys under his charge. He preferred the strong-willed street child prepared to fight the imposition of discipline because, in his view, 'they invariably became more industrious'. For Neitenstein it was the institutional regime which created the conditions for this 'earthquake'.[51]

The industrial school system ran on a strict time-table. Children awoke at set hours, mustered, performed physical drills, went to classes, cleaned the institution, took religious lessons, and had library hours and meals at set times. The routines of the day were organised to mirror the patterns of the day for industrious workers. Children were educated, given moral instruction and trained in industrial occupations such as carpentry, baking, painting, iron work and farming for boys and sewing, laundry work and the domestic arts for girls. To ensure that they bowed to the moral authority of their teachers strict rules of discipline applied. Neitenstein divided his charges into seven grades, each grade corresponding to particular privileges, responsibilities and diets. Children who misbehaved went to lower grades and those who responded to discipline were promoted.

These patterns of work and discipline were common to all types of reformatories, asylums and schools for children from the poorer classes. In the institution the children could be isolated from the corrupting influences of street life and trained to be self-reliant workers and domestics. It was the enclosed environment which was the linchpin of the moral reform movement. Institutions were designed to be factories for the production of good citizens and workers. This was a bold philanthropic vision and one that shaped the endeavours of those who hoped to stem the tide of idleness and poverty in the colonies.

4 Workers' welfare

In 1850 John Lamb, a spokesman for the anti-transportation movement, declared that 'a feeling of hostility was springing up between the gentry and the middle class, while the passions of the lower orders were becoming inflamed'.[1] This conflict erupted firstly over transportation and later over the composition of colonial parliaments, suffrage, the eight-hour day and land reform. These struggles helped forge alliances between the labouring and the middle classes, led by men such as Henry Parkes, John Robertson, John Dunmore Lang, George Higinbotham and Charles Cowper. These men established colonial liberalism as the dominant political discourse of late 19th century Australia and their message was carried on by liberals such as Charles Pearson and Alfred Deakin. At stake was political power and the right to determine the future direction of colonial settlement. Also at stake were measures to combat poverty. For philanthropists selective charity and moral reform were the means to overcome the evil of idleness which caused poverty. But for radicals and liberals, supported by the emergent labour movement, a prosperous economy, property ownership and a fair day's pay were the best means to ensure that Australia was a 'workingman's paradise' free of the poverty that plagued the 'old world'.

The conflict between philanthropic solutions to poverty and the strategies of liberals, radicals and labour was most acute in the face of the 1890s depression. In 1891 leading philanthropist Rev. J.D. Langley argued that widespread unemployment was best tackled by renewed emphasis on work tests to discourage pauperisation. In the same issue of the *Sydney Quarterly Magazine* prominent liberal B.R. Wise put the opposing view: 'the bulk of poverty cannot be traced to personal vices but are attributable to industrial causes for which the sufferer is not responsible'. The real solution, according to Wise, was trade unionism, land taxation, the minimum wage, and worker co-operatives.[2] This view challenged the philosophy of philanthropy. For liberals, radicals and the labour movement charity might be made redundant, except for an unfortunate few, if reforms with respect to land, labour and wages ensured the prosperity of the labouring classes.

Colonial yeomen

Opening up the land to small farm settlement was one of the significant reforms and great tragedies of 19th century Australia. Many of the immigrants of the 1840s and 1850s were hungry for land. They left a Britain torn apart by industrialisation in search of a life of independence. Many were inspired by the radical and Chartist struggles of the period which pressed the claims of the 'industrious classes' against those of the 'idle propertied classes'. In their view the propertied classes drained off the wealth of workers in the form of rent. Instead the industrious classes should keep the fruits of their labour by working for themselves rather than masters and some imagined that the colonies offered this opportunity. They recalled (but really imagined) a past age, before industrialisation, when yeoman farmers attained a manly, independent existence, and supported a family in reasonable comfort. This ideal inspired the cry of 'unlock the lands'. It was only by breaking the tyranny of the squatters and establishing a yeoman class that the colonies could become 'strong, healthy and populous'.[3]

In the 1860s colonial legislatures passed Selection Acts to facilitate the settlement of a yeoman class. Colonists could select 320 to 640 acres of unimproved land before survey and purchase the land, on liberal financial terms, from the government. The colonial liberals who controlled the parliaments also saw it as a means of ending the hold of the squatters on the land and recouping revenue from its sale. Inadequacies in the legislation suggest that the urban liberals were more concerned with undermining the power of the squatters than with creating a yeomanry.[4] Whatever the real purpose, selection was a financial and human disaster. Many squatters simply bought the land they held as leasehold (a considerable windfall for colonial governments) and others resorted to dummying and peacocking to ensure that they retained the best tracts of land. Contrary to the spirit of the acts, many squatters consolidated their holdings. In Victoria three squatters secured 50000 acres, while in Queensland two controlled 100000 acres near Roma. These practices denied selectors access to decent farming land. Worse, many prospective selectors had little experience of farming and no capital to improve their property or tide them over lean seasons.[5]

H.C. Frederick, who selected land on the Darling Downs in the 1870s, had more resources than most. He had sufficient capital to

Survivors—a selector family near Katoomba, 1900. Those that survived on the land lived in poor circumstances but did their best to maintain an image of respectability, especially on Sundays. (Photo courtesy Mitchell Library)

gain two selections (1280 acres) and begin improvements. His efforts were defeated. He chose the land for its grass cover and its proximity to a number of wells. His annual rent was £192 and he spent £500 on a house, and £240 on fencing. The land had no natural water and his attempts to sink his own well proved fruitless. At 300 feet, at a cost of £1 a foot, he reached brown tepid water which animals refused to drink. After rain his land became a large muddy pond, unsuitable for animals, agriculture or habitation. After spending £1000 on useless improvements he had nothing left and began to fall behind in his payments. He was not alone. With 26 other local selectors, he petitioned the Queensland government for help. He was luckier than some. The government decided he was 'respectable' and did not require him to pay back the money he owed.[6]

Frederick had a head start on some selectors. He had capital and some knowledge of farming but poor land was his downfall. There were many similar stories. In New South Wales, six years after the first Selection Acts, 16 000 selections had been taken but less than half the selectors remained on the land and only 1100 were up to date in their payments. In all the government was owed £4 million by selectors. The success of selection in increasing land under cultivation varied considerably. In South Australia the land under cultivation increased fourfold between 1854 and 1880 but in New South Wales the effect of selection was negligible.[7] But the real costs were human. Many lost their life savings, laboured long hours for no reward and eked out a miserable existence in rough slab huts. Many left their selections, indebted, while others died, suffered serious illness, went mad or committed suicide.

The enormity of the tragedy of the selectors has left its mark on Australian culture. Literature provides some of the most poignant records of the experience. Henry Lawson's 'Settling on the Land' charts the impact of drought, flood, pestilence and conflict with local squatters on a new selector, Tom Hopkins, who eventually goes mad. Barbara Baynton highlighted the plight of women on selections in such stories as 'The Chosen Vessel' and 'Squeaker's Mate'. Women had to help around the farm as well as cook, maintain the house and rear the children. They risked injury, desertion and attacks from passing workers. These grim realities affected many rural families. Struggling selectors, unable to make a living from the farm, left for long periods in search of shearing and labouring work, leaving women to carry the burden of maintaining family and farm. One visitor to the country remarked that selectors' wives 'grow lean and bronzed and hard, prematurely old and sad'.[8]

The yeoman ideal was an image of independence and social stability of broad appeal. But it was out of step with the market. Increasing domestic and international demand for produce favoured larger farms that could concentrate on cash crops, reduce overheads and produce for a mass market. The viability of the independent self-sufficient farm and the small township was undermined by complex changes in the relations between the country and the city. The railway boom of the 1870s and 1880s in New South Wales and Victoria opened up the country to city influences. This created boom and bust conditions for towns sited at rail heads which prospered, then died when the line was extended further. Local flour milling, tool making and clothing industries were undercut by goods from city factories, now easily and cheaply transported to outlying districts. Tradesmen in rural towns found that their prospects for employment contracted.

Railways made it easier for men to travel quickly from district to district following seasonal work, but easy transport of goods to the city encouraged concentration and mechanisation of production in agricultural industries to meet the demand of city markets. In some areas of Victoria there was a fivefold increase in the use of farm machinery in the late 19th century, allowing some farmers to ease the burden on their wives.[9] But for labourers it meant a contraction in employment in agricultural districts. People left the country in search of employment in the cities and this process was accelerated by the serious droughts and rabbit plagues that afflicted eastern Australia from 1894 to 1903. Between 1891 and 1911 Sydney, Melbourne and Brisbane increased their proportion of their States' population by up to 10 per cent, accounting for a third, and in Melbourne's case, two-fifths of the State population.[10] Not everyone prospered there.

Working for a wage

Despite the tragedy of selection many commentators and visitors believed Australian workers were well off. Anthony Trollope, visiting in the 1870s, declared that the 'wages of a labouring man in Australia are about double the wages of his brother at home'.[11] High wages were sustained by an expanding economy and a scarcity of labour. People, then and now, have described the years from 1860 to 1890 as the colonial 'long boom'. The evidence is impressive. In these years Gross Domestic Product trebled. Sustained growth came from the pastoral and agricultural sectors. In the same period the harvest of wheat increased tenfold, the number of beef and dairy cattle trebled and the production of wool increased sevenfold. The rapidly increasing colonial population also fuelled growth in construction and manufacturing industry. In 1860 only 17 966 people were employed in factories, and by 1890 this number had increased to 149 000, 17 per cent of the adult workforce. Underpinning economic growth were high levels of foreign investment, extensive government borrowings to finance the infrastructures for trade (railways, wharves) and urbanisation (roads, sewerage, housing) and increasing productivity.[12]

In this economic climate many workers prospered. Unemployment was low and wage rates high. In the 1880s skilled tradesmen could earn 11s a day, unskilled labourers 7s to 9s a day and domestic servants, with full board, 10s a week.[13] The scarcity of skilled workers drove up wages in some trades but did not always force employers to pay more for labour. In parts of northern Australia and Queensland, labour was scare and employers turned to Aborigines and Pacific Island labourers instead. Aborigines were a vital part of the workforce in the pastoral industry, many becoming expert stockmen, and Kanakas were used extensively in the sugar industry. But racist beliefs in the inferiority of 'native' labour were used to justify poor wages and conditions for these workers. Between 1863 and 1904, 63 000 Kanakas were brought to Australia. They worked long hours for low pay, poor rations and miserable accommodation. The death toll was high, the Melanesian labourer mortality rate being more than three times the average for Europeans in Queensland.[14]

High wages and the scarcity of skilled workers encouraged many employers to seek alternative ways of reducing labour costs and increasing profits. One way was to utilise machines and a greater specialisation of tasks to make more employees unskilled workers. In the 1880s the greatest concentration of manufacturing was in Victoria where there were 59 000 factory workers, a third of the Australian total factory workforce and 20 per cent of the colony's entire workforce. In this decade 40 per cent of Victorian factories employed less than six people. They were usually places where skilled tradesmen gathered under one roof. But large factories and yards were appearing. By the 1880s there were 31 factories employing more than 200 people. A similar trend was apparent in the other significant manufacturing colony—New South Wales. Between 1881 and 1891 the average number of people employed in Sydney factories rose from 18.1 to 29.9. There were some very large enterprises. By 1890 Mort's Dock and Engineering Company employed 4000 men.[15]

The emergence of large manufacturing concerns eroded the market for many skilled tradesmen. Machines meant more employment for unskilled workers and less for some tradesmen. In the 1890s investment in manufacturing equipment in New South Wales increased 30 per cent. The impact of machinery varied greatly. Many trades were unaffected but there were new well paid jobs for engineers and supervisors and in the late 19th and early 20th century can moulding machines undermined tinsmithing, linotype machines eliminated large numbers of compositors, ironmoulders were largely replaced by machines, as were some workers in the baking and brickmaking industries. Other trades were undermined by new production techniques. The increasing use of concrete reduced the call for stonemasons and the replacement of wooden by iron ships eroded employment for shipwrights. Machines were not always necessary. By bringing a few trades under one roof and dividing the production process into a series of simple operations, employers could turn a skilled trade into a few semi-skilled tasks without the purchase of expensive equipment. This was the fate for many joiners and plasterers.[16]

It is difficult to assess to extent to which unskilled labour replaced skilled. There were no general statistics gathered on this problem and the rate of replacement varied from industry to industry and even from firm to firm. Fitzgerald argues that the proportion of unskilled labour in manufacturing in Sydney increased from 10 per cent to 15 per cent between 1861 and 1881. But this was before large-scale mechanisation. A more telling figure is her assessment of occupational mobility. In late 19th century Sydney nearly 30 per cent of sons had less skilled and less highly paid occupations than their fathers.[17]

Not all employers resorted to machinery to increase profit. Just as Australia's reliance on the export of primary produce created casual and seasonal rhythms in the lives of many workers, Australia's dependence on imports of manufactured items, largely from Britain, built casual and seasonal rhythms into work in domestic manufacturing. Many colonial manufacturers merely supplemented overseas orders, filling gaps when there was high demand or a shortfall in imports. This was particularly apparent in clothing and footwear industries. There workers laboured for long hours to meet demands in peak seasons and were then laid off once orders had been filled. In these industries it was unprofitable to risk investment in large plants or machinery. An alternative was to employ cheap female and juvenile labour. The prevailing Victorian ideal of separate spheres for men (work) and women (home) helped justify lower wages for women. Women's work was more likely to be defined as unskilled. Coghlan estimated that half the women in colonial Australia worked at some point in their lives, and a fifth remained workers throughout their lives. Half of these women worked as domestic servants, a quarter in industrial employment and an eighth in shops and offices.[18]

Attempts to assess the extent of female employment are fraught with problems. Census figures suggest that the majority of women workers were single and went in and out of the workforce depending on whether they were needed at home to help with domestic tasks and childcare. These official figures state that only a tenth of all married women worked outside the home, but these figures underestimate the extent of wage work undertaken by married women. They often picked up extra work sewing, ironing and washing to supplement their husbands' poor wages, or to support their children if they were deserted or widowed. These occupations were rarely recorded in official employment statistics.[19]

Although the official rate of women's participation in the workforce remained relatively steady, in the late 19th and early 20th centuries an increasing proportion of these women chose to work in manufacturing. In 1871, 29.6 per cent of women workers in Adelaide and Melbourne were employed in manufacturing and by 1881 this figure had risen to 37.3 per cent. Although there was a slump in the 1890s Depression, the proportion of women in manufacturing rose again to 43.6 per cent by 1911. This increase corresponded to a decline in the attractiveness of domestic service. The proportion of women working as domestics fell from 56.5 per cent in 1871 to 30 per cent in 1911. Women disliked the long hours, loneliness and close supervision of their work as domestics, many preferring the 'freedom of the factory'. Most women in manufacturing were employed in the clothing, food and drink industries where they could earn 15s to 20s a week, less than half the rate for unskilled male labourers.[20]

Women workers lacked the protection of unions, making them an easily exploited workforce. Employers had a range of strategies to cut the wages of their female employees. Some made women work for three to twelve months without pay on the grounds that they were learning a trade. At the end of this period they qualified for a wage of a few shillings a week, thereafter rising annually to a wage of between 15s and 20s a week. Sometimes women had to work for four or five years before they received the standard wage in their industry. In peak periods women factory and shop workers usually worked ten- to fifteen-hour days, six days a week in the clothing trades, in poorly ventilated and ill-lit rooms. In the off season they could be laid-off altogether. Pay was deducted if the women were sick or late for work.[21]

Low wages and poor conditions were not the only problems faced by women workers. In 1891 Miss Leahy, a Brisbane saleswoman, worked from 9 in the morning to 9 at night, six days a week, and after several years her wage had increased to 15s a week. She was paid fortnightly but her employer sometimes refused to pay. At one point she was owed six weeks pay and it became apparent that she would not be paid at all. She was forced to get another job with no means of recovering her loss. Miss Jones, a Brisbane clothing factory worker, experienced a different problem. She earnt 15s a week and paid 5s a week for board, so to save money she walked home from work in the city to New Farm and twice she had been harassed by men on the way. She became too frightened to walk home and had to pay fares.[22]

Outwork was another means of exploiting women workers. Women were sometimes required to take work home or were contracted by middle men to work at home making and finishing clothes. They were paid according to the number of items completed. Shirt finishers could earn 8d to finish a dozen shirts, and coatmakers 1s 9d to make a coat. This was a useful arrangement for mothers who had to care for children or daughters needed at home to help with the chores, but the time and effort involved was enormous. By some estimates a coatmaker took nine hours to make a coat and earn 1s 9d. It is doubtful that anyone could maintain this pace for long and still earn a living. Middle men sometimes deceived outworkers about the price they should receive or took the goods without paying the full amount owed. They could threaten to cancel future orders to keep earnings low for outworkers.[23]

Children were an important source of labour. Families needed children to help with domestic chores or with work around family farms. This fact was recognised by the legislatures which introduced compulsory schooling in the colonies in the 1870s and 1880s. This legislation allowed children to combine schooling and work. In South Australia children only had to attend for 35 days each quarter and there were liberal exemptions to allow children to work at home and help with farm work.[24] But waged work for children was also important. In the 1880s a sixth of all children aged under fifteen were breadwinners. In Victoria in the 1890s 14 000 children had certificates exempting them from school attendance.[25] Boys commonly found work in the tobacco, leather and brick industries, and girls in tobacco, wool and clothing factories. Their main tasks involved carrying materials, packing and picking wool. Some of this was hard work. 'Puggers-up' in brickworks carried 50 pound weights of clay to tables where adults made the bricks.

The wages of children and youths were important to families without a male breadwinner. Percy Blessington, aged eleven, earned 8s a week in a tobacco factory, a sum that helped his widowed mother support her other children. Similarly Edward O'Keefe, ten, worked in a leather factory to help his widowed mother, a laundress, support four other children. James Papp, eleven, contributed 6s a week to the family income. Adelaide Burke, eleven, was even more important to her family's income. Her 4s a week as a worker in a tobacco factory was the sole income for herself and her widowed mother.[26]

Employers could exploit the powerlessness of young workers. As in the case of women workers, some employers refused to pay children and youths wages in their first year of employment and only raised their wages slowly thereafter on the grounds that they had not yet learned the trade. Others just refused to hand across the money, leaving young workers with little recourse but to seek another job. These abuses rarely came to light. One that did was only revealed because the boy involved was a state ward. In 1875 Captain Mein, Superintendent of the juvenile training ship *Vernon*, moored in Sydney, apprenticed one of his charges to a farmer on the Richmond River. The employer allowed the boy's wages to accumulate to £38 without ever paying him and then began to beat him and deny him food. Eventually the boy ran away and the master felt no obligation to pay. In this instance Captain Mein

The sweated outworker. The anti-sweating movement represented the plight of these women in melodramatic terms but their remedy for these low wages and horrific working conditions was to stamp out the trade without providing alternative work for the women dependent on these miserable wages. (*Lone Hand*, March 1911)

believed the boy and took action to recover the wages. Few boys would have had official backing to recover wages if treated in a similar fashion.[27]

The knowledge that women and children were working long hours in noisy, poorly ventilated factories and at home as 'sweated' outworkers provoked cries of outrage from churches, trade unionists, philanthropists and liberal reformers. Anti-sweating, early closing and protectionist associations were established to publicise the plight of exploited juvenile and female labour and to press for regulations to limit their hours of work and improve working conditions. In 1885 the Victorian legislature passed a Factory and Shops Act aimed at reducing the working hours of women and children. But the legislation had no effective mechanisms to enforce its provisions and sensational accounts of exploitation continued in the colonial press throughout the 1890s.[28]

Despite the evident prosperity of many colonial workers there were marked inequities in the labour market. Seasonal and casual labour reduced the earnings of workers whose livelihood depended on high prices and buoyant trade in primary produce. By the 1880s, however, it was apparent that the colonial economies were facing more serious problems. Productivity was declining and this encouraged some employers to seek cheaper labour (women and juveniles) or invest in machinery and equipment to increase production at the expense of skilled tradesmen. More serious problems were also evident with the return of significant unemployment, after more than a decade when unemployment had been negligible.

In 1884 a recession and sharp rise in unemployment in New South Wales prompted the government to investigate measures to ease the condition of the urban unemployed. The Colonial Secretary wrote to magistrates and councils in country districts urging them to provide work for the urban unemployed. The government promised to provide railway passes to enable workers to travel to country districts. The replies were not encouraging. Of the 200 country councils and magistrates that responded only 45 agreed to accept any labourers and then only on the condition that funds were provided for public works. Dubbo Council employed a few men on ring-barking, while Molong Council found a farmer in need of two labourers during harvest time. Most reported sufficient local labour to meet demand or local unemployment. The replies point to regional economic differences; unemployment and underemployment were high in some rural areas despite general colonial prosperity. In Gosford several dozen men were out of work, and in Wyong labourers had to agree to work for local farmers for rations. In Gunnedah, despite a good season, many men were out of work, so it was 'a poor look-out for any man on the tramp'.[29]

In 1887 another rise in unemployment led to the establishment of the Casual Labour Board to coordinate government relief efforts. It received applications for work and organised public works in country districts to employ able-bodied labourers. In two years the Board received 5677 applications and nearly 2000 of these men had wives and children to support. In the first fourteen months the men cleared 31 680 acres of land, built 522 miles of road and constructed

Ridiculing the struggle of the unemployed for assistance. The unemployed fought for concessions in a hostile climate of opinion. (*Illustrated Sydney News*, 2 August 1884)

175 bridges and culverts, earning 2s a day, less than a third of the usual rate for unskilled labouring. The year before a similar agency had opened in Brisbane and in its first six years 7053 men applied for work.[30] But some unemployed did not benefit from these relief measures. Married men were often reluctant to apply for employment that took them up country away from their families and preferred to struggle for work in the city. Despite this the Brisbane and Sydney Labour Boards found they could provide limited work for only half the applicants. Public relief work was expensive and governments could not provide for all. These failings became more evident with the onset of the 1890s Depression.

The 1890s Depression

In the early 1890s tensions between unions and employers erupted in a series of prolonged strikes in the maritime, pastoral and mining industries. Picket lines and mass demonstrations by workers were smashed by police to allow non-union labour to work and striking unions suffered a series of bitter defeats. At the same time a series of international economic disasters, particularly the dramatic fall in world commodity prices and the collapse of the London bond market, plunged Australia into a severe depression. It is impossible to calculate accurately the extent of unemployment. The only available figures refer to unemployment amongst trade unionists, some of whom failed to register because of the 'shame' of their condition. Unemployment was probably as bad, if not worse, amongst non-unionised workers. For trade unionists unemployment rose from 4 per cent to 28 per cent between 1890 and 1893, two-thirds of whom were unskilled workers. Wages for those still employed fell by 20 to 40 per cent in many trades.[31] Others had to become part-time workers as employers wound down their operations. The collapse of some building societies and banks in 1893 robbed workers and small investors or their life savings. Only Western Australia escaped the worst effects of the depression. The discovery of gold there in 1891 precipitated an exodus from eastern Australia. Over 40 000 people left the other colonies to seek their fortune. Not many found it and many married men left their families destitute and dependent on charity.

Charities were inadequate to the task of relieving distress. Many could not meet the increased demands on their services. In the climate of economic insecurity many subscribers were reluctant to continue their contributions and governments found it difficult to maintain their previous levels of subsidy. The Melbourne Ladies'

Benevolent Society admitted that it could not cope and was forced to turn deserving applicants away. The Melbourne Charity Organisation Society claimed to be investigating five times more cases in 1893 than in previous years. The New South Wales Benevolent Society provided out-door relief for 681 families each week in 1893 and by 1897 this figure had risen to a new height of 1196 families. The Committee of the Benevolent Society claimed that never 'has so much distress been relieved'. By some estimates 20 000 families in Melbourne alone received charitable assistance during the depression. Some societies tried to reduce the call on their services. The Charity Organisation Society's rigorous investigation procedures, however, only found that about fourteen per cent of applicants were undeserving. Some hospital committees examined their in-patients to see if any could be discharged. In 1892 the Victorian Parliament passed an amendment to the Police Offences Act making imposture an offence liable to two years imprisonment.[32]

In Melbourne, Sydney and Brisbane there were large street marches by the unemployed. The 'long processions of pipe-smoking men' petitioned parliaments for the right to work. In Melbourne a torchlight procession of the unemployed sang 'La Marseillaise' and stoned the shop of an auctioneer who had seized the goods of families behind in their rent. These protests angered and alarmed prominent citizens. Jacob Goldstein, Melbourne philanthropist, dismissed the unemployed as 'loafers', and sarcastically added that they were led by activists from 'the local Nihilistic Club, the Social Democratic Society and the League for Teaching our Grandmothers How to Suck the Political Egg'.[33]

In this climate of social tension governments acted to deal with the plight of the unemployed and defuse unrest. Governments accepted that some unemployed citizens had a right to assistance. Some, like the 1894 South Australian Select Committee on the Unemployed, believed that unemployment was 'not the fault of the individual'.[34] The traditional recourse to public relief work, however, was severely hampered by the collapse of the overseas bond markets. Colonial governments could not raise the loans they had in the 1880s to finance expensive public relief schemes. Often the men were paid low relief wages for work that was of no value. In South Australia the unemployed had to break stones. But this was quite skilled and they were paid by the quantity of stone broken. Ill, tired and weaker men found this heavy work difficult and received less assistance. One politician, D.M. Charleston, condemned these schemes as only providing 'an animal existence'.[35] These schemes punished the victim and failed to address the causes of distress.

The punitive approach was reinforced when colonial governments cooperated with charities to provide relief work. Philanthropists favoured the extension of work tests in labour colonies, modelled on German experiments, as a means of disciplining labour. This fostered philanthropic beliefs that many unemployed were undeserving and assistance should only be given to those prepared to earn it. In Victoria the Charity Organisation Society, in cooperation with the government, established the Leongatha Labour Colony in 1893. Later the same year a similar colony was opened at Ultimo in Sydney. There men chopped wood and broke stones, usually for no other purpose than to pass the work test, earning between 1s 6d and 4s a day. Leongatha had 3451 admissions in its first year.[36] Men who were unable to participate were denied the opportunity to work for a small dole and had to seek other work or charitable assistance.

Some colonial governments used labour bureaus as a means of coordinating relief work and removing the urban unemployed to the country. In 1892 the Victorian government opened one in Melbourne and in two months 13 000 men had registered. But the Melbourne Bureau failed to find employment for many men and it closed in 1893. In 1892 the New South Wales government replaced the old Casual Labour Board with the Government Labour Bureau, and within a year 18 000 men were registered. The Bureau notified applicants of work in the country and provided railway passes for the successful. Each day 400 to 600 men arrived to read the notices and in the first year 8000 men found positions. But this figure is deceptive. City workers complained that by the time they had travelled up country to take up their position it had been taken by unemployed rural workers, who desperate for work, accepted lower rates of pay. Usually the work was temporary, so at the end of the job the city worker found that he had to spend his savings returning to Sydney to again apply for work at the Bureau. Many employers exploited the circumstances of the unemployed and paid wages well below the going rate for unskilled work. Men became frustrated with the failure of the Bureau to police these practices and the focus of their anger became the Bureau superintendent, Joseph Creer. Whenever he arrived for work the men outside groaned loudly.[37]

Labour bureaus were also designed to discipline unruly labourers. Police investigated applicants and known agitators were rejected as well as 'drunkards, beggars and vagrants'. In Sydney 399 men were struck off the Bureau register after police investigation. Forcing the unemployed to go to the country in search of work diluted labour unrest in the cities. But the system was also used by some employers to undermine the strength of unionists in country areas. In 1892 there were over 700 men locked out of the mines in Broken Hill by mine owners who then advertised at the Sydney Bureau for workers. Prominent members of the labour movement J.C. Watson and

Alf Lindsay declared the Labour Bureau to be 'a positive menace to country workers'. Employer organisations, notably the Pastoralists Union led by Whitely King, also established private employment registry offices in Sydney. They hoped to expand the pool of rural labour, drive down wages and enforce freedom of contract on unionists. They charged the unemployed between 10s and 30s to register and then encouraged them to go down to the government bureau, lie about their private success, and obtain a railway pass.[38]

The actions of police, employers and governments angered workers. They resented the hurdles that prevented them from gaining adequate assistance and the belief that unemployment was the fault of the worker, which justified these punitive actions. In this context the works of English radicals like Henry George, and socialists such as Edward Bellamy, became popular texts for the Australian labour movement. These texts traced poverty 'to the deep wrongs in the present constitution of society'. William Lane's novel *The Workingman's Paradise*, published in 1893, was a powerful indictment of colonial capitalism. For Lane, capitalism impoverished workers, denied men the right to a manly independence and prevented men and women from contracting marriages based on mutual respect.[39] But other sections of the labour movement rejected radical solutions to the plight of workers and their families. They believed that a stronger parliamentary voice for labour was needed to ensure that the needs of workers were met. Their aims chimed in with the growing belief amongst some philanthropists and reformers that charity was inadequate and unemployment not the fault of the individual. In this context, colonial liberals such as B.R. Wise, Alfred Deakin and C.C. Kingston moved to improve the lot of workers as the means of resolving the bitter divisions between capital and labour.

Helping workers

Colonial liberals had never been strict adherents of the doctrine of laissez-faire. Since the 1850s they had intervened to foster prosperity in the colonies by regulating the economy through public investment and tariff policy. Underpinning these policies was an optimism about colonial wealth and progress. By the 1880s this optimism had to be tested against evidence of continuing poverty, unemployment and labour unrest. Some colonial liberals argued that further legislative efforts were needed to guarantee more widespread prosperity. This conclusion was influenced by a broader reassessment of the liberal tradition in Britain, where poverty and labour unrest at home and heightened imperial tensions abroad cast doubts on the legacy of free market liberalism. The limits of imperial expansion seemed to have been reached and some began to question the confident social Darwinist assumptions that progress to higher stages of evolution was inevitable.

There was a lurking anxiety in the liberal mind of the late 19th century. What if the highest stage of evolution had been reached? The British people might be on the point of decline, conforming to an older law of the rise and fall of empires. In this climate of opinion some British liberals, notably T.H. Green, called for a reinvigorated liberal tradition to ensure progress through greater levels of state intervention aimed at achieving genuine social justice. The social crisis of the 1890s increased pressures on colonial liberals to adopt a 'new liberal' program of state intervention. Federation provided a further impetus to establish institutions of lasting importance for the new nation. The resulting industrial and welfare reforms of the late 19th and early 20th centuries earned Australia a reputation as the 'social laboratory of the world'.[40]

High on the new reform agenda were measures to improve the wages and conditions of workers. The two pillars of the liberal program were the white Australia policy and tariff protection. There was considerable pressure from the labour movement to stop cheap Asian labour from undercutting acceptable wage rates. Fear of racial decline from possible intermingling of the races and the threat of Asian invasion gave the white Australia policy a broad appeal. The erection of tariff barriers to foster Australian industry aimed to increase profits and provide the conditions for employers to pay sufficient wages. Other reforms involved the regulation of the labour contract to guarantee decent conditions for workers. These measures were opposed by many employers, who feared the erosion of profits, but curbing the worst excesses of labour exploitation was a high priority for liberals and the labour movement.

In the 1890s and 1900s New South Wales, Queensland, South Australia and Western Australia suppressed the 'truck system' which had been a source of considerable profit for employers and robbed workers of their earnings. Other legislation in the colonies attempted to guarantee rural workers decent accommodation, to ensure that workers owed wages had first call on the assets of bankrupt firms and to make employers liable for injuries to workers. Factory and Shop legislation required employers to improve work conditions to reduce workplace accidents. In 1910 these measures were supplemented by worker's compensation legislation.

In a typical year such as 1913, 52 workers were killed on the job and a further 1087 suffered injuries that laid them off work for more than fourteen days.[41] While some of these workers were assisted

A new and improved factory—Vicars Woollen Mills, 1922. Using machinery and female labour were means of increasing productivity and lowering the wage bill. (Photo courtesy NSW Government Printing Office)

by Friendly Societies, not all workers, particularly casual workers, could afford to protect themselves and their families from the consequences of serious illness and injury. Worker's compensation was an important safeguard for those families threatened with destitution from the death or injury of the male breadwinner.

Protecting juvenile and female labour was a continuing concern. By 1890 only Victoria had passed Factory and Shop legislation to limit the hours of employment and improve working conditions for women and juveniles. In the 1890s and 1900s extensive Factory and Shop legislation was enacted in the other States. There was widespread concern that long hours of labour in dangerous, poorly ventilated and unsanitary conditions robbed families of their mothers and undermined the health of women and juveniles. In the 1900s these fears were exacerbated by revelations about the decline in Australia's birth rate. Many concluded that national vigour was being undermined and the future of the race threatened by the poor health of women workers and their refusal to fulfil their duty as mothers. At the 1911 New South Wales inquiry into female and juvenile labour doctors argued that long hours and poor working conditions were responsible for a high incidence of ulcers, varicose veins, pelvic inflammation and tuberculosis amongst factory workers, burns amongst laundry workers, lead poisoning amongst blind makers and serious infections amongst women in the furniture trades. The report concluded that 'the present working week was too great a strain on women and boys'.[42]

Concern about the future of the race and mounting medical evidence of illness and injury gave impetus to efforts to extend protection for juvenile and female workers. By 1914 employers were required to prevent women and boys from using dangerous machinery and had to provide clean, sanitary work conditions, special meal rooms, toilet facilities, drinking water, and to prevent the premises being used as sleeping quarters. Children under the age of fourteen, except in South Australia where the age was thirteen, could not be employed in factories. In particular trades, such as typesetting, brickmaking, glass melting, salt making, lead manufacturing, silvering of mirrors and mercury processing the minimum age of employment was usually sixteen for boys and eighteen for girls. Boys under sixteen and women could not work between 6 in the evening and 6 in the morning, although some States extended the time to 9 in the evening for women. Children under sixteen could not work for more than five hours without a break and there were limits on the amount of overtime that could be worked. Similar hours applied to women and juveniles serving in shops with exceptions in the case of tobacconists, druggists, newsagents, food outlets and hairdressers. Inspectors were appointed under the Acts to police these regulations and recommend fines for infractions.[43]

The increasing regulation of female and juvenile labour encouraged some employers to turn to outwork to maintain profits. Factory and shop inspectors found this practice difficult to police. Although the Acts required employers to keep a register of all outworkers and their wages, and in Queensland and Western Australia sub-letting was forbidden, these regulations were difficult to enforce.[44] Women had little interest in reporting exploitative masters or subcontractors as outwork was one of the few ways they could earn a living and look after their children.

In 1911 Annie Duncan, New South Wales Factory Inspector, found many women workers 'helpless through poverty and want of cohesion and legislative protection, [outwork] is made large use of by manufacturers and warehousemen, at most inadequate rates of pay'.[45] But she also found that outwork was an important source of income for many families. Annie B, the wife of a plumber seriously ill with lead poisoning, managed to support her family by working at home. Another widowed mother supplemented the few shillings she received from the government to support her children with home work, and managed to support them 'by dint of long hours of toilsome work at the machine'.[46] Justifiable attempts to stamp out outwork threatened to rob some families of their livelihood, because they were not matched by efforts to safeguard their employment and pay them a decent wage.

The poor wages and conditions for many women workers prompted private solutions. In 1900 feminist trade unionists in Adelaide formed the Working Women's Trade Union and opened the Women's Co-operative Factory and Women's Mending Bureau. Through these organisations women were given sewing, darning and other work in the clothing trade for a wage of 25s a week. The Union organisers recognised that these wages were lower than they hoped because of competition from commercial manufacturers, but they were still 5s to 10s more than the prevailing rates for women workers and the Union provided a sick pay scheme. The Union attempted to establish links with philanthropists and prominent women citizens to encourage them to buy from the Factory and the Mending Bureau.[47] These efforts aimed to provide women workers with decent wages and conditions, but they ran counter to other efforts to reduce women's employment.

Underpinning Factory and Shop legislation was the belief that women and children should not be working. Their place was in the home supported by male breadwinners. If this ideal were to be achieved mechanisms to ensure wage justice for men were vital. This was an important platform for the labour movement and part of the liberal social reform program. Alfred Deakin argued that 'permanent prosperity can only be based upon institutions which are cemented by social justice' and that this was best achieved through 'an impartial tribunal with the state behind it'.[48] The 1896 Victorian Factory and Shops Act established wages boards to determine minimum wage levels in the 'sweated' industries. The principle was extended in 1900 with wages boards for a wide range of industries. South Australia (1900) and Queensland (1908) adopted a wages board system. New South Wales in 1901 and, in 1904, the Commonwealth established conciliation and arbitration systems, administered through special courts.[49] This was an unwieldy and complex set of institutions but they provided the means for labour to negotiate a measure of wage justice.

The 1907 Harvester judgment of H.B. Higgins has been seen as the landmark decision in the Australian arbitration system. Higgins attempted to establish a minimum wage that would be sufficient to allow male workers to support a wife and three children in 'frugal comfort', and determined that such a wage was 7s a day. The concept of a minimum 'living' wage was opposed by many employers. One South Australian manufacturer argued that it would deprive 'the weak of earning a living up to their capabilities'. Others argued that industries could not afford to pay. Such objections were undermined by the gradual introduction of the living wage principle in all wage tribunals at State and Federal levels. But the introduction was slow, fought on an industry by industry basis, ensuring that powerful unions won early decisions while unskilled and poorly organised workers, those most in need of assistance, were the last to achieve benefits. By 1914 barmen, dairymen, cooks, farriers, ironworkers and many others received less than the Harvester minimum. It was not until the 1920s that the 'living wage' became applicable to a significant majority of male workers.[50]

The living wage was a powerful instrument for wage justice but it had serious flaws. Higgins had given little thought as to whether 7s was adequate and workers complained that increases in the minimum wage failed to keep pace with the rising cost of living. In 1920 the Hughes government, under mounting pressure from the labour movement, established the Commonwealth Basic Wage Royal Commission to determine adequate measures for a minimum wage. The Commission undertook a detailed investigation of the cost of the basic items deemed necessary for 'frugal comfort'—rent, food, clothing, fuel, school and medical fees, household items and recreation—and concluded that an adequate minimum wage was £5 16s a week, more than £1 above the actual minimum wage level used in the Federal arbitraton court. The Commission was attacked by employers for its extravagant estimations of family needs while the labour movement considered them too frugal.[51] Although the Commission's findings were never implemented, its report revealed that the living wage was closer to a subsistence level than one of frugal comfort. Added to this was that the needs of workers with large families were ignored under the Harvester system, which only allowed for three children.

The living wage principle did not assist women workers. In Victoria attempts by the Wages Board to eradicate 'sweating' resulted in only small wage rises for women. The 1908 Victorian Minimum Wage Act set wages at 4s a week for milliner and dressmaker apprentices, well below the male Harvester minimum. At the Federal level Justice Higgins was also instrumental in establishing different principles for women's wages. In the 1912 Fruit Pickers case he set the 'living wage' for women at half the male rate and in 1919 the Commonwealth reaffirmed this ruling by declaring the female basic wage to be 54 per cent of the male rate. These decisions assumed that women did not have dependents to support. In some industries, however, unionists pushed for equal pay for women. In 1909 female cutters in the clothing industry were granted equal pay but this meant they were no longer a source of cheap labour.

Raising women's wages, limiting the hours they could work and improving working conditions made female labour less attractive to employers. Unions pressed to have women's work defined as unskilled and poorly paid, or fought for equal pay to exclude them from a trade while men struggled to define their work as skilled, with commensurate wages. Underpinning these struggles were prevalent beliefs that a woman's place was in the home while for men it was unmanly to perform women's work or be supported by them. Men were meant to be the breadwinners.[52] Protective wages and hours legislation served to cement this ideal. But this legislation failed to address the problems of families without a male breadwinner.

5 Pensions and pills

In 1895 Professor Edward Ellis Morris, President of the Melbourne Charity Organisation Society, confidently stated that the best means of combating poverty was private philanthropy. Investigation and work tests were essential to encourage self-reliance because 'demoralisation occurs from giving alms'.[1] There was nothing new or surprising in such a statement but Morris' insistence on the necessity of philanthropy masked considerable anxiety. He believed that philanthropy was in a state of crisis, undermined from within by charities too willing to provide assistance and challenged from without by socialists and liberals who turned to the state to solve society's ills. The roots of this crisis lay earlier in the 19th century.

By the 1860s philanthropists and reformers were questioning the effectiveness of asylums as instruments of moral reform and urging greater government intervention to assist neglected and delinquent children. By the 1880s the persistence of poverty, crime and drunkenness suggested to many that the causes of these problems lay deeper than early 19th century reformers and philanthropists had imagined. What was the solution? For some the answer lay in renewed evangelical efforts to improve the poor and Morris was in the forefront of this movement in Australia. But Morris' call for renewed philanthropic endeavour was uttered against a tide of opinion which believe that poverty was due to social and economic conditions, rather than idleness.

The lessons of unemployment and labour unrest in the 1880s and 1890s were crucial. Liberals began to focus on the imperfect workings of the market as the origin of poverty. Radicals and labour activists turned their attention to the exploitation of workers by the better-off classes. These arguments and the failure of many charities to alleviate poverty also had an impact on some clergy and philanthropists. At the 1890 Charity Organisation Society Conference Rev. A. Macully of Melbourne argued that 'those who blame the victim and treat the subject in this off-hand fashion have given it little attention ... depressions are a major cause'. Even some city missionaries, one of the most committed evangelical groups, began to doubt that immorality was the sole cause of destitution. In 1898 Frederick Leak and Thomas Harkness, two Adelaide city missionaries, found want of work to be a major cause of poverty.[2]

These arguments represented a small but decisive break with the colonial charity tradition. While some like Morris reaffirmed their faith in private solutions, a growing body of opinion turned to the state to remedy poverty. This paved the way for the industrial and wages legislation which aimed to improve the lot of poorer workers. But the state was also seen as an instrument to be used to better manage the problems of other poor populations, such as the aged, dependent women, the ill, and neglected children. Increasingly governments turned to direct payments to the poor as the solution. During the 1890s liberal and labour opinion began to support the idea of pensions for the aged and infirm in preference to charity. In supporting the 1900 New South Wales Old Age Pensions Bill, William Morris Hughes argued that 'the basis of this Bill should be that all men, by reason of their citizenship, should be entitled to a pension'.[3] This was an important break with philanthropic beliefs that assistance was a benevolent gift granted to the deserving only.

Philanthropy faced other challenges. In 1911 the editor of the *Australasian Medical Gazette* urged doctors to assert their role in diagnosing and solving social problems: 'as the most important and largest organised scientific body in Australia, we should make some endeavour to guide public thought along scientific lines'.[4] Medical science was seen as an alternative to the moral focus of philanthropy, offering new ways of seeing old problems and new methods of social intervention. Science became an attractive solution because moral reform seemed to have failed to alleviate many social problems. By the turn of the century the philanthropic belief that poverty was best relieved by encouraging self-reliance and moral improvement was being questioned from many quarters; by a few philanthropists, whose faith in traditional methods of poor relief and moral reform declined, by those who believed assistance should be a universal right not a form of selective benevolence, and by doctors who argued that many social problems associated with poverty had medical solutions. These challenges altered the face of poor relief and social reform in 20th century Australia.

New charity

In 1890 Edward Ellis Morris organised a charity conference in Melbourne to provide a forum for discussion of the ills of charitable relief and the 'new' methods needed to combat pauperisation. As a young man in England, Morris had been influenced by the founder of the Charity Organisation Society, C.S. Loch, who believed, like many other philanthropists, that charities should assist the deserving and not the undeserving, to prevent pauperisation. But in his view charities were failing in their duty to police imposture, and a more rigorous and centralised system of investigation was needed to ensure that the undeserving were not helped. In 1878 Morris arrived in Australia determined to pursue this aim. The establishment of the Charity Organisation in Melbourne in 1887 was one step. The charity conference, and a subsequent conference in 1891, were aimed at spreading Morris' message about the need for 'scientific' or 'new' charity.[5]

What was wrong with the provision of out-door relief in the colonies? Morris and other conference participants found too many small charities all doing the same work with little cooperation to prevent double-dipping. Morris argued that the 'old idea of charity as a local endeavour' of the better-off classes was 'impractical, wasteful and ineffective'.[6] Charity allowed too many loopholes. A centralised charity authority would coordinate the activities of different charities and provide the means for a general register of charity recipients to guard against imposture, and help in the search for wife deserters and others who neglected their social obligations. Those who valued giving alms for the sake of giving undermined the higher purpose of charity. For Morris, women in the Ladies' Benevolent Societies were particularly to blame. He argued that they were indiscriminately generous and incapable of clearly distinguishing the deserving and the undeserving. Women were useful helpers in the role of visitors but they were less skilled at making the crucial decision about entitlement. Morris' scientific charity was an attempt to wrest control of alms-giving from the hands of worthy ladies and put it under the control of male, scientific experts.[7]

There was nothing very new about 'new charity'. Its concern with philanthropy as an instrument of moral reform echoed evangelical concerns that had been voiced for many years. What Morris offered, however, were new methods and techniques to make the old tasks of investigation more efficient. Morris believed that volunteers to visit families receiving relief were weighed down by too many cases and incapable of investigating each case in detail. Visitors needed to concentrate their activities, take a smaller case load, and study the circumstances of each case in depth. Nor was it adequate to appoint visitors merely because they were worthy citizens prepared to help. Visitors needed training to understand the best means of encouraging self-reliance. For prominent Charity Organisation Society philanthopist, Col. Goldstein, this training had to be in sociology because 'socialism is theoretical but impracticable ... sociology is scientific and must be practicable'.[8]

The science of sociology supposedly taught that individuals were formed by their environment, revealed the nature of those environments and provided guidance on the best means of changing the environments that bred pauperism. Conference delegates such as H.L. Jackson, Goldstein and Morris affirmed that scientific charity was the key to reviving charity as a means of moral reform, purged of the loopholes that had undermined philanthropic endeavours in the past. A scientific approach would obviate the need for indiscriminate government intervention, which might foster pauperism, would restore the spirit of self-reliance and counter the disturbing growth of socialism as a solution to society's ills.

Morris' campaigns for charity coordination were thwarted by sectarian rivalries and fears by some charities that organisation would rob them of their poor relief role. At the first charity conference Catherine Helen Spence, prominent Adelaide philanthropist, praised the intentions behind 'scientific charity' but argued that South Australia had no need for a coordinating body as the government's Destitute Board already performed this function.[9] Representatives of the New South Wales Benevolent Society, the colony's dominant charity, demonstrated little enthusiasm for plans to coordinate their activities. Nor did the Catholic Church have any interest in bringing their activities under the umbrella of Morris' Protestant movement. Although the Charity Organisation Society articulated widely held philanthropic beliefs it was only in Victoria, where there was a plethora of small charities, that the Society had an important practical role. Despite this Morris and the new charity movement were symptomatic of larger tensions and anxieties.

In late 19th century Britain, America and Australia there were growing fears amongst the middle classes that poverty, crime and illness were increasing and socialism was being seen by workers as the solution to their misery. In this context there were renewed philanthropic and evangelical efforts to combat poverty and restore the spirit of self-reliance amongst the working classes, and the number of charities began to multiply, contrary to Morris' conviction that more centralisation was necessary. In the 1880s and 1890s important new charities and church organisations, notably the Salvation Army, St Vincent de Paul Society, Central Methodist Mission and the Queen's Jubilee Fund were established in the Australian colonies. In addition the number of small local charities proliferated. These charities and churches operated a diverse range of services—children's homes, night shelters, soup kitchens, hostels for the homeless, food distribution depots and prison gate brigades.

The beginnings of private charity in Western Australia. The new Ministering Children's League Home. (*Cyclopaedia of Western Australia*, 1913)

Local factors sometimes accelerated these processes. During the 1890s gold rush in Western Australia the colony's population trebled, providing the impetus for the growth of private charity. In that decade many new church organisations and local charities, such as the Ministering Children's League, began to assist the colony's poor, supplementing existing government efforts.[10]

Some evangelicals and philanthropists, however, believed that increasing charitable work or improving its efficiency would not tackle the cause of much poverty and misery. In their view the real problem was the man who drank too much, who wasted his earnings on drink, failed to provide for his family, was violent and often deserted his family, leaving his wife and children to seek charitable assistance. By the 1890s Miss Selina Sutherland, secretary of the Melbourne Ladies' Benevolent Society and energetic charity worker, accepted, like many other philanthropists, that moral weakness was the cause of poverty but increasingly she focused on the male 'sinner'. Like-minded reformers thought the temperance movement offered the best means of lasting moral reform.

The first colonial temperance movement flourished in the 1830s and 1840s. These reformers considered drunkenness a vice, cured only by abstinence, and to this end temperance reformers sought to persuade people to take the pledge. The movement lapsed but revived again in the 1880s. The second wave of temperance was one of the largest social reform movements of the century. The new temperance groups found the old strategy of moral suasion ineffective and instead lobbied governments for legislation to restrict access to drink. They were condemned by brewers, workers, and radical journals such as the *Bulletin* as 'wowsers', but their campaigns for prohibition, local option and early closing legislation drew considerable support from Protestant churches, a few radical workers, such as William Lane, and the thousands of women who joined the Women's Christian Temperance Union. In the experience of many women, reformers and philanthropists, drink, and more importantly the male drinker, was the cause of much poverty and misery and the temperance movement attempted to address this problem.[11]

Some women viewed these problems in a different way. Nineteenth and early 20th century feminists agreed that women and children suffered at the hands of drunken husbands but believed that the problem was not just drink but broader structures that left women unprotected against the more aggressive male sex. Feminists, such as Rose Scott and Vida Goldstein, believed that men's power to dominate women and their lesser control over their instincts, or what Scott called 'the animal in man', meant that women were the victims of male passions. The cost of leaving women unprotected could be counted in the seduction of young women, abortion, illegitimacy, prostitution and family desertion, all of which meant women and children were the bulk of the poor. In this context feminists campaigned on many issues to safeguard women and children: to ensure that husbands with property provided for their family in their will, to raise the age of consent from fourteen to sixteen years, to improve women's access to maintenance from deserting husbands, to improve employment prospects, wages and conditions for women workers, and to secure the appointment of women police and prison officers so that 'fallen women' would not be mistreated by male officers. The struggle for the vote was the means to these ends. The vote would give women the power to influence the legislatures to act in the interests of women and children.[12]

Feminists and temperance advocates turned to the state as the only authority with sufficient power to bring about reforms unattainable by the private methods of philanthropists. Their diagnoses of the cause of poverty and misery differed, as did their solutions, but they were part of a broader stream of opinion dissatisfied with philanthropic efforts to combat poverty and related social problems. This reflected a broader conflict between those, like Morris, who believed private efforts were still the answer and the many who turned to the state as an important instrument of social improvement. Two important areas of struggle were child welfare and pensions.

Child welfare

In 1867 the children at the Brighton Reformatory School in Adelaide were moved to the Exhibition Building to provide quarters for the military. Conditions at the Exhibition Building were inadequate. Children were forced to sleep four and five to a bed and lack of staff meant that bedding and clothing were rarely changed. The food was poor and diarrhoeal disease was endemic. Children were left in their beds in a 'filthy state' for many days, some became severely emaciated and a fly plague spread eye infections. Other diseases took their toll. Three or four children developed gangrene of the mouth after contracting measles and died. It was an affair that shocked Adelaide's liberal and philanthropic elite, the more so because few attempts were made to arrest the situation.[13]

The fate of the children at the Brighton School was an alarming revelation of conditions in a 'child-saving' institution but it was not the only report that unsettled colonial philanthropists. In the late 1860s and early 1870s newspapers reported poor conditions, inadequate attention to reform and even riots at asylums such as the St Kilda Industrial School and Biloela Girls' Reformatory in Sydney. Investigations concluded that these institutions were little better than prisons, where children were massed together with little thought of education or reform. The 1873 Public Charities Royal Commission in New South Wales, chaired by prominent lawyer and reformer William Charles Windeyer, investigated conditions at Biloela further and found the asylum bleak and objectionable. Worse was the violence meted out to the girls by staff. Black eyes, bruises and bloody noses seemed to be common and staff resorted to gags and jackets to control inmates. The Commissioners visited the institution a few days after a riot and found some of the offenders locked, half-naked, in cells. This was far from the reformatory ideal of philanthropists.[14]

The evidence uncovered by these inquiries did not indicate a sudden decline in asylum standards but a new consciousness that made asylum conditions a more urgent focus of concern. By the 1850s and 1860s the persistence of poverty and juvenile crime led some British philanthropists to question the efficacy of asylum reform. They began to document abuses of the asylum ideal and offered in its place a scheme of placing children with families. In the colonies this proposal met early resistance. In 1866 the Committee of the Hobart Queen's Asylum for children had 'grave doubts' about the benefits of the 'farming out' principle.[15] Others, however, were attracted to the idea and turned a critical eye on the colonial institutions. Their reports of riots, ill-treatment and horrible conditions in colonial orphans asylums, industrial schools and reformatories paved the way for reform.

In South Australia Emily Clark and Catherine Helen Spence were outspoken critics of reformatories in the colony. They were instrumental in inviting Miss Clark's cousins, Florence and Rosamund Hill, to Australia. The Hill sisters were noted British philanthropists particularly concerned with child reform. In 1873 they toured the colonies and their reflections, published two years later, were less than flattering. The Randwick Destitute Children's Asylum was a target of particular criticism. In their view reform was impossible in an institution where 'several hundreds are massed together'.[16] Windeyer agreed. The problem was more than poor facilities or cruel staff; it lay, as the Hills saw it, in the nature of institutional life. The Public Charities Royal Commission concluded that 'the barracks bred barrack children', adapted to the rhythms of institutional life and not to the rigours of being a useful worker in the wider society.[17]

These arguments were not a radical break with earlier views that reform was best achieved by removing children from the street environment that bred vice and immorality. The dispute was over the best environment for reform. Critics of reformatories still believed that reform was possible, but not by sending children to an asylum where they were treated like criminals and were more than likely to lapse into 'bad habits' upon release. The best environment for reform was the family. The Hill sisters argued that 'home influences are essential for reform' and without such influences neglected children, orphans, waifs and delinquents 'would not become useful members of society'.[18] The key to reform for Clark, Spence, the Hill sisters, Windeyer and others was boarding-out. Children still needed to be removed from the corrupting environment of the city slums but instead of being placed in asylums they needed to be boarded-out, either in small cottage homes which conjured up a family atmosphere or with actual foster families. There children would benefit from the civilising influences of 'proper' mothers.

The first boarding-out experiments began in South Australia. In 1872 Emily Clark convinced the Destitute Board to transfer 200 children in the Board's institutions to cottage homes. In 1881 a more ambitious experiment was initiated by Mrs Windeyer, Mrs Garran and Mrs Jefferis. They successfully persuaded the New South Wales government to establish a new authority, the State Childrens Relief Board, charged with implementing a boarding-out policy for children in government orphanages and industrial schools. Families which accepted boarded-out children received 5s a week for each child in their care, while the Board used the services of paid inspectors and lady volunteers to inspect these homes to ensure that the children were properly cared for.[19] Other colonies took longer to adopt the boarding-out system. In 1900 boarding-out was still in its infancy in Western Australia because government officials believed that there were not enough suitable homes in the colony.[20]

Boarding-out, however, greatly increased the number of children under some form of state supervision. In 1881 there were just over 3000 orphaned, neglected and delinquent children in government industrial schools and reformatories. By 1911 there were 17 731 children receiving direct state assistance in Australia and three-quarters of these were fostered. The remaining quarter were kept in institutions but the character of the institutions was also changing. The large institutions were closing. By 1914 most of the juvenile naval training ships had closed and in 1916 the Randwick Destitute Childrens Asylum shut its doors. They were replaced by small institutions, cottage homes and farm colonies, usually for repeated delinquents and physically and mentally handicapped children.[21]

Foster care was not the only policy responsible for the decline of institutional care. Arthur Renwick, President of the New South Wales State Childrens Relief Board (1881–1902), found that there were not enough suitable foster parents and cottage homes to cope with the number of neglected and delinquent children apprehended by police and philanthropists. In the absence of suitable boarding-out facilities, Renwick concluded that it was better to maintain children at home than in an institution. In 1896 the government introduced a boarding-out allowance, so that instead of removing children the government would assist impoverished, deserted and widowed mothers to maintain their children at home. This was certainly a cheaper alternative than foster or cottage home care. The allowance for mothers was usually 2s 6d a child, a meagre sum, only half that provided to foster parents, and applicants were subjected to interviews and visits from the Board's officers to ensure that they were deserving.

Some mothers feared state interference. Mrs Roberts, a widow with four children, rented a small, dilapidated two-room house in Chippendale, Sydney, at a cost of 5s a week. The family received food from the Benevolent Society and a rent allowance of 2s 6d a week. She earned 12s a week, but one of her children was ill and

PENSIONS AND PILLS 93

The new cottage home. These smaller institutions became the model for child savers in the late nineteenth and early twentieth centuries. (Dalwood Home, *Annual Report*, 1921)

her eldest boy, who had lost an eye in an accident, was kept home from school so he could supplement the family income by collecting rags and bottles for sale. They had few blankets or clothes. A neighbour occasionally gave them some wood, especially during the winter months.

In 1898 the Public Charities Royal Commissioners visited and found them 'in a pitiable state of destitution'. The Society's relief was clearly inadequate and the Commissioners urged Mrs Roberts to apply for the boarding-out allowance. She had not heard of the benefit but feared that her children would be taken away.[22] Her suspicions may have been unfounded but ignorance of the allowance and understandable concern about official scrutiny prevented some families receiving assistance. But many others were desperate for help, even the meagre allowance, and this allowed for a significant expansion in the number of children under some form of state surveillance. By 1914, in addition to over 4000 children fostered and in institutions, the State Childrens Relief Board maintained 5000 with their own mothers.[23]

The exception to these policies was Aboriginal children. In the late 19th century, governments in Victoria and New South Wales attempted to minimise the costs of maintaining able-bodied Aborigines on government reserves by refusing rations to Aborigines of mixed descent aged under 34 years. This was a policy of forced assimilation. Many believed that the Aborigines were a dying race, doomed to extinction because of their failure to 'civilise'. Reserves became places for 'full-blood' Aborigines to spend their 'dying' days while others had to be absorbed into the wider community as useful workers. In 1909 and 1915 the New South Wales government furthered this policy under the Aborigines Protection Act by allowing 'neglected' Aboriginal children of mixed descent to be removed from their parents and placed in an institution. Girls were sent to Cootamundra Girls Home (1911) and boys to Kinchela Boys Home (1924) in Kempsey where they were trained as domestics and farm labourers respectively. Between 1909 and 1938, 2000 Aboriginal children in New South Wales were taken from their parents.[24]

The establishment of government departments to oversee child welfare policies represented a significant intervention of the state into areas traditionally the preserve of private charity. This was a further move away from the division of public finance and private benevolence and an assertion of the need for direct government control. Revelations of ill-treatment and abuse of children, poor conditions in institutions, overlapping between charity, church and government provisions and continuing poverty, neglect and delinquency prompted calls for greater state intervention in all areas of poor relief. In the 1880s and 1890s colonial governments appointed inspectors or superintendents of charity to inspect and report on all charitable institutions receiving government subsidy. The 1890 Victorian Royal Commission into Charitable Institutions recommended the establishment of a central charity board to oversee the distribution of funds. It also supported the idea of a greater government voice on the boards of subsidised charities and hospitals, a move strongly resisted by many charities. The 1898 New South Wales Royal Commission into Public Charities urged that subsidies be withdrawn from charities that continued to house orphaned and neglected children in large institutions. Governments also began to take a greater role in the administration of hospitals, beginning the transformation of charity hospitals into public hospitals.[25] Through these measures governments hoped to influence the direction of philanthropic intervention and bring the activities of private societies into line with government policy.

Some charities and churches ignored government attempts to impose the boarding-out and cottage home system. For evangelical reformers like George Ardill, and for many churches, the key to helping children was a proper Christian education and this was best achieved in a church institution. In the late 19th and early 20th centuries new private children's homes were established by such groups as the St Vincent de Paul Society, the Salvation Army, the Central Methodist Mission and the Roman Catholic, Anglican and Presbyterian churches. Some of these church and charity institutions were large. The St Vincent Boys Home at Westmead in Sydney, run by the Marist Brothers, housed over 200 boys in 1900.

Church and charity institutions were more flexible than government departments and were prepared to take children for short periods, when illness or unemployment made it impossible for parents to care for their children. When the crisis passed parents could remove the children again. Other parents could not afford to keep children despite boarding-out allowances and charity and church homes provided a means of solving this problem. Despite the government boarding-out policies the number of children admitted to private institutions increased. In New South Wales the number of children in private homes trebled between 1881 and 1911. Many charities and churches feared that increased government control would undermine the Christian reform message and they acted to preserve the relevance of their mission.[26]

Pensions

Government concern with stricter regulation of the operation of charities and institutions also extended to the care of the aged and infirm. These groups were cared for in benevolent and government asylums but a series of embarrassing inquiries into asylum conditions produced abundant evidence that the aged and infirm were not receiving the humane treatment that was the cornerstone of philanthropic rhetoric about care for the deserving poor. An 1884 inquiry into conditions at Dunwich Benevolent Asylum in Queensland found inmates denied baths and sufficient food. Some patients were beaten by warders and deliberately given wrong medicines. One man, suffering from diabetes, was beaten, denied food and water, and left to die in his cell.[27] Three years later investigations into Newington and Parramatta Asylums for the Aged in Sydney revealed similar conditions. Patients had been beaten, dragged round courtyards and forced to sleep outdoors in winter. Patients who complained about conditions were denied food or threatened with expulsion from the asylum. Some ill-treatment was more perverse. Warders stuffed one inmate's mouth with excrement. At the Parramatta Asylum the warders appointed an epileptic to shave the other inmates. William Roy, a blind and feeble inmate, was deliberately placed in a ward at the top of a long flight of stairs, making him a virtual prisoner.[28]

These were undoubtedly extreme cases and although allegations of staff cruelty and neglect were commonplace, most were dismissed by officials as unfounded, or the product of aggrieved staff dismissed for misconduct. What distinguished these inquiries was the acceptance by investigators that the complaints of patients were substantially true. Men like William Roy were found by investigators to be respectable gentlemen fallen on hard times and revelations that men of their own class suffered such treatment fuelled calls for reform. Other philanthropists noted an understandable reluctance on the part of the deserving aged to enter asylums, despite the inadequacies of charity relief.

Mrs Hill was a widow, aged 76, living in a room in Redfern in 1898, at a rent of 2s 6d a week. She received food and rent money of 1s 6d from the Benevolent Society but the Society's visitor noted:

[she] is a feeble woman, and her room a dirty hovel. There was reason to believe that for several days she had been partially starved. She made the following statement: 'I do not get enough food, and I cannot work. The society's ration only lasts until Saturday. A poor neighbour sends me dinner on Sunday, and I saved part of it for Monday. Since Monday I have only had a little bread and jam. Today I have had no breakfast, nor shall I have anything this afternoon' ... When asked whether she would not rather go to Newington Asylum ... She answered. 'I would sooner have my liberty and live even as I do'.[29]

The independent aged poor. Life in these destitute circumstances was preferable to that in an institution for this couple in western NSW around 1900. (Photo courtesy NSW Government Printing Office)

Serious ill-treatment of the infirm aged may have been rare but mounting evidence that it occurred, and revelations that people were understandably reluctant to seek help, prompted the search for alternatives.

The problems of invalids and their families were equally pressing. Mr B, aged 33, had a wife and five children, the eldest aged nine and the youngest new-born. They lived on the top floor of a small house, in three rooms, including the kitchen, in Barker's Lane. Mr B was bedridden with asthma. He had been seriously ill for twelve months, unable to work, and had spent some time in hospital. The family was helped by the Benevolent Society. They received 2s 6d rent subsidy but their rent was 5s a week. They also received food from the Society to the value of 2s 3d a week, well short of the family's needs. Mrs B was surviving on a diet of tea, had few clothes and no shoes and was too weak to earn more than a few shillings a week. Doctors ordered medical comforts for her husband which she was unable to afford. Occasionally a local clergyman called in and left a shilling. Sometimes friends dropped by with some leftover food, a shilling, or cast-off clothes. The children went down to the markets each week and the carters allowed them to pick up any potatoes that fell from the carts. When pressed about her situation Mrs B replied: 'Well, you see, we have not large appetites ... and a cup of tea almost satisfies me now'. Such conditions concerned the government Commissioners, who called in on this family unannounced. It was clear that the Benevolent Society allowance was inadequate.[30]

Pensions were proposed as the solution to the problems of asylum ill-treatment and impoverishment amongst the aged and invalid. Underlying this proposal was the demographic pressure of the ageing of the mass of immigrants who arrived in the colonies in the 1850s and 1860s. Between 1861 and 1911 the proportion of the white population aged over 60 rose from 2.75 per cent to 6.4 per cent.[31] Inquiries into the condition of the aged revealed considerable hardship. In 1898 12 per cent of those aged over 60 in Victoria were found to be penniless. But this was probably an underestimate. Three years later inquiries in New South Wales found 29 per cent of all those aged over 65 without means.[32]

The growing numbers of impoverished aged strained asylum resources. In the 1890s the Queensland government introduced an indigence allowance of 5s a week to assist the infirm aged to remain at home rather than seek admittance to the seriously overcrowded Dunwich Asylum. In Sydney, reformers such as Arthur Renwick and Rev. F.B. Boyce formed the Old Age Pensions League to lobby for the introduction of pensions. Government inquiries in New South Wales (1896), Victoria (1898) and South Australia (1898) further investigated the plight of the aged and the feasibility of pensions. Witnesses condemned prevailing asylum methods of care as 'unsuitable ... to a civilised society'. There was widespread acceptance that many deserving cases were being denied assistance. The South Australian Commissioners found that the respectable aged were too ashamed to apply to the Destitute Board for help. James Main, a Sydney City Missionary, found that many sober hardworking men were unprepared for old age because illness, unemployment or lack of forethought meant they had not joined a Friendly Society. These men refused government assistance because they would 'rather go out and die in the street like a dog than go to a Benevolent Asylum'.[33]

Pensions began to be seen as a just reward for hard-working

citizens, not a benevolent gift to be bestowed at the whim of a philanthropist. Some philanthropists protested that pensions would undermine self-reliance, but these familiar objections were swept aside by the liberal and labor politicians who supported the new legislation. They praised pensions as a universal benefit free of the stigma of charity. The lead was taken by New Zealand, which passed an Old Age Pensions Act in 1898. New South Wales followed suit in 1901. The other States moved more cautiously but in 1908 individual State initiatives were superseded by the Commonwealth Old Age Pensions Act.[34] This legislation provided a pension of 10s week for men aged over 65 years and women aged over 60, provided they did not have income of more than £52 a year or property worth more than £310. In 1910 a further Act made pensions available to invalids. This was a significant extension of government assistance to the poor but it was not entirely free of philanthropic ideas. Pensions were denied to Asiatics, some Aborigines, people who had deserted their spouses, and people who had not been resident in Australia for 25 years, or five years in the case of invalids. Magistrates had to be satisfied that applicants were of 'good character' before they could receive a pension; applicants could forfeit the pension if convicted of drunkenness or a felony. Despite these restrictions there were 82 943 old age and 13 700 invalid pensioners by 1913.[35] But the character qualifications point to the strength of philanthropic principles. Pensions in practice were not a universal right but a form of 'state charity'.[36]

Pensions did not solve the problem of the infirm aged in asylums. R.T. Paton, Chairman of the New South Wales Old Age Pensions Board, charted the fate of a number of asylum inmates. They used the pension as a reason to leave an asylum but many found they were incapable of caring for themselves or affording medical care and were forced to return.[37] Pensions did not mean the end of asylum care. On the contrary charities began to increase their provision of asylums for the infirm aged and invalid. In New South Wales six new church and charity homes for the aged and invalid were opened between 1901 and 1911 and the number of admissons to private asylums rose from 1496 to 5303 between 1881 and 1911.[38] Charities and churches continued to work against the grain of government policy and found no shortage of applicants for their assistance.

Government payments were seen as the solution to other problems. The first decades of the 20th century were ones of heightened anxiety about the future of 'the race'. In 1903 New South Wales Statistician Timothy Coghlan revealed that Australia's birth rate was declining and the infant mortality rate was high. This provoked

A young volunteer helps an aged inmate at Dunwich Asylum in Queensland in 1920. Despite the pension philanthropists continued to assist the aged poor in asylums. (Photo courtesy John Oxley Library)

alarm amongst people who believed that Australia might be vulnerable to invasion from overpopulated Asian nations. In this climate of opinion Commonwealth legislators sought to encourage medical attendance at birth by paying all mothers an allowance of £5 for every 'viable' birth regardless of their 'character'.[39] The maternity allowance was the first genuinely universal government welfare benefit.

Pensions and the maternity allowance were financed from government consolidated revenue. In formulating the pension scheme, legislators, on the recommendation of various commissions of inquiry, had rejected the German model of insurance as the means of funding welfare payments. Insurance was considered unsuitable for Australia, where many workers were already making regular payments to Friendly Societies in return for medical benefits and others were too poor to afford insurance. In opting for a non-contributory system of pension benefits legislators proclaimed the superiority of pensions which used the tax system to ensure that those on higher incomes contributed to the welfare of those who were less well off. The uniqueness of this system heightened Australia's reputation as a 'social laboratory'.

Medicine

Government payments to the poor were not the only challenges to the traditions of philanthropy. Philanthropic beliefs that poverty, and the 'related conditions' of crime, insanity, drunkenness, prostitution and delinquency, were the consequence of vice and immorality were increasingly questioned by doctors. New medical theories prompted new views about medicine as an instrument of social reform. In the mid-19th century some prominent doctors, notably Francis Campbell, superintendent of Tarban Creek Lunatic Asylum (1848–67), argued that much crime, insanity and drunkenness was caused by moral weakness. This was in accord with prevailing philanthropic views. By the late 19th century the bulk of the profession believed that disease and faulty heredity were the causes of these social problems. Underpinning this change was the impact of social Darwinism which posited that the natural laws of social evolution would guarantee progress to higher stages of civilisation. By the 1890s this proposition seemed questionable in the light of continuing poverty, rising rates of crime, delinquency and insanity, high rates of infant mortality, and disease. Doctors believed they had a role to play in the formulation of new solutions.[40]

Philanthropists inadvertently contributed to the triumph of med-

Nerves at Breaking Point

WHEN your nerves are constantly "on edge" and you feel "run down" and depressed, it is a sure indication that your daily dietary is not providing sufficient nerve-restoring nourishment.

What you need is delicious "Ovaltine". Made from malt, milk and eggs, "Ovaltine" is supremely rich in the nourishment which builds up the nervous system.

New-laid eggs are liberally used in "Ovaltine" because of their valuable nerve-building properties. That is one of many reasons why "Ovaltine" definitely stands in a class by itself. Reject substitutes.

TRIAL SAMPLE: A generous trial sample of "Ovaltine", sufficient to make four cupsful, will be sent on receipt of 3d. in stamps, to cover cost of packing and postage.

PRICES:
1/9, 2/10, 5/-.
AT ALL CHEMISTS AND STORES.

'OVALTINE'
Builds up Brain, Nerve and Body

A. WANDER LIMITED, 218 KENT STREET, SYDNEY

The idea of healthy lifestyles was paralleled by the introduction of new nerve cures to ensure that the curable patient (usually a woman) could be treated at an early stage. (*Australian Woman's Mirror*, 2 June 1936)

ical ideas. E.E. Morris' belief that renewed philanthropic rigour (scientific charity) was the key to diminishing social problems contained the seeds for the decline of philanthropy as a widely accepted discourse on the nature of society. By stressing science Morris implied that experts might be more appropriate than benevolent volunteers. Some clergy and philanthropists were more explicit. Rev. H.L. Jackson, a participant at the 1890 charity conference, made an urgent plea for scientific experts to be employed by charities in fighting social disease.[41] Increasingly the metaphor of disease was displacing that of vice in the description of social problems. From the 1890s an increasing number of doctors joined the boards of charitable societies, marginalising the voice of evangelical philanthropists.[42]

Drink had long been seen as the root of many social problems. Philanthropists, clergy and reformers blamed drink for inebriety, poverty, family violence, insanity, crime, delinquency and illness. In their opinion drink was an evil which, left unchecked, became an uncontrollable vice. This was the view of W.B. Ullathorne, Benedictine prelate and vicar-general (1833–34), who declared the drunkard to be 'a self-made wretch', and drunkenness a vice that warranted punishment. This was also the view of Sir Alfred Stephen, Chief Justice of New South Wales (1845–73), who argued that drunkards were confirmed sinners with little prospect of reform. Colonial doctors supported this conclusion. Francis Campbell argued that inebriety began as a sin, but once it became a habit there were definite physical effects with the end result an incurable disease.

Common to all these viewpoints was the belief that the origin of drunkenness was a moral problem: a loss of will and an inability to control the craving for drink. Drunkenness was thus situated within the ambit of mid-19th century beliefs in moral reform. The solution to inebriety, for medical practitioner and lay reformer alike, was to convince drunkards to take the pledge or, if they proved reluctant, to place them in asylums for extended periods to allow their weakened will to be strengthened by the reformative regime of institutional life.

By the early 20th century doctors had distanced themselves from these programs of moral reform. The growing popularity of the germ theory in the 1880s and 1890s pointed in the direction of distinct environmental influences, not morality, as the causes of disease. This theory played an important role in constructing a new medical discourse on inebriety. It was a disease caused by toxins. In 1906 Dr Ramsey Smith, later chief adviser on public health to the South Australian government, argued that the moral view was inadequate and 'kindness and fanaticism' failures as treatments. He favoured the use of anti-toxin drugs such as bichloride of gold or sulphate of atropine, which countered the toxic effects of alcohol and destroyed the physical craving for drink. An alternative, although less popular view, was that inebriety was a psychological craving. Melbourne psychiatrist C.G. Godfrey and New South Wales physician J.M. Creed believed that inebriety was a psychological problem best tackled by the use of hypnosis or suggestion therapy. All these doctors, however, treated inebriety as a curable disease. A long confinement in an asylum was not necessary, except for criminal inebriates. Instead new clinics, private practices and hospitals became the places where inebriates stayed for short periods to receive medical treatment.[43]

Similar ideas influenced policies for the treatment of the insane. The germ theory was the means for reconceptualising the causes of mental illness. In the mid-19th century alienists such as Francis Campbell believed that two thirds of all cases of insanity were moral in origin, one third physical. But early 20th century psychiatrists believed that these ratios were reversed and that many of the physical cases could now be cured with drugs or surgery. The problem confronting these doctors was why some people exposed to toxins succumbed to mental illness. In 1911 W. Beattie-Smith, prominent Melbourne psychiatrist, encapsulated the problem. Why did two patients drinking to excess have very different problems? One might develop cirrhosis of the liver, the other mental disturbance. The answer to this quandary was heredity. Patients who developed mental illness had an hereditary predisposition. This seems a pessimistic conclusion but for doctors it was the rationale for a special role.

Doctors, it was now thought, could offset hereditary predisposition through drug and surgical treatments if the problem was caught in the early stages. New treatment facilities such as special clinics, hospital admission wards and out-patient services were needed for the curable patients in the early stages of their problem. Two patient populations were being forged: the curable, treated in clinics and hospitals, and the incurable—those with serious physical conditions or whose disturbance had remained untreated for too long. This latter group were those whose hereditary predisposition could not be affected and who required confinement for the remainder of their lives. This group were kept in the old lunatic asylums, no longer seen as institutions for moral reform, but as repositories for the incurable. Conditions in the old asylums deteriorated. Fewer staff and an increasing resort to strait-jackets were the consequences of the decision to make the asylums dumping-grounds for the hereditarily unfit and incurable.[44]

In early 20th century Australia many reformers were concerned about the effects of heredity on the character of the population. They echoed the fears of eugenicists in Britain and America. The 1903 Royal Commission into the Decline of the Birth Rate warned of the dangers of Australia's small population. Asian hordes, hungry for land, were the imagined foe and pro-natalists like Octavius Beale and Sir Charles Mackellar cried 'populate or perish'. But eugenicists had a different worry. They were more concerned with the quality, not the quantity, of the population and feared that the decline in the birth rate was primarily amongst the better-off, healthy middle classes, while the socially undesirable and criminal poor, who were now considered hereditarily deficient, were out-breeding the fit. Prominent eugenicists, such as Richard Arthur, physician and politician, A.G. Stephens, literary critic, and R.J.A. Berry, Professor of Anatomy at Melbourne University, envisaged a future society composed entirely of morons.

These fears were exacerbated by revelations about the unfitness of English enlistments for the Boer War and the defeat of Russia by Japan in 1905. Some believed that western nations were in decline and drastic measures were needed to arrest this deterioration and promote national efficiency. These were international fears and although many Australians believed that the new world was free of the problems of the old, some argued that Australia could not afford to be complacent. In 1914 an Australian medical congress committee warned: 'In Australia few people outside the medical profession realise the gravity of the problem of the mentally deficient, its relation to crime, and to the multiplication of the unfit in the community'. A small, influential group of doctors, academics, teachers, philanthropists and politicians sounded a warning about the threats to the social fabric and the need for efficiency.[45]

In this context the claim by some doctors to have preventive treatments for hereditary deficiencies was particularly important. What was required were measures to differentiate the incurably unfit from the curable. The former needed to be shut away in institutions or farm colonies to prevent them spreading their deficiency to the wider society. The latter needed to be placed in hospitals or clinics where they could be treated by doctors. At the turn of the century new tests were developed to assist in diagnosing these different populations. This meant medical examinations involving new techniques such as anthropometrics (body and skull measurements) and IQ tests. Harvey Sutton, Director of the Victorian School Medical Service in 1911 argued that the interests of national efficiency were best served by 'more precise forms of intelligence testing ... the extension of surveillance into schools and the extension of the concept of hereditary deficiency beyond that which is physically apparent'. These tests defined different classes of deficiency: idiots and imbeciles, who required confinement; morons (or the feeble-minded), who might be trained to have a limited role in society; and the moral imbeciles (later called psychopaths), who had no hereditary deficiency but had social or psychological problems which inhibited their education. This last group could benefit from education and psychological counselling. Without such measures, the *Medical Journal of Australia* warned, 'a nation of unhealthy weaklings, have nothing to expect but continued and continuing decadence'. The doctors who supported these ideas married a belief in heredity with an optimistic faith in medicine and education as the means to social improvement.[46]

These ideas, tests and treatments were increasingly influential in early 20th century Australia. Child welfare was one important area. The late 19th century supporters of boarding-out believed that parental neglect and an impoverished home environment were the causes of delinquency and placing children in a proper home would assist reform. Sir Charles Mackellar, medical practitioner, politician and head of the New South Wales State Children's Relief Board (1902–14) was an enthusiastic advocate of boarding-out. He supported the introduction of the Children's Court (1905), where experts could discuss the best course of treatment and probation would ensure that children coming to the attention of authorities were not institutionalised. But Mackellar was increasingly influenced by new medical ideas and became convinced that some delinquents, by virtue of their hereditary deficiency, were not amenable to reform and were best kept in cottage homes and farm colonies. To this end a doctor was appointed to the Children's Court in 1912 to examine children apprehended by police, determine their IQ and recommend whether they should be institutionalised or placed out on probation.[47]

The 19th century ideal of the asylum had undergone a radical change by the early 20th century. Institutions were increasingly seen by doctors as places for the hereditarily unfit, the deficient or the incurable, while those groups who were thought capable of improvement were sent to homes, clinics, schools or hospitals for treatment and education. The old language of moral reform and the dangerous classes was being supplanted by a new one of medicine, disease and the deficient classes. Doctors, using new tests, were charged with the responsibility of diagnosing the different classes of patient. Institutionalisation was increasingly seen as a life sentence for the incurable. South Australia (1913), Victoria (1920) and Tasmania (1922) were the first States to introduce 'mental defectives' legislation to ensure that those diagnosed as deficient could be detained indefinitely.

The other side of the national efficiency problem was to ensure that people, especially children, had to be helped to achieve their full capacity. People needed to be educated in healthy lifestyles. Doctors, teachers, politicians and philanthropists turned their attention towards improving the race. Baby health centres, kindergartens, child guidance clinics, school medical services and educational pamphlets and lectures on child feeding, proper child care and the psychological aspects of raising children became important in the early decades of the 20th century. Governments introduced milk services for school children to improve their health. Social purity, White Cross, physical education societies, and organisations such as the Father and Son Movement focused on inculcating habits of physical and moral hygiene. In inner city areas district nurses were appointed to visit mothers and educate them in proper hygiene and infant feeding. Psychologists were used in schools to help diagnose those children suffering education problems.[48] Through these means it was hoped that social problems might be averted in the early stages. The 19th century philanthropists usually waited until a problem had occurred, but the new reformers hoped to intervene before problems developed. Their program was one of preventive medicine and social hygiene.

6   One long Depression

'Depression! I never knew nothing else! The 1920s was just as bad' declared Harry Hartland, recalling his days as a bushworker.[1] The interwar years have usually been seen as a time when a new Commonwealth convulsed by the traumas of war finally emerged as a renewed and self-confident nation. A decade of growth and optimism, however, was shattered by the 1930s Depression. These are. familiar landmarks in Australia's history. What is less remembered is the continued poverty, regardless of boom or bust, which shaped the lives of many Australians in the early 20th century. Charitable societies still had many applicants for relief, urban slums were still obvious to those who traversed the inner-city areas and many workers and their families struggled to survive on low wages and the meagre fruits of intermittent work. In contrast a few were very wealthy. A 1915 census of wealth revealed that only 0.5 per cent of Australian men owned 30 per cent of Australia's wealth. Although individual Australians were not as rich as their counterparts in Britain and America, the concentration of wealth in a few hands was three times greater in Australia than in the United States.[2]

In the early 20th century some sectors of the economy flourished while others slumped. Although Gross Domestic Product increased fourfold between 1901 and 1929 there was little growth in the mining sector. In the west the mining towns of the Golden Mile, between Kalgoorlie and Boulder, suffered a serious recession in the 1920s. Mines were closed and sacked miners became prospectors. In the coalmining towns of the Hunter Valley many collieries only operated for a hundred days a year and a fifth of the miners earned less than the basic wage from this infrequent work.[3] These regional patterns were not obvious in national economic statistics.

A new century

In the early 1900s the Australian economy began to recover from the crisis of the 1890s Depression. Although the serious droughts,

Chippendale—Sydney in the 1920s. Slums were still a feature of urban life and reformers sought out this evidence to press for clearance programs. (Photo courtesy NSW Government Printing Office)

which continued until 1903, meant that rural areas recovered more slowly, in the years leading up to World War I wages increased for many workers and unemployment fell. Despite these signs of improvement some Australians lived in slums little different to those in the mid-19th century. Archdeacon F.B. Boyce of the Sydney Diocese was a tireless campaigner for slum reform. On his tours of the inner-city in 1912 he found tenements in Chippendale where eight people lived in two small rooms, and houses in Athlone Place under four feet of water during heavy rains.[4] Melbourne police found similar conditions. In 1913 Constable George Scott found many two-roomed houses in East Melbourne rented for 10s a week and 'not one bath in sixty of them'. Arthur Pearson of the Melbourne Housing Crusade Committee found houses in Queensbury and Little Pelham Streets built of palings and old iron, rented at 7s a week and 'not fit to keep a pig in let alone respectable people'. Two years later police inspections of South Melbourne found numerous dwellings with no sheds, coppers or yards. Houses in Tinpot Alley were tin sheds, miserably hot in summer and freezing in winter and similar conditions were found by other constables in Fitzroy, Richmond, the city centre and Bendigo.[5]

The shift of the population from the country to the city exacerbated the housing problem. The proportion of people living in capital cities increased by nearly 7 per cent in the first two decades of the 20th century and housing construction failed to keep pace with population growth, allowing landlords to charge high rents. In 1913 Robert Irvine, Professor of Economics at Sydney University, investigated the problem and concluded that the housing famine created rents which absorbed as much as one third of the basic wage. Landlords could charge exorbitant rents for hovels while others let their houses as brothels to maximise the return on their investment. High rents forced families to seek alternatives. A common solution was to take in a lodger. Irvine found one five-roomed house accommodating a mother and five children, the lesees, and also a married couple, another married couple with three children and two single men, fifteen people in all. Some families were forced to squat in the hills near Long Bay. There, nearly 150 people lived in huts made out of galvanised iron, kerosene tins, packing cases and sacking. These huts at Eucalyptus Town, as it was known, were highly prized and people paid as much as £10 to occupy one. In Melbourne settlements flourished around the Bay near Frankston where families lived in ill-ventilated and overcrowded tents with open pits for toilets, Health officers were concerned about the lack of sanitation.[6]

Conditions for many Australians worsened with the onset of war. The interruption to trade and the uncertain future prompted employers to close down operations and unemployment almost doubled during 1914, reaching 11 per cent. The war also forced up prices, as imports became scarce and transport costs escalated. The cost of important food items outstripped wage rises; bread rose 50 per cent, flour 87 per cent and butter 63 per cent. Added to this was the financial burden of the war effort. The federal government introduced war loans, raising £250 million.[7] The diversion of government funds to the war effort and the similar concentration of the London bond market on financing Britain's war effort meant that there was little money available, and no likelihood of raising loans to finance public relief schemes to help the unemployed and destitute.

The war meant tightening belts for ordinary Australians but reports of war-time profiteering angered many. It seemed that profiteers and 'boodlers' were prospering while workers were making the sacrifices, exacerbating social tensions already strained by the conscription referenda. These tensions erupted in 1917. Trade unions organised major strikes, the number of working days lost almost trebled to four and a half million, and in Melbourne women organised protest marches over food prices. In September one of these erupted into a riot, windows were smashed and the damage bill exceeded £5000. Governments responded harshly to signs of civil disorder and protests about falling living standards. Prominent labour activitists, notably members of the International Workers of the World group, were gaoled on trumped up charges of arson. Police and special constables smashed picket lines and arrested trade unionists, eventually forcing the strikers into submission, and a number of the women involved in the food riots were arrested.[8]

Returning soldiers

Australian politicians proudly proclaimed the feats of the ANZACs, but these were achieved at great cost. Australian forces made a 'blood sacrifice', suffering the highest casualty rates of any allied nation: 60 000 dead and 150 000 wounded, accounting for 65 per cent of the AIF sent overseas. Raw statistics do little to convey the physical and mental suffering of the injured men who returned from the war and the families that had to look after them. Limbless soldiers were a common sight in towns and cities after the war. Many suffered worse ailments and injuries—paralysis, blindness, disfigured faces, chronic lung complaints from the effects of gas, tuberculosis, crippling forms of mental illness, debilitating heart ailments and recurring neuroses resulting in stammering, speechlessness, phobias, suicidal depression or uncontrollable violence. Some of these problems did not become apparent till years later. In the 1930s doctors diagnosed a problem known as the 'burnt-out soldier': tired, depressed and incapable of holding down a regular job although there was no obvious physical incapacity. Investigations into the health of ex-soldiers concluded that their life expectancy was four years less than those who had not served overseas.[9]

Some soldiers returned with health problems that threatened other Australians. At the end of the war a major outbreak of influenza—the Spanish flu—swept Europe, killing fifteen million people in twelve months. Health authorities in Australia feared that returning troops would infect the population, but stringent quarantine measures failed to prevent the spread of the virus and 12 000

Australians died. Venereal disease—the 'red plague'—was another problem. Despite lectures and an ample supply of prophylactics army doctors estimated that 50 000 troops contracted venereal diseases while on overseas service and 5000 returned to Australia still carrying the disease, potentially spreading it to wives, girlfriends and the rest of the community. This prospect concerned public health authorities, who lobbied to make venereal diseases subject to compulsory notification, a system enacted in Western Australia (1915), Queensland (1916), New South Wales (1918) and South Australia (1920).[10]

There were other problems associated with war service. Rowland Lording was only sixteen when he joined the AIF in 1915. A year later, serving on the Western Front, he was ripped apart by machine-gun fire and hovered close to death for almost six months. His condition was complicated by tetanus and he had to have a number of blood transfusions. His problems were long-term. In the fifteen years after his return he had 52 operations to rectify recurring problems with his recovery. As a consequence he became addicted to morphine, and stole to support his addiction. He was later arrested for theft.[11]

The plight of returned soldiers concerned many Australians. Contributions to charitable funds to assist soldiers and their families were generous. New organisations, notably Legacy, were established to help the families of deceased soldiers. Friendly Societies provided free medical care for the widows and children of deceased soldiers. Community sympathy was also apparent in the treatment of soldiers charged with serious crimes. In the 1920s a number of returned soldiers murdered wives, de factos and girlfriends who had left them. At the trials, soldiers often complained of headaches, dizziness and blackouts since their return and this was taken as evidence of war neurosis. These were seen as mitigating circumstances and the defendants were usually found not guilty, or convicted on a lesser charge.[12]

Governments were committed to assisting soldiers and the families of those who had died as a result of their service to the nation. The range of benefits was impressive. Repatriation hospitals provided care for the sick and injured, special army mental hospitals were established to provide psychiatric treatment without the stigma of certification, education funds were provided for the children of deceased soldiers and by 1936, 19 597 children had been assisted under this scheme. Over 30 000 soldiers received a special sustenance allowance while undergoing training schemes to become skilled tradesmen and professionals. Governments provided artificial limbs for over 3000 soldiers disabled through war injuries and by the late 1930s nearly 40 000 homes had been built or financed under the provisions of the War Services Homes Act.[13]

Pensions were an important form of relief for disabled returned soldiers. Australia introduced one of the most extensive war pension schemes of any nation. Anyone assessed to have a disability of more than 5 per cent qualified, whereas in England the lowest limit was a 20 per cent disability. As a consequence many qualified for a pension. Throughout the 1920s and 1930s between 70 000 and 80 000 incapacitated soldiers received a pension each year and when the dependants of these men, and war widows and children who also received a pension are added, the number of Australians supported by war pensions totalled a quarter of a million. The peak year was 1931, when 283 322 people were assisted.

In 1936 a new pension scheme was added to those already operating. Service pensions assisted the 'burnt-out' soldier and in this category a further 15 000 pensioners were added to the total in receipt of war pensions benefits by 1940. War pensions, unlike old age and invalid pensions, were not subject to a means, assets, residence or morals test; they were a right guaranteed to those who had fought for their country. Australia may have had liberal qualification criteria but the level of benefit was comparatively low. The maximum pension for a private was just under half the average weekly wage. The equivalent pension in Britain was 74 per cent of the average weekly wage, Canada and the USA 62 per cent and France 65 per cent. Widows received less than half the male rate.[14]

The most ambitious but tragic attempt to assist veterans was soldier settlement.[15] Modelled on the 19th-century selection and closer settlement schemes, this was yet another attempt to recreate the yeoman ideal on Australian soil. As late as 1915, government investigations found closer settlement a failure but there was no attempt by the promoters of soldier settlement to rectify the errors of the past. How could politicians pursue such a foolhardy course of action? Some worried, as many had done before, that the cities were breeding grounds of moral decay and believed that the future of Australia lay in the country. Rural Australia was idealised as a healthier environment for future generations. Others, particularly after the 1917 Russian revolution, were concerned about the congregation of large numbers of single returned soldiers in the cities. Giving men a stake in the land was a means of instilling commitment to the existing social order. Many returned soldiers wanted to settle on the land. After years at the front, the idea of being self-sufficient landowners held great appeal.

The soldier settlement scheme allowed men to buy farms at low rates of interest. Governments, keen to see men on the land, allowed them to purchase with no deposit, mortgaged to the full value of the property. Initial repayments were waived for the first year, sometimes two, to assist in establishing the farm. Soldiers rushed to join. By 1922 nearly 28 000 soldiers had been accepted into the scheme. In all 40 000 men became soldier settlers, taking with them 60 000 dependants, but by 1925 it was apparent that serious problems existed. Soldiers and their families were leaving the land and many of those who stayed were behind in their repayments. Few measures were taken to solve these problems.

By 1929 the situation was too serious to ignore and a Commonwealth inquiry headed by Mr Justice Pike concluded that the system was a failure. Over half the soldiers had left the land, only one-tenth were up to date in their repayments and the accumulated debt from the scheme was £23 million. The Commissioner highlighted four major reasons for this failure—lack of capital, lack of homes, unsuitability of the settlers and the drop in the price for farm products.[16] It was a familiar story. Although some settlers prospered, most settled on poor land, had little knowledge of farming and insufficient capital to tide them over poor seasons. Governments exacerbated this problem by settling families on blocks of land that were too small to be viable. Men with disabilities which prevented them from working hard and families with few financial reserves were also permitted to take up farms.

Individual stories of tragedy abound. Settler families without any savings lived in tents for years at a time, while many laboured for long hours on land that was unsuitable for agriculture. Material poverty was acute and this placed extra strains on families. Ethel Lester's husband selected a dairy farm in Victoria and took his wife and three children there. The farm did not prosper and Ethel found that she had to help out with the farm work in addition to the domestic chores and child rearing. As the debts mounted her husband became violent and abusive, knocking her down when she made a mistake while fencing. Eventually, fed up, she took her children and deserted the farm; she later sued for divorce.

The material poverty and cycle of debt took its toll on the domestic life of many soldier settlers. Some became angry and violent, their wives exhausted and depressed; others left to follow general labouring work to provide an income. Families struggled for years to make the farm viable and still other families broke apart under the stress of these circumstances. The yeoman ideal of manly independence expired in the face of the realities of farm life.[17] In this context of accelerating failure, governments were persuaded not to pursue those soldiers who defaulted and deserted their farms. They had suffered enough.

The roaring 20s

In the 1920s the Australian economy began to recover from the effects of war shortages and inflation. Unemployment began to fall, declining to 6 per cent by the mid-1920s. From 1923 the new Nationalist Country Party government led by Stanley Melbourne Bruce and Earle Page pursued a policy of economic growth under the banner of 'men, money, markets'. They encouraged State governments to borrow heavily on overseas markets to facilitate growth and sought to expand international, mainly imperial, markets for Australian goods. Considerable emphasis was placed on expanding the agricultural and manufacturing sectors of the economy. Vital to these schemes was migration. In the 1920s, 260 000 (mainly British) migrants came to Australia, three-quarters of whom received assisted passages. The policy of expansion achieved some success. The workforce in the manufacturing sector grew by 100 000 people, and production by £100 million in the decade.

In the cities the significant growth in the metropolitan populations underpinned increases in domestic consumption and a growth in employment associated with home building and the provision of urban services to Australia's expanding suburbs. But not every scheme succeeded. The Western Australian scheme of assisting migrants to settle on the land confronted the same obstacles as soldier settlement. Optimistic migrants found themselves marooned in a harsh and unfamilar environment with no money to tide them over early lean seasons. Many defaulted and the accumulated government debt reached £64 million by 1924. The rural economy, as a whole, suffered from the downturn in world prices for primary products.[18] Overall the economic indicators suggested that Australia had entered a decade of prosperity in the 1920s but the recovery was uneven and fragile.

Not everyone prospered. Jean Brett was a young child when her mother died of pneumonia. Her father was away fighting in World War I and Jean, along with her brother and sister, was placed in an orphanage. When her father returned from the war the family was reunited and for the next decade led a peripatetic existence, moving from the house of one relative to the next as jobs and circumstances changed. Eventually Jean's father remarried and the family settled in Port Melbourne. Conditions were hard. Jean's stepmother favoured the newborn children; her father drank and, although he gained regular employment on the wharves, conditions at home were far from salubrious. All the children slept in one room infested by rats. In the 1930s, after Jean had left home, her father committed suicide.[19]

The Bretts were not a chronically impoverished urban family. Jean's father earned a regular income; they did not have to rely on charity to survive and relatives helped out when times were tough. Their lives were shaped by the personal crises of death, illness and the upheaval of war, but in general their circumstances were poor and typical of inner-city working class families. Some were more prudent than the Bretts and lived better but many others were in similar circumstances and only able to afford cramped, overcrowded houses with few amenities.

Some migrants found that the reality of Australia did not live up to their hopes and dreams. Edith McBride, divorced with a fifteen-year-old son, lived in Glasgow, Scotland, when she discovered that she had become pregnant to a man keen to go to Australia. He went ahead and Edith and her new-born daughter Mary followed in 1924. The man refused to see them after they arrived in Sydney and they were left to fend for themselves. Edith was a skilled worker. She had been a tracer at the John Brown Ship Yards in Glasgow and during the war a tracer at the British Aircraft Factory. She could find no employment in her trade and became a domestic. Edith, however, could not work if she had a child and was forced to place Mary in an orphanage. They met on Edith's infrequent days off. She remained a domestic for many years until knocked down by a car, making her a permanent invalid.[20]

Australians in remote parts of the country sometimes lived in 'comfortless and disordered' circumstances. In the tropical regions of northern Australia many European Australians lived in poorly constructed wooden and iron houses which were unbearably hot in summer. Most dwellings were poorly ventilated and many had kitchens on the side of the house facing the sun. In Townsville a survey of 400 homes revealed that only 15 per cent had ceilings, a third had no water in the kitchen or ice chests for food, three-quarters relied on kerosene lamps for light and a third had an inadequate supply of mostly cracked and broken kitchen utensils. Half the houses surveyed had yards full of rubbish, old newspapers, tins and garbage. Most of these had uncovered drains and the yard was often used as a toilet. Similar conditions were found in Cairns, Atherton and Cloncurry. Water supplies to these towns were often polluted. These were the homes of the employed. In 5 per cent of homes, where the husband was habitually unemployed or alcoholic, there were no comforts and insufficient food. Doctors noted a high incidence of a syndrome termed 'tropical neurasthenia', marked by depression, irritability and occasional bursts of exuberance, amongst locals. They concluded that it arose from indolence, the heat and the monotony of hard work.[21]

Impoverished circumstances but an independent existence for this Aboriginal woman and child at Billila on the Darling River, c.1920. (Photo courtesy Mitchell Library)

Aborigines in northern Australia faced different problems. They were an important source of labour for the pastoral industry but in 1928 Queensland Chief Protector, J.W. Bleakley, surveyed conditions for Aborigines in Northern Australia and found that black workers received very low wages, were provided with uninhabitable accommodation and had to pay exorbitant prices for food. These Aborigines, however, were well-off in comparison to the older Aborigines who could no longer work or gather sufficient food. They lived in indigent camps in a state of semi-starvation, surviving on food supplies from working Aborigines and the left-over offal from cattle slaughtered for market. When times were desperate they tramped to police stations, telegraph offices or mission stations to receive food handouts.[22]

Government policies did little to address the problems of Aborigines. In 1897 Archibald Meston, appointed by the Queensland government to investigate conditions of Aborigines in North Queensland, reported that drink, disease, opium and the exploitation of Aboriginal workers by employers was destroying the 'native population'. He recommended that government reserves be established to protect the Aborigines from the ravages of 'civilisation'. Legislation governing Aborigines in Queensland (1897), Western Australia (1905), South Australia and the Northern Territory (1911) aimed to encourage Aborigines to go to reserves and mission stations. This was intended as an act of humane paternalism but it placed severe restrictions on reserve Aborigines (about 50 per cent of the total Aboriginal population of Northern Australia), governing their personal freedom, forcing them to work on reserves without remuneration and allowing them to be contracted out as workers to local employers at exploitative rates of pay. These regulations ensured that reserve Aborigines were a pauperised class.

In the 1930s protective legislation governing Northern Australia's Aborigines was strengthened, preventing freedom of movement, forbidding marriage between the races, extending control over Aboriginal property and earnings, denying Aborigines the right to vote, drink or carry guns, and authorising governments to remove 'half-caste' children from Aboriginal parents so they could be placed in homes to be trained as labourers and domestics.

These policies cut at the root of Aboriginal culture and some Aborigines did not passively submit to the imposition of government and missionary controls on their lives. During the 1930s Aborigines at the Coranderrk and Cumeroogunga reserves in Victoria and New South Wales went on strike for better conditions. Leading activists, such as William Cooper and William Ferguson, lobbied governments for measures to grant Aborigines full citizenship and the rights accorded to other Australians, organised protests against government legislation and led the Aboriginal Day of Mourning at the 1938 Sesquicentenary Celebrations. They petitioned governments, arguing that Aboriginal voices needed to be heard in the formation of policy. They were largely ignored.[23]

Old age and invalid pensions improved the prospect for many infirm, incapacitated and aged white people. In the 1920s people overcame their reluctance to receive 'state charity' in ever-increasing numbers. In 1912 there were 90 000 old age and invalid pensions in Australia and by 1929 this number had increased to 200 000. But pensions were a help, not a guarantee of comfort.

Between 1920 and 1925 the pension rose from 15s to 20s a week but rents for slum houses were rarely below 10s and rooms in run-down boarding houses 4s a week, usually more. For those without other sources of income or help from relatives and neighbours, being forced to rent meant there was little money left over for other necessities. Investigations in the 1930s estimated that as many as 70 per cent of pensioners did not own their own homes or other forms of property.[24]

Other people in need failed to qualify for pensions. Mrs B.L. Spire, an England migrant and recently widowed, became a chronic invalid. She had kept a few boarders in her Coogee home until her health failed her. Her application for an invalid pension was rejected firstly because she had not lived in Australia for five years, and secondly because her boarders were taken as evidence that she could earn a livelihood even though she now felt incapable of keeping them. Doris Cameron was struck off the invalid pension after three convictions for drunkenness. She had no means of support. Governments received many letters from aged people in desperate circumstances who failed the assets test because their home was assessed to be a few pounds above the asset limit.

Legislation to allow deserted mothers to sue husbands for maintenance failed to help many families. Between 1899 and 1919, 39 667 cases of mothers seeking maintenance were brought before the courts in New South Wales, but orders in favour of the mother were only granted in 60 per cent of cases and in the same period there were 30 408 cases of non-compliance.[25] Mrs Nettling lived in Junee with her two children. She had been deserted for five years and earned 12s a week as a laundress. Frequent maintenance orders and appeals to the police had brought no result because her husband could not be traced. Edith Cassidy of Scone had been deserted by her de facto, who left her 'without a penny and two baby girls to support'. A few months later he was found and imprisoned for stealing, making him incapable of paying maintenance. Edith had to rely on an allowance from the Child Welfare Department. Mabel Gannon had come from Queensland with her husband and children but after a 'drinking binge' he had sold the car and run off. She had no money but was refused assistance because she was not a resident of New South Wales. She had no money but was given a railway pass to return to Queensland.[26]

Despite government pensions and allowances many Australians were still dependent on help from private charities. New charities, notably the Smith Family, were established in the 1920s and other long-standing organisations continued to run extensive operations. In this decade the St Vincent de Paul Society, an organisation of over

The continuing work of private charity. A food distribution depot at Pyrmont, Sydney. (*Sydney Mail*, 9 January 1929)

4000 lay Catholic churchmen, made 30 000 home visits and assisted over 8000 families each year. The Salvation Army distributed 300 food parcels a week to families in Brisbane and 400 a week in Melbourne. In New South Wales the Benevolent Society continued to provide food and some rent assistance to nearly 2000 families each week. The South Australian Destitute Board provided food for over 7000 people and indoor care for a further 700 a year in the later 1920s. Some families still struggled to survive on the goods provided. The Blanchard family of Zetland, Sydney, consumed their rations within four days, leaving them another three days before they could turn up at the Benevolent Society to tide them over each week.[27]

The poor often received more help from friends and neighbours than charities. The Presbyterian deaconesses who visited the inner-city slums of Melbourne in the 1920s found a strong community spirit amongst the inhabitants. Neighbours shared food when one family was in dire need and pooled savings to spare a neighbour the shame of a pauper's funeral. Occasionally, when a family was sick, neighbours called charities in the hope that they could arrange for a doctor. There were other forms of help. Mrs Baines had seven children and her husband was up country in search of work when she fell seriously ill. She was sent to hospital and neighbours boarded the children. As one declared 'ye know ye 'ave to 'elp each other when there's trouble'. One deaconess was convinced that 'charity ... is a mere bagatelle as compared with the aggregate amount of relief which the poor are at times providing for themselves'.[28]

Awareness of self-help networks did not stop philanthropists from pursuing their aims but some resented charitable interference. When Melbourne Presbyterian deaconesses visited one home they found a drunken husband collapsed in a chair, four children camped in one narrow bed and an exhausted mother tending a dying baby, which was lying in a cot fashioned from two fruit boxes. The husband aggressively asked the 'busy-bodying Church women' to leave but the mother fearing for her child pleaded for medical assistance. It came too late. Lewis Rodd recalled that when two ladies from the Benevolent Society called round to his home to leave a food parcel his blind father picked up the food and threw it in the street, shouting 'here's your charity. Take it and your investigations somewhere else'. Some charity workers went to extremes to assist and trampled on the sensibilities of the poor. Late one night a Presbyterian deaconess in Melbourne broke into the house of a woman who had consistently refused to answer her calls.[29]

In contrast liberal reformers tried to tackle the problem of poverty by improving housing. Slums were considered the breeding-grounds of crime, disease and poverty. Doctors and urban reformers, such as J.W. Springthorpe and J.B. Barrett in Melbourne, were attracted to the British ideal of garden suburbs. In 1913 they declared: 'Beautiful healthy suburbs, real homes, standing amidst their own gardens—these are the birthright and the possibility of even our poorest'.[30] These ideals motivated the designers of the Daceyville garden suburb in Sydney. In 1912 the McGowen Labor government commenced building workers' homes in this garden setting. In Queensland the Premier William Kidston was an advocate of a scheme to build cheap, clean housing for workers. He introduced and passed the 1909 Workers Dwellings Act which provided cheap housing for workers. This Act and the Daceyville scheme, however, failed to tackle the problem of slums. They provided decent housing but successful applicants had to be in regular employment and this disqualified poorer families.[31]

The Sydney Home Mission Society and Melbourne Housing Crusade Society were more directly concerned with the plight of the slum dwellers. These societies tried to publicise conditions in the

Melbourne street children in the 1920s. Photographs such as these were designed to publicise the need for greater support of philanthropy. (From A.E. Pratt, *Letting in the Light*, 1933)

slums in the hope of convincing local councils to require landlords to improve properties and State governments to introduce slum clearance programs. These actions were not always welcomed by those who lived in the slums. When Archdeacon Boyce took Sydney's Lord Mayor on a tour of Chippendale in 1905 they were met by heckling locals, 'six of em ... ought to be stuffed in a bag' cried one resident. Residents knew from experience that improvements meant rent rises. When one landlord was persuaded by reformers to improve his Melbourne tenement he 'slapped' on a coat of paint and raised the rent for each family by 2s a week.[32]

In the war and interwar years some governments attempted to contain spiralling rents by setting rent limits. New South Wales (1916) and Queensland (1920) introduced Fair Rent Acts but some found ways round these Acts by charging extra money for the renters to get the key to the property. Others made it a condition of tenancy that the tenants buy old furniture and fittings in the house. Then a year or two later the tenants were advised that the house was for sale. Because of the cost of removal many poorer tenants left the old furniture behind and a short time later new tenants were moved in on the condition that they purchased the furniture. Not all tenants submitted to these practices. In 1923 tenants brought 1198 actions against landlords for breaches of the Fair Rents Act in New South Wales.[33]

Despite evidence of continuing poverty, governments made few attempts to introduce new forms of income or social security. At the turn of the century Australia had earned a reputation as a 'social laboratory of the world' with the introduction of pensions, worker's compensation, arbitration and the baby bonus. After the 1912 Maternity Allowances Act, however, with the exception of some benefits for Commonwealth public servants, there were no new Federal government initiatives in this field until the 1940s. Some State governments introduced new schemes. In 1923 the Theodore Labor government in Queensland passed the Unemployment Relief Act, dubbed the 'loafer's paradise bill' by the press, to assist seasonal labourers during periods of temporary unemployment. In 1925 the Lang government introduced widow's pensions into New South Wales and two years later child endowment. These were important but limited schemes. The Queensland unemployment system only covered workers for temporary unemployment. The widow's pension was really a limited supporting mother's allowance, paid to widows with dependent children aged under fifteen. Child endowment was only paid to families receiving the basic wage and was tied to a restructuring of the 'living wage', defining the family unit as two people, man and wife, instead of four or five. Thus the basic wage was cut and only increased by an endowment of 5s a week for each child. This limited measure meant that only 28 000 children were supported in the first year of the scheme.

Overall the social policy record of Australia during the 1920s and 1930s was dismal. In comparison to the rest of the western world Australia was being 'left behind'. In 1911 Britain had introduced a more comprehensive social welfare system, encompassing pensions, unemployment and health benefits. It would be too simple to blame Australia's inertia on the dominance of the conservative parties at the Federal level of government. Government initiatives were hampered by the war debt and the expense of providing extensive social welfare schemes for returning soldiers. But there were other problems, ones of policy and principle. Australia's pension schemes were financed from consolidated revenue. This had been seen as a progressive policy requiring the better paid to contribute more in the form of taxes and allowing casual labourers and other workers, who paid few taxes, to receive benefits. But as early as 1909 leading liberals, such as Alfred Deakin, were questioning the wisdom of this principle. Pensions were proving to be a bigger than expected drain on consolidated revenue and the prospect of having to increase taxes made governments reluctant to embark on further welfare schemes. More significantly the 1911 British Act was based on the insurance principle, thereby following the famous German system. For some this was taken as evidence that Australia, by moving early, had gone down the wrong track. The Australian system seemed to have been rejected by the rest of the world in favour of insurance.

In the 1920s the Bruce–Page government supported the idea of national insurance as the only means of expanding the range of welfare benefits. The 1923 Royal Commission into National Insurance reported favourably on the insurance principle and in 1927 the government introduced a National Insurance Bill making provisions for sickness, invalidism, old age, widows and orphans. But the Bill was criticised, by trade unions and the Labor Party for being based on insurance, by Friendly Societies which feared that it would undermine their operations, and by some business leaders who objected to provisions for employers to also contribute to the insurance scheme. The Bill lapsed. The 1920s was a period of considerable debate but little action in the field of social welfare.[34] As a consequence Australians had few safeguards against the effects of the Depression.

The 1930s Depression

The signs of impending economic collapse began in the late 1920s. By 1928 the fall in world prices for primary products was significant and the unemployment rate was again in double figures. In Perth a crowd of unemployed men angrily protested about the inadequacy of government relief measures. In 1929 further falls in world prices and the Wall Street stock market crash signalled the dramatic collapse of the world economic system. The Australian economy was particularly vulnerable. Economic growth in the 1920s had been built on the foundation of large overseas loans but when export income began to fall and world credit tightened Australia's capacity to meet interest payments was undermined, plunging the country into major economic crisis.

In 1930 the Bank of London sent Sir Otto Niemeyer to advise Australian governments on the appropriate measures to ensure that debts were paid. His conclusions were blunt. Australians had been living beyond their means. Wages and government expenditure had

ONE LONG DEPRESSION 125

"One of our pledges is that the nation shall live within its income."—J. A. Lyons

UNEMPLOYED: "I don't mind living **WITHIN** an income, but I'm tired of living **WITHOUT** one."

The labour movement's caustic comment on J.A. Lyons' pledge that the nation would live within its income. Unemployed man: 'I don't mind living *within* an income, but I'm tired of living *without* one.' (*The Australian Worker*, 3 February 1932)

to be cut and budgets balanced. Although these prescriptions for recovery were opposed by many trade unions and Labor leaders such as E.G. Theodore, and rejected outright by New South Wales Premier, J.T. Lang, in May 1931 the Premiers Plan, which charted a course of significant wage and expenditure cuts, was adopted as the basis for government economic policy. As a result government expenditure was cut by 20 per cent. The basic wage was also reduced by 20 per cent and pensions by 12.5 per cent but these cuts were partly offset by falling prices for food, clothing and rent.[35]

The unemployed bore the brunt of the economic crisis and official statistics suggest that unemployment was worse in Australia than in any other western nation except Germany. The full dimensions of unemployment, however, can only be guessed at. Governments did not collect unemployment statistics and those that exist are from trade union records of unemployed members. The 1933 census is the only other measure of unemployment. But these two measures probably underestimate the extent of unemployment. Workers who were not members of unions were probably as vulnerable to unemployment as their unionised counterparts and investigations show that some census respondents were ashamed to admit to being unemployed. Even with these limitations the peak of trade union unemployment in 1932 was 28 per cent, significantly higher than the equivalent highs in Britain and the United States of 22 and 25 per cent respectively.

There were important regional variations. Unemployment was worst in heavy industry and building sectors. This meant that the effects of unemployment were felt mostly in the cities, and the more heavily industrialised States of Victoria, New South Wales and South Australia. Queensland, with its largely rural economy, was the least affected but even this State had an unemployment rate of 18 per cent at the height of the Depression.[36] Underemployment was another indicator of distress. Many firms wound down their operations by employing workers for only one or two days a week. At the 1933 census two-thirds of all male employees and three-quarters of all female employees were either unemployed or earning less than the basic wage, indicating that they were only working part-time or accepting lower wages in preference to unemployment.[37]

Charities played an important role in assisting poor families during the Depression. Although some charities found that many former subscribers were unable to maintain contributions others managed to meet the extra call for assistance. In 1931 the St Vincent de Paul Society provided food for 25 000 families. The Salvation Army distributed food to 600 families in Sydney, nearly 600 in Melbourne and 400 in Brisbane each week. Other charities were subsidised to distribute government sustenance relief, significantly expanding their activities. In 1930 the Sydney Benevolent Society provided food for 167 806 people. The number of clients assisted by the South Australian Public Relief Department (the old Destitute Board) rose from 6000 in the mid-1920s to 88 000 in 1931.[38]

The extent of the distress required government efforts to assist the unemployed despite wider economic imperatives to reduce expenditure. State governments introduced sustenance doles, consisting of food coupons drawn against local shops, government stores or charity depots. Only in Western Australia were doles paid in cash: 7s a week for single men, 14s for married men. In country districts police were responsible for the distribution of sustenance doles. Applicants for relief had to register at government labour bureaus or police stations and local council dole officers or the police interviewed and visited applicants to ensure that they were 'genuine'. In Queensland applicants were forced to sign a declaration confirming their pauper status.

In the peak year of 1932, 600 000 received sustenance doles. But many applicants resented the long queues and humiliating interviews they were subjected to and others complained about the punitive attitudes of officials. One dole officer in Adelaide earned the nick-name 'Black Mack', because of his high-handed attitudes to the poor. Workers in country areas complained that they were 'not criminals' and should not have to report to police.[39] Local police had considerable power and could use this power to refuse rations. In Wallerawang, New South Wales, the local constable refused to hand out food to men he found drinking. He also refused to feed those men he suspected of committing petty offences in order to get an overnight meal in gaol.

Joan Cook of Tamworth was married with seven children and her husband had been out of work for months. She received child endowment for five of her children but her two eldest girls were aged seventeen. The dole officer refused to provide any food for the two girls, arguing they were now old enough to support themselves, but he also refused to give them adult doles until they were 21. In addition he refused to provide any food for the rest of the family in the weeks when Joan's endowment cheque arrived. In other weeks she had to join the queue at the local police station but found that the police officer accused them all of being 'lazy and indolent' when handing out the ration.[40]

Some families explored any avenue of work rather than submit to the indignity of applying for the dole. Edith Taylor, a mother of eight, was married to an unemployed Melbourne waterside worker. He refused to accept government charity, preferring instead to

Relief for the unemployed near Sydney, 1933. This was a concession wrung from governments after a long period of protest. Many men wanted work, not the dole. (Photo courtesy NSW Government Printing Office)

borrow money to buy a horse and cart to collect and sell bottles and bags of manure. Neighbours sometimes helped out with offerings of fruit from backyard trees and tradesmen did not always demand payment. This assistance was not sufficient. A day's bottle collecting netted only 6d. After a year, and no longer able to support themselves, they had to swallow their pride and apply for the dole. As a consequence they had to accommodate inquiries from council dole officers. On one visit Edith's husband was away and she responded angrily to some of the officer's questions. Some time later she learnt that the officer had reported that her husband did not want to work. Only the intervention of a friendly local council officer prevented them being thrown off the dole.[41]

Unmarried unemployed men were subject to special conditions. Governments hoped to diffuse the potential threat from disgruntled men gathering in the cities by giving them railway passes to go to country districts in search of work. In Queensland single men could only receive the dole for one week in any district and had to move to the next district to apply for rations. In Perth the single unemployed had to move to a camp at Blackboy Hill to qualify for the dole. Sometimes these policies backfired when locals protested about large groups of unemployed moving into their district, running down supplies and possibly taking jobs. In 1932 local citizens of

Cairns evicted 150 men from the unemployment camp at the showground. Conflict was particularly intense in Wollongong. In 1930 a camp of 200 unemployed was established near Port Kembla. Locals feared that the employment of these men on public relief schemes would undermine local jobs. Under pressure from ratepayers the local council cut rations to single men in the hope of forcing them to leave for other areas. When this failed the police were called in to break up the camp.[42]

Many applicants found the actions of police and dole officers capricious. These officers seemed to make up regulations to deny people assistance or place humiliating hurdles before people could get the dole. The unemployed were often abused and harassed by officers. In this climate many unemployed protested about the inadequacy of sustenance doles. Organisations such as the Unemployed Workers Movement and the United Front Councils coordinated their activities and large marches were organised. In 1930, 2000 of Perth's unemployed marched on the Treasury Building. Similar large marches occurred in other capital cities and marchers often carried banners declaring 'We Demand the Right to Live', 'Work not Dole' and 'We Demand Work or Basic Wage Maintenance'. Sometimes these marches erupted into violence. In 1931 a large protest in Adelaide over harassment from 'Black Mack' and the meagreness of the dole ration ended in a riot and police were called in to quell the disturbance.[43]

Protest by unemployed workers pressured governments to introduce public relief work even though this was more expensive than the dole. To fund relief work the State governments introduced special unemployment taxes on all workers earning more than £2 a week. In 1931, the first year of these taxes, £10 million was raised, although the cost of relief work was £15 million. In return for a wage of between 1s 6d and 2s 6d a day men were engaged for three or four days a week to build roads, bridges and dams, repair existing facilities, dig irrigation canals, landscape parks and plant gardens. Sometimes it was work for the sake of appeasing the desire of the unemployed to receive wages rather than the dole. Gangs of men cleared land only to replant the land again or broke stones that were not used for construction.[44]

The dole or a relief work wage was meagre and many families had to be resourceful to survive. Tent cities sprang up around the country, accommodating those who could not afford rent or had been evicted from their homes. At the 1933 Census there were 9000 such camps housing 33 000 Australians. The inhabitants of these camps hunted and fished to supplement rations and received handouts from soup kitchens. Underground mutton (rabbit) became a staple food for many. Sometimes vegetable gardens were planted. Other times the unemployed raided the gardens and fruit trees of property owners. Many had no blankets and slept in their clothes to ward off the cold. Parents fashioned children's clothes out of old flour bags. Some families were assisted by friends and neighbours who provided extra food or board.[45] There was much local sympathy for evicted families that sometimes erupted in spontaneous protest. When bailiffs turned up to evict families they were often met by angry crowds which sometimes suceeded in blocking evictions. In 1931, 60 men guarded a house in Granville for two weeks and 100 men picketed a house in Wallsend. Other locals broke the windows of landlords and bailiffs who had evicted neighbours.[46]

In these difficult times Australian women took action to further reduce the size of the family. The birth rate had been declining for many years but in the early 1930s it dropped sharply, from 21.3 births in every 1000 of the population in 1929 to 16.4 in 1934. Women were delaying marriage and public health experts also blamed abortion for this decline.[47] In the early years of World War II a survey of women who had contributed to the fall in the birth rate during the 1930s revealed the motivations underlying practices which limited the size of families. One women pleaded 'you ... say populate or perish! Well I have populated and I have perished'. Another was more direct, declaring 'we women are on strike and we will stay that way until we get a fair deal'. Economic insecurity was a major concern. One woman argued that the basic wage was insufficient to keep a family and another sadly reflected, 'children keep you poor and no matter how fond of them you are no woman feels proud to see them wanting the necessities of life'.[48]

In the 1870s women were having eight children but by the 1930s this average had fallen to three. This dramatic action by women reflected the impoverishment that large families faced in Australia. In the Depression years many more women decided that times were too tough to have more children.

7 A welfare state?

By the late 1930s there were signs that the economy was recovering from the Depression. Politicians and economists took the decline in the unemployment rate (officially down to 9 per cent by 1937) to mean that the worst was over. But some social commentators believed that there were lessons from the Depression that could not be ignored. Australia's social security and unemployment policies had proven inadequate to the task. In 1939 F.A. Bland, Professor of Public Administration at Sydney University, declared that 'once famed as pioneer workers in the social laboratory, we have fallen far behind, smugly satisfied with our achievements'. For G.V. Portus, Professor of Politics at Adelaide University, social unrest during the Depression indicated that this might be a dangerous smugness. For him social security benefits were 'the insurance premiums which capitalism pays on its life policy'.[1]

During World War II there was a significant expansion in Australia's social security system. In the space of a few years the Commonwealth government attempted to catch up with the rest of the world, beginning with the Menzies government national child endowment scheme in 1941. But it is the subsequent Labor administrations of Curtin and Chifley (1941–49) that have been credited with laying the foundations for the post-war welfare state. They introduced pensions for widows and deserted mothers (1942), increased maternity allowances (1943), introduced funeral benefits (1943), unemployment, sickness and special dependency benefits (1944), free hospital treatment for low income earners (1945) and pharmaceutical benefits (1947).

Improved social security benefits were only part of Labor's 'light on the hill'. The Curtin and Chifley governments hoped to ensure that Australians would never again suffer the effects of serious recession. They envisaged a stable post-war society where government regulation of the economy would guarantee general prosperity. Full employment was the key to this vision but social security benefits were there to act as a 'safety net' for the few who could not—due to illness, age, bereavement, family breakdown or temporary unemployment—gain the full fruits of the market.[2]

Conditions in post-war Australia seemed to confirm this vision. Australia entered a long period of economic growth after the war, fuelled by immigration, the growth of manufacturing, high world prices for agricultural and pastoral produce and after 1960 a booming export market for minerals. The volume of goods and services produced in Australia trebled between 1939 and 1969, and unemployment between 1940 and 1970 rarely exceeded 2 per cent, a rate unmatched even in the long boom of the late 19th century.[3] Australia was experiencing a previously unknown period of prosperity. By the 1960s, however, evidence of continuing poverty began to accumulate. It was obvious that the 'safety net' had a disturbingly large number of holes in it.

Making a welfare state

Social security again became an important area of political debate in the late 1930s. There was a consensus that Australia needed a more extensive welfare system to avoid the hardships of the past, but how was this system to be funded and what social values should it reinforce? Over these issues there was sharp division. The Lyons government revived the idea of social insurance. Prominent members of the government, notably Frederick Stewart and R.G. Casey, drew strength from support for the insurance principle in Britain, Europe and New Zealand. They persuaded the government to commission reports on national insurance and unemployment insurance by British experts, Sir Walter Kinnear and Godfrey Ince. The two reports, presented in 1937, agreed that Australia lagged behind the rest of the world in welfare benefits and concluded that 'it is now universally agreed that National Social Insurance Schemes should be on a contributory and compulsory basis'.[4] Advocates of national insurance believed that this policy would provide funds for new welfare benefits and reduce the burden of the pension bill. By 1938 old age and invalid pensions cost taxpayers £16 million a year, 18 per cent of Commonwealth budget expenditure. Casey, the Treasurer, painted a grim picture of a further decline in the birth rate, an increase in the proportion of the aged in the community and a sharp rise in taxes to pay for pensions. He curtly retorted to critics that 'if the government could draw money from the skies it could do anything'.[5] It couldn't, so the preferred option was to persuade people to contribute to their future welfare.

Labor, led by John Curtin, condemned the contributory principle as 'class taxation'. It forced those on lower incomes to contribute most to paying for welfare. Labor considered social security funded from consolidated revenue, the basis of existing pension schemes, more equitable because those on higher incomes contributed more to general revenue under progressive tax scales. Curtin argued that welfare should not just be a matter of finance but also one of social justice.[6] But Casey, Stewart and other supporters of insurance were also moved by ideals of social improvement. Kinnear's report on insurance stressed that the contributory principle's aim was to encourage thrift and self respect. As a universal system people receiving assistance would no longer feel ashamed or suffer the stigma of charity because they paid their own way and received benefits as a right. It would encourage Australians to work harder and save their income in order to participate in the scheme.[7] Insurance was a new means of achieving the old philanthropic goal of producing thrifty and industrious habits amongst the labouring classes.

After Casey presented the National Insurance Bill to Parliament in 1938 more practical problems emerged. Curtin and the Labor Party argued that the scheme was far from universal in application because it excluded the unemployed, farmers and the self-employed from benefits, had a lower scale of benefits for women and maintained a distinction between those on lower incomes, receiving government benefits, and higher income earners expected to contribute to private insurance and friendly society schemes.

There were other critics. Some business leaders resented proposals that employers should also contribute to the scheme and friendly societies feared the erosion of their position and pressured the government into the private insurance provisions of the Bill. Doctors were also disturbed by the health insurance scheme. They believed that it would result in fixed fees and rob doctors of the right to provide the best service for each patient. Despite these objections the National Insurance Act was passed in 1938. It faced immediate obstacles. Some provisions were found to be unworkable and doctors refused to cooperate with the scheme. The Act was never implemented and within a few months the outbreak of war created a new set of demands.[8]

How could governments ensure that Australians committed themselves to the war effort? This was an urgent question. Politicians did not want a repetition of the industrial strikes and upheavals of conscription which divided the nation in World War I. If governments were to demand 'equality of sacrifice' for the war effort then Australians had to be persuaded that they would be rewarded for this sacrifice. In the early years of the war investigations pointed to problems of morale. The 1941 Melbourne social survey, undertaken by a Melbourne University team, found some families in older working-class suburbs struggling to make ends meet where, despite improved employment prospects in war-time industries, some had given up the search for work. In 1942 a government funded survey of the Sydney suburb of Redfern found that many families 'had never recovered initiative and hope after the Depression'. Worse, some who were in employment were uncooperative and resistant to the need to increase production. In this context governments sought to rekindle faith in the nation by promising a stable and prosperous social order. Prime Minister Menzies supported the national insurance scheme, hoping it would convince people that Australia was 'a place worth working and fighting for'.[9]

Welfare historians have asked whether the war was the crucial context for the creation of a welfare state or merely a period when more long-term trends towards increased social security benefits were realised.[10] The debates about insurance and the enactment of the National Insurance Act suggest that there were long-standing pressures to catch up with the rest of the world in the welfare field. On the other hand the war provided a unique context to dramatically accelerate the program of expanding the social security system. Similar pressures operated in other countries, notably Britain, where social reformers and politicians laid the foundations for post-war prosperity complemented by more extensive welfare schemes. In Australia the war provided the necessary stimulus to create incentives for the war effort. It also provided the means for changing the relations between the Commonwealth and State governments which had inhibited a coordinated and national social security system.

In 1941, after the failure of the national insurance scheme, the Menzies government set out to secure greater benefits and a commitment to welfare. In that year the government passed the Child Endowment Act, granting 5s to mothers for every child, except the first, aged under sixteen. This was a small assistance to supporting mothers but it was of less immediate assistance to many families because the government used endowment to prevent an increase in the basic wage. But the government made a further gesture towards improving welfare services through the appointment of a joint Parliamentary Committee of inquiry into social security. The Committee eventually published nine reports on aspects of welfare such as unemployment, housing, hospital and medical services, preventive health programs and national fitness. The Committee started from the premise that 'a considerable proportion of Australia's citizens are poorly housed, ill-clothed and ill-nourished'. The government's objective, according to the Committee, should be a 'better standard of living for the great majority of the Nation and in particular for the lower wage earners'.[11]

Some critics have suggested that the Committee reports are shallow documents, full of practical policies but devoid of the visionary social philosophy that characterised the contemporary British welfare reports of Beveridge, which provided a sound rationale for government intervention based on principles of equity and justice.[12] These criticisms ignore the new liberal ideals, in the tradition of Alfred Deakin, which underpinned the Australian reports. The Committee argued that, 'for so long it was held that poverty was the fault of the individual. More modern opinion is that poverty is mostly not the fault of the individual but of the environment in which he lives'.[13] The Committee hoped to break with the philanthropic tradition that had dominated amelioration of poverty arguing that new forms of state intervention were required to improve the social environment and ensure that all citizens were provided for. In this context the laws of the market could not run their course, rather the economy had to be guided to achieve social justice. By forcefully articulating a new liberal philosophy of paternal state intervention the Committee helped forge a political culture committed to social welfare and smoothed the path for specific policies. The Curtin government inherited and fostered this new liberal welfare philosophy.

The Curtin government made post-war prosperity the key to mobilising Australians for the war effort.[14] Labor drew on the advice of a group of brillant young economists and bureaucrats, such as H.C. Coombs, Richard Downing and Roland Wilson, to plan war and post-war reconstruction policy. These men drew their inspiration from English economist John Maynard Keynes, whose theories of regulated capitalism and full employment were profoundly influential for the next 30 years. These men lived in the shadow of the Depression, and it is not surprising that full employment was seen as the best safeguard against poverty. It was in this context that social security benefits were relegated to the role of safety net for those who through some misfortune were not employed. At the same time the government skilfully used the rhetoric of equality of sacrifice and reconstruction to sweep aside the opposition that had stalled the introduction of welfare schemes. In three years (1942–45) the Curtin government introduced new benefits for the sick, widows and deserted mothers, and the unemployed and increased benefits for the aged and invalid.

The war provided not just a rationale for reform but also a

practical means for securing the financial basis for new social security benefits. Labor's opposition to social insurance forced the government to look for another source of funds. Before the war the State governments were responsible for the collection and spending of income tax revenue. In 1942, as a war-time measure, the Commonwealth government assumed from the States the power to levy income tax. This significantly altered the relations within the Federal system. The Commonwealth now had the fiscal means to regulate the Australian economy and provide new services on a national scale. But to provide the necessary funds the government decided to broaden the tax base by reducing the minimum taxable income from £156 to £104, and under this system Commonwealth tax revenue rose from £90 million in 1939 to £257 million in 1943. A proportion (a quarter) of all income tax revenue was paid into a National Welfare Fund—a financial reserve for the payment of benefits. In effect there was a hidden contributory element to the new welfare state, despite Labor's opposition to contributory schemes. On the other side Labor sought to minimise the tax burden by reducing outlays through a means test for pensions.

This policy perpetuated long standing divisions and resentments in the community, between those stigmatised as recipients and those who paid their taxes but were excluded from benefits. In addition a greatly increased administrative machine was needed to inspect the recipients to ensure that they did not lie about income and impose on the social security system. In important ways Labor's new welfare state failed to fully extricate itself from the 19th century charity tradition.

After the war Labor's reform campaign stalled. Opposition to further social welfare benefits emerged. In 1945 the Australian branch of the British Medical Association successfully challenged the constitutional validity of the 1944 Pharmaceutical Benefits Act. Even though the Act was redrafted and passed in 1946 the Association advised doctors not to cooperate with the scheme. In 1949 surveys found that only 155 doctors out of 8000 were prepared to write prescriptions under the new system.[15] The medical profession was equally implacable in the face of government efforts to introduce a comprehensive hospital and medical benefits scheme. They opposed any suggestion of government control over remuneration and conditions, retaining their faith in the ideal of the family doctor and the fee-for-service principle. The Association argued that this system provided the best service and, in answer to critics, pointed out that doctors generally waived fees when treating the poor. For the rest of the population the Association advocated private insurance.

These proposals were not welcomed by the government or the National Health and Medical Research Council, which argued that the individual family doctor system left many people in isolated areas without medical services and inhibited the development of coordinated preventive health campaigns.[16] Only in Queensland did the State government succeed in introducing free hospital treatment for all. Elsewhere doctors preferred their traditional role as benevolent, but paternalist, professionals. This meant that medical care was not a right. People too distant from doctors and hospitals, too fearful of the cost or without a family doctor could miss out an essential services.

By the late 1940s Australia had a greatly expanded social security system. The Labor government had managed to redress the years of inaction in the welfare field. Commonwealth spending on social security rose from 2.8 per cent of Gross National Product in 1938–39 to 4.2 per cent in 1949–50. By 1946 there were 320 000 old age and invalid pensioners, 42 000 widow's pensioners, 140 000 claims for unemployment and sickness benefits in that year, 156 000 maternity allowance claims and families received child endowment for one million children. For nearly 400 000 people, 5 per cent of the population, social security payments were their sole source of income. But the failure to introduce a comprehensive hospital and medical benefits scheme meant that Australia still lacked important welfare services common in other western nations.

Australia's reliance on benefits available only to those who satisfied a means test differentiated its welfare system from other countries which endorsed the insurance model. As a consequence social security was not a universal right in Australia and recipients were still the subject of inspection. In 1946, 22 per cent of invalid pension, 17 per cent of widow's pension and 9 per cent of old age pension applications were rejected.[17] Australia had established a unique framework for its welfare state but did it substantially improve the lives of poor Australians?

A community observed

The immediate post-war years were difficult ones for many Australians. The concentration of production on the war effort had diverted investment from sectors of the economy such as construction and by 1944 there was a housing shortfall of 257 521 dwellings. The return of soldiers and the arrival of the first refugees placed even greater pressures on the housing market. Government rent controls meant many landlords charged 'key money' for new tenants to move into controlled premises. Some families were forced to do without furniture after using all their savings to buy the key. Migrants faced particular difficulties after their stay in government camps.[18] They had still not resided long enough (five years for widow's or invalid's pension, twenty years for old age pension) to qualify for social security benefits.

The majority of Australians, however, did qualify and these benefits provided a buffer against hardship. But not all prospered. In 1946 Mona Ravenscroft, an experienced sociological researcher, was commissioned by the Department of Post War Reconstruction and the University of Sydney to investigate living conditions in the inner city Sydney suburb of Newtown,[19] a poorer working-class suburb. In addition to families who had lived in the area for a few generations, the suburb was populated by recently arrived families attracted by cheap rents and single labourers seeking lodgings. Housing conditions were poor.

The majority of houses in the area were small run-down three-room cottages with few windows and postage-stamp backyards. There were three boarding houses in the area for single men and pensioners. Some, however, lodged with local families. Ravenscroft found that a third of Newtown's dwellings were inhabited by families sharing with lodgers. There were also extended family networks. The 'Mattingley clan' were scattered in a number of houses in the one street. In one house lived two brothers, their wives and children, a sister (deserted by her husband) and her children and a male boarder. Two doors down lived another brother and sister with their respective spouses and children. Inadequate wages forced many to share their homes and, as a consequence, dwellings were found to be seriously overcrowded, averaging one and half persons for every room in the suburb, nearly twice the national average. Facilities were also poor. In a sample of 371 houses Ravenscroft found only ten with coppers for washing.

Although the national economy was sound, many of the male breadwinners in Newtown were unskilled labourers working in casual or seasonal employments. They could ill afford rents on unprotected properties. Those on social security benefits were the worst off. After single pensioners paid 10s to 12s a week (out of a total benefit of 32s 6d) for a room in a family home or boarding house there was little left over for daily expenses or emergencies. Some deserted and widowed mothers found the pension so inadequate that they threw it in and took up full-time work to support their families. This conformed to the self-help ethos of traditional charity but it meant that children were left alone for long periods, with only neighbours and friends to 'keep and eye out' for them.

Those families in arrears of rent and facing eviction did 'midnight flits', taking furniture and other items. Others hoped to stay in the community and neighbours sometimes came to the rescue. Mrs G was a young married woman who had had four children in the first five years of marriage. One of the children contracted mumps and her husband was also seriously afflicted. He was laid off work and they got behind in the rent. They were evicted and slept in a park for a few nights. A few days later a woman going into hospital to have a child offered to let Mrs G and her family stay for a while if they helped with the cooking and housework. Twenty people lived in a small four-bedroom house for the two months it took Mrs G and her family to find another home.

Help from friends and neighbours suggests that there were community bonds. Some benefited from neighbourhood sympathy. Widowed and deserted mothers on a pension who worked under assumed names to supplement their income were helped by neighbours who 'kept an eye out' for well-dressed strangers, thought to be government inspectors, and offered the information—'Mrs so and so is in town today'. But there were also clear divisions in the community. Many, despite impoverished circumstances, valued their respectability and viewed with contempt and suspicion those living in back streets who were known to gain their livelihood through theft and prostitution. Another despised group were the 'charity mongers', not considered by locals to be 'genuinely' needy, who span a 'facile tale of woe to a gullible welfare officer'.

Families were not always united in the fight against poverty. Conflicts erupted over the distribution of income in the home and at the centre of these disputes was the husband's 'pocket-money'. It was customary for husbands to retain part of their wage for gambling, drinking and other pastimes. Ravenscroft's inquiries revealed that most husbands took pocket-money and one fifth retained half or more of their pay packet. Some families, even those with a supposedly reasonable income, suffered because wives had to feed and clothe the whole family on a fraction of their husband's wage and this made child endowment an important income supplement for mothers. But some husbands viewed endowment as an excuse to take more for their own pocket-money.

Women's awareness that they were 'losing the economic battle' prompted actions to reduce the number of births. Although some women attempted to induce their own abortions Ravenscroft found that the services of the local midwife were well-known and well-patronised. One woman explained that she had had five miscarriages, three spontaneous and two induced, and each had become septic leading to a long hospital convalescence. Her husband had eventually left her, an action viewed with relief, even though she had to support three children; 'I think I'm lucky my husband's gone. Even when he was here I had to work'.

Ravenscroft argued that local welfare services were inadequate and little patronised by Newtown residents. Men found the local Employment Bureau alienating and disliked the close scrutiny and questions from officers when they applied for unemployment benefits. Locals also avoided medical services, except as a last resort. They hated the outpatients department at Royal Prince Alfred Hospital because they had to wait for long periods 'like sheep in a pen' for any help and were then placed in a bed 'when there was so much work to be done at home'. Mothers avoided Baby Health Centres because they had 'too much to do' but Ravenscroft suspected that they disliked being patronised and made to feel incompetent by the trained nurses.

The only service accepted by locals was the District Nursing Association. The nurses visited homes free of charge, sometimes helped with the housework, provided health counselling and put people in touch with doctors. In one year the nurses made 40 386 home visits and assisted 2274 Newtown residents. Sometimes they discovered terrible cases of destitution. One old pensioner who had not eaten for a week was found in a boarding house room lying on a wire bed with no mattress, suffering a severe case of bronchitis. Although the service was free some grateful families slipped the nurses a few pence. People appreciated the district nursing service because it was local, personalised and did not force people to be treated in large, intimidating institutions.

Ravenscroft's study suggested that Labor's welfare state had failed to provide an adequate safety net for many poor Australians. Social security was designed to supplement the savings of those unable to find regular employment, but income supplements are crude social policy devices. They take little account of conflicts within families, the assertion of masculine prerogatives that disadvantage mothers and children, the burden of more children than the family income can sustain or the embarrassment that some face applying for benefits. Despite the efforts of reformers many poor Australians still viewed security payments as a form of charity and preferred to do without rather than accept their entitlement. But the study did suggest improvement. Despite evidence of great privation Ravenscroft found fewer instances of the abject destitution that charitable workers had found so often in 19th century colonial cities. The effect of government benefits in the 20th century seems to have been the eradication of chronic destitution and the construction of poverty as relative hardship. The distinction is a fine one, of little concern to those struggling to survive, but important in charting the historical dimensions of poverty.

The helping professions

After 1942 the Commonwealth government provided most of the funds for social security but State governments retained responsibility for organising many social services and distributing funds. State governments continued to provide services for the sick, the mentally ill, Aborigines, the homeless and neglected, orphaned and delinquent children These services were extensive. In 1946 there were 42 286 public hospital beds in Australia catering for 667 927 patients throughout the year, 26 520 beds in mental hospitals, 35 384 children under various forms of state supervision and 28 207 Aborigines maintained on reserves or placed in institutions. These services cost over £15 million. By 1965 the cost of hospital services alone had risen to £180 million, funding 64 477 public hospital and 34 000 mental hospital beds.

In the post-war years slum clearance and the provision of public housing became important policy areas. Between 1944 and 1966, 247 051 homes were constructed under public housing schemes, and a further 10 000 homes a year were built under War Service schemes. As a consequence the number of people living in the old inner-city areas declined. In 1933, 16 per cent of Sydney's population lived in the inner city but by 1961 this proportion had fallen to 8 per cent.[20] The dispersal of inner-city communities, however, also disrupted the neighbourhood support systems that had been significant in the survival of many poor families.

Private charities and church welfare services were vital in the provision of welfare services. The number of societies grew after 1945. By 1970 there were 20 000 to 30 000 different charitable organisations in Australia, many government subsidised, to the tune of $131 million by 1976. These church and charity organisations operated a large number of hostels, homes for the aged, child welfare homes, kindergartens, hospitals, soup kitchens and refuges for the poor, much as charities had done in the 19th century. Many of these were small societies but there were also a number of large societies which continued to operate, and even expand their services, in the post-war period: notably the Smith Family, Central Methodist Mission, Dr Barnardo's Homes, St Vincent de Paul Society, Brotherhood of St Laurence and the Salvation Army. By 1965 the St

Vincent de Paul Society, one of the largest charities, had nearly 10 000 active members and they provided food, clothing and rent subsidies for 149 839 people at a cost of half a million pounds.

Churches and charities relied heavily on volunteer workers and were thus able to provide assistance more cheaply than if it had been distributed directly by governments. In the 1930s charities sought to coordinate their activities by forming State Councils of Social Service. The first was established in New South Wales in 1936 and in 1956 the Australian Council of Social Service was established to provide a point of national coordination. Through these councils, charities and voluntary agencies became important lobby groups for improved funding and services for the poor.[21]

The system of state and private social services for the poor retained much of its colonial character. Governments had assumed greater control over such services as health and hospitals but in the 20th century the old charity model of private benevolence and public subsidy continued to be the basis for much poor relief. In other respects, however, the model was changing. The lady visitors and police who had been the inspectors for colonial charities were being replaced by a new professional workforce—the social workers. Along with this new profession there was a gradual abandonment of moral ideas of poverty and the emergence of social and psychological theories.

The origin of the social worker lay in the case work practices pioneered by the Charity Organisation Society in the late 19th century.[22] This system had been designed to overcome the indiscriminate alms giving of the 'lady bountiful'. In Britain, Australia and America the scientific casework approach was grafted onto the role of the hospital almoner and the new idea of the social worker emerged. In the 1920s charity organisations began to press for the establishment of social work training courses at universities. Sydney, Melbourne and Adelaide Universities responded but the demand was small. By 1941 there were only 95 university qualified social workers employed in Australia, half of them with private agencies, the rest in public hospitals and government departments. In the post-war period, however, the growth of government and private social services created a greater demand for social workers and a significant expansion in funding for tertiary education facilitated their training. The growth in the profession was gradual, small by world standards, but by the mid-1960s there were over 400 university trained social workers in Australia.

Social workers in Australia were trained on a British model. This focused on the social aspects of poverty in contrast to the American emphasis on psychology. Australian social workers studied econo-

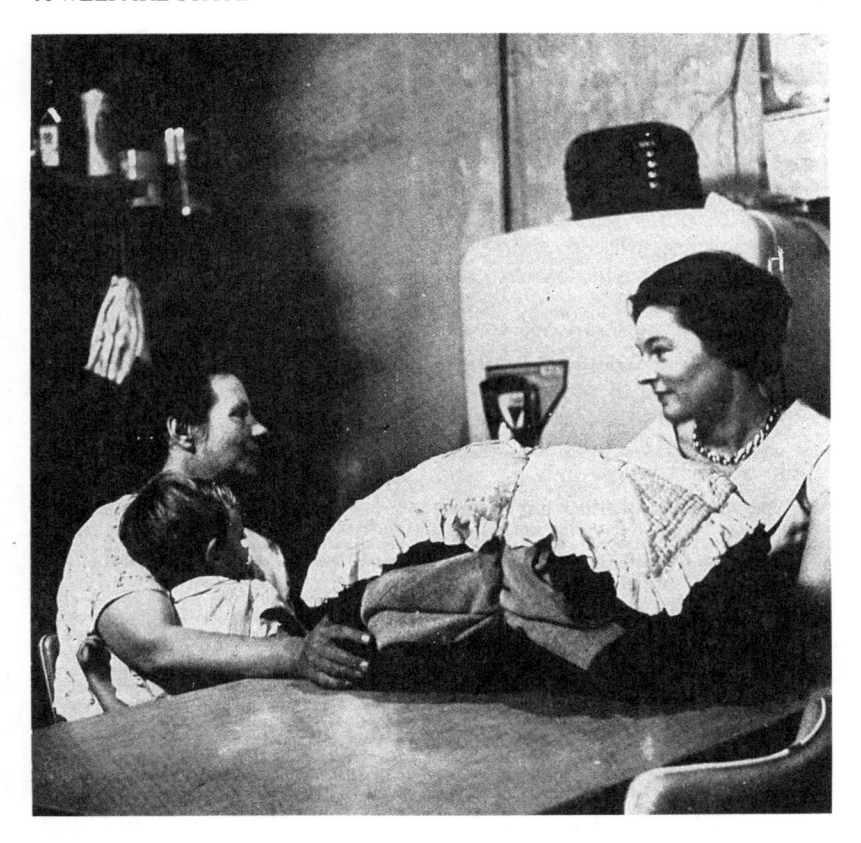

The emergence of the social worker, Melbourne 1958. The professions arrived not only to provide material assistance but advice and guidance. (Photo courtesy Brotherhood of St Laurence)

mics, sociology, political science, psychology, biology and history. They were taught to see poverty as a consequence of unemployment, illness, family breakdown and lack of access to services. Their role was to mediate between the needs of the client and available services; identifying people in need, advising them of help available, contacting services and arranging employment or home care. The emphasis on connecting people to services was a significant break from the charitable tradition of investigating applicants to weed out the undeserving. But some traditional practices lingered on. Social workers and departmental officers still investigated applicants for assistance and many found to be 'of bad character, dirty, slovenly or with a criminal record' were denied assistance.[23]

Another significant transformation in the character of social services in post-war Australia was the growing influence of psychiatry in the treatment of particular social problems. In the 1940s psychiatrists warned that Australia faced a serious public health problem from the return of soldiers suffering from war neurosis. This had been the case after World War I and medical authorities had been unprepared for the extent of this problem. In 1946 Melbourne psychiatrist Reg Ellery warned, 'without mental hygiene developed and disseminated throughout the length and the breadth of every community there can be no hope for preserving a stable and lasting peace'.[24] To assist in this public health program psychiatrists advocated the opening of more clinics where patients could receive treatment without the fear of certification and compulsory confinement in an asylum.

Psychiatrists concentrated their efforts on treating the curable neuroses and mild psychoses in private clinics, outpatient facilities of general hospitals and the special admission wards for voluntary patients at mental hospitals. Through these means psychiatrists hoped to treat patients in the early stages of the illness when they were supposedly more curable. To facilitate this process psychiatrists argued that knowledge of mental illness and available treatments needed to be spread more widely in the community.

Part of the problem, according to psychiatrists, was that mental illness was far more prevalent than had been recognised. It was not just the 'socially maladjusted' who needed treatment but a broader range of people not previously considered ill. In the 1940s psychiatrists stressed the idea of 'psychosomatic illness' to argue that many patients consulting general practitioners had mental not physical problems. Others argued that many forms of social behaviour were really the product of 'mass neurosis'. In 1948 Alan Stoller, prominent Melbourne psychiatrist, suggested that the manifestations of neurosis could be seen in 'family disruption, crime, sex disorder, alcoholism and social neuroses, in racial prejudice, industrial conditions, poor housing, overt maladjusted behaviour, aggression, accidents, strikes, racketeering'. The *Medical Journal of Australia* announced that psychiatry could be a means of curing absenteeism.[25] Psychiatrists sought to re-define many forms of behaviour as mental in origin with the aim of extending the scope of psychiatric treatment in the interests of 'social well-being'.

The psychiatrists' arguments were bolstered by the drug revolution of the 1950s. In this decade a range of anti-psychotic and tranquilliser drugs were developed, hailed by psychiatrists as the first real alternative to incarceration for the insane. As a consequence the number of private psychiatric clinics began to grow, more psychiatrists were attached to child welfare and community health services and new legislation made it easier for patients to seek psychiatric treatment. The psychiatric message also filtered into popular culture. Newspapers and women's journals carried stories on suburban neurosis and headlines such as 'Neurosis Rules Today's Family', 'The Psychology of the Child' and 'Everyone Suffers from Fits of Depression'. On the same page there were usually advertisements for drugs, tranquillisers and new psychotherapies.

People were sensitised to the psychological stresses of everyday life and the treatments available for common problems but there was little discussion of the serious side effects of long-term drug taking. By 1970 nearly 13 million prescriptions a year, a fifth of all prescriptions, were for tranquillisers and anti-psychotic drugs. The target of much of this literature was women and this was reflected in treatment statistics. By the 1960s, 60 per cent of all patients undergoing psychiatric care were women, a far cry from the 19th century when the majority of patients had been men.[26]

Drugs allowed many more people to be treated outside the old mental hospital system. Between 1946 and 1970 the annual number of patients treated in psychiatric clinics rose by 60 000. Added to these were the thousands treated with drugs who remained at home. The style of treatment in the old mental hospitals also changed. Increasingly people were admitted for short periods, pacified with drugs, then released before they were diagnosed as recovered, only to be readmitted at a later date. The average length of stay of patients fell from 56 days in 1946 to 24 days in 1970 but the rate of readmission rose from 15 per cent to 60 per cent in the same period. Critics suggested that the move to an open-door policy had become a revolving door policy. Those left in the mental hospitals were considered incurable and faced declining conditions. In the 1950s and 1960s a series of inquiries into mental hospitals revealed a picture 'of mass overcrowding, with a general level of custodial care with little active treatment'.[27] In the post-war period psychiatrists had an increasing role in defining and treating many social problems but their traditional clientele, generally older and poorer patients, languished in prison-like institutions.

The growth of social work and psychiatric services in the post-war period had a significant impact on the provision of help for the poor and dependent. Although social work's emphasis on the social environment and psychiatry's stress on individual psychology ran counter to each other some social welfare experts argued for the virtues of a teamwork approach to deal with 'multi-problem' families.

Social and psychological intervention in tandem might better cope with families suffering the effects of alcohol, violence and stress and related problems such as delinquent children. Even in the prosperous times of the 1950s and 1960s charities and government social services found there was no shortage of applicants for assistance and they turned to the new professions in the hope of providing permanent solutions to the social problems associated with poverty.

Prosperity and poverty

The 1950s and 1960s have been seen as years of significant economic growth. High levels of investment, buoyant world trade, good prices for Australian produce on overseas markets and a rapid growth in the domestic market, largely due to unprecedented levels of immigration, were some of the key factors in Australia's post-war boom. In the two decades after the war over two million migrants arrived and Australia's population rose from seven and a half million in 1945 to eleven million in 1966. In the same period overseas investment rose from £500 million to £5000 million, the number of factories in Australia doubled, the real value of manufactured goods trebled, export income from manufacturing increased tenfold, wool and wheat production doubled, average weekly earnings increased sevenfold and although inflation undercut these gains unemployment averaged only one per cent. This was an unprecedented period of prosperity for Australians. But some evidence suggests that not every Australian shared in this prosperity.[28]

In 1950 Melbourne *Herald* reporter John Hetherington ran a story under the headline 'Is Old Age a Crime?'. He detailed the 'squalid, filthy and sordid' conditions in which some old age pensioners lived. This story prompted an inquiry by the Victorian government and the Brotherhood of St Laurence into the problems of Melbourne's old age pensioners. The inquiry found that 15 000 pensioners in Melbourne, the majority of whom were women, were unable to buy sufficient food and were forced to live on bread and butter supplemented by the occasional tin of soup. The same people could not afford sufficient clothes and lived in run-down houses, with leaking roofs, damp walls and poor ventilation. Nearly 2000 pensioners' homes had little or no water supply. One man was found living in a corrugated iron hut with no windows and a canvas sheet to protect him against the rain. Only a small proportion (2 per cent) of Melbourne's pensioners lived in nursing homes or private institutions but some of these residences were found to be in a poor state of repair with few facilities and terrible meals. Government attempts

A WELFARE STATE?

Poverty in the 'lucky country'. A poor family in a government housing camp near Brisbane in 1956. (Photo courtesy John Oxley Library)

to improve pensioner housing in the light of this report fell short of demand.[29] By 1963 waiting lists for subsidised housing were long and many private organisations demanded donations before providing accommodation, thus depriving the very poorest of assistance.[30]

Widowed and deserted mothers were another impoverished group despite the pension. A 1961 survey of widows, sponsored by the NSW Council of Social Service, found that 14 per cent of widowed mothers had no money left after paying rent and food while a further 38 per cent had less than £1 left each week after these basic expenses. Some widowed mothers complained that they received 'a starvation pension' and, forced to live 'on the breadline all the time', they had no money to meet extra burdens such as school fees, medical expenses or unusual problems such as special shoes for flat-footed children. Some were forced to live in cheap slum housing infested with rats and social workers reported a high incidence of juvenile delinquency amongst children raised in these circumstances.[31]

Unemployment, intermittent and casual work or the illness of a breadwinner continued to be important factors in plunging some families into poverty. Unemployment benefits did not alleviate this situation. In 1961 the Brotherhood of St Laurence calculated that reasonable food and living costs for a family of five were 5s a week more than the unemployment benefit.[32] Problems for these families were compounded by the delay between applying for and receiving unemployment benefits, a delay for which they were not compensated. If a family lacked savings they could get behind in rent and face eventual eviction. These families lived in 'constant anxiety' over how to pay the bills. Most bought household items on hire purchase, getting into debt beyond their means, and had to cut down on food to avoid repossession. This made them more vulnerable to illness, for which they had no insurance. It was a vicious circle. The Piper family were typical. Mr Piper had a wife and seven children and only worked for twenty weeks during 1960. The family lived in a two-bedroom brick home in Melbourne, the gas had been cut off after they failed to pay the bill and they had almost no furniture after being evicted from their previous home. Mr Piper went looking for work every day, had no medical insurance and was £100 in debt. He admitted to being depressed but stoically declared 'it's up to you'.[33]

Migrants faced particular hurdles in sharing Australia's wealth, particularly if they could not speak English. Between 1947 and 1980 half a million migrants came from Southern Europe (18.5 per cent of all migrants in this period) and a further 380 000 (13.3 per cent) came from Eastern Europe, most arriving before 1970. Upon arrival these migrants generally found employment in the poorer paid sectors of the workforce, particularly in the expanding manufacturing industries. Migrants from these regions averaged lower incomes and higher rates of unemployment than Australian born workers, English migrants and migrants from Northern Europe. Not all migrants from Southern or Eastern Europe struggled, many prospered, but in times of crisis arising from unemployment, illness, widowhood or advancing age these migrants faced acute problems. Many had no relatives to assist them and the language barrier prevented them from seeking government or charitable assistance to which they were entitled. Some succumbed to the stress of settling in a new culture.

From the 1950s Australian psychiatrists noted a high incidence of mental breakdown amongst newly arrived migrants from Southern and Eastern Europe. New arrivals also found that they were not always entitled to assistance available to others. Mrs T, a 60-year-old Russian widow, arrived in Australia in 1964. Two years later her sponsor became ill and she was let alone. Crippled by arthritis, she could only perform small tasks and was forced to live in a small shed at the back of a hotel. She had no light, electricity or water, cooked on a primus stove, carried water from a nearby laundry and used the toilet facilities of the hotel. For a few chores she earned $8 a week, only a quarter of the female minimum wage and $5 less than the pension, while her rent was $4, and because she was newly arrived she was ineligible for an old age pension.[34]

In the early 1960s a few social commentators began to draw these threads of evidence together. In 1963 Ray Brown, lecturer in social administration at Adelaide University, argued that poverty was not restricted to a few small pockets in inner city slums. He believed that 5 per cent of the population lived in chronic poverty.[35] Two years later similar arguments were published by David Scott, Director of the Brotherhood of St Laurence in Melbourne. He declared that serious poverty existed amongst aged and invalid pensioners, widowed and deserted mothers and the families of the unemployed.[36]

These studies drew their inspiration from the studies of British poverty by Townsend, Titmuss and Donnison, which found that 14 per cent of Britain's population was poor, and Hutchinson's famous 1963 study *Hidden America* which argued that 20 per cent of the population of North America lived in poverty. The Australian figures were not as high but they highlighted a stark contrast between the average sized family supported by a male breadwinner and pensioners, the unemployed, families supported by a female breadwinner and large families. American revelations of widespread poverty had prompted President Lyndon Johnson to declare a 'war on poverty' but Australian politicians were reluctant to admit that there was a problem. In 1965 Harold Holt, Deputy Leader of the Liberal Party, could not 'accept the implication that Australian standards of social welfare are low'.[37]

One of the most forceful statements on poverty in Australia was made by John Stubbs in his 1966 work *The Hidden People*. He set out the evidence in stark detail. In his view half a million Australians, 5 per cent of the population, were living in chronic poverty and most of these received welfare benefits. As many as 45 000 Australians lived in tin sheds and huts, 25 per cent of all aged pensioners lived below a subsistence living standard and in Melbourne alone, 5000 lived on 'skid row'. Stubbs cited cases of pensioners buying dog meat for themselves. They lived in boarding house tenements with no electricity or water and were forced to urinate in bathtubs. One aged couple were found living in an old stable in the Sydney suburb of Rockdale. They had no gas, water or electricity. The evidence was overwhelming. Stubbs concluded that Australians had deluded themselves in thinking that they had one of the fairest societies in the world and that Australia's social welfare provisions were unequalled by any other country.[38]

Stubbs' work was a powerful indictment of the social security system but his estimates of the extent of poverty were based on rather impressionistic evidence. In 1966, however, the Melbourne University Institute of Applied Economic and Social Research, headed by Professor Ronald Henderson, set out to quantify the extent of poverty in Melbourne. This study introduced a new concept into the Australian social welfare debate—the poverty line. By fixing a minimum income level for an acceptable standard of living (the poverty line), it was possible to assess how many people lived in poverty. But what was the minimum acceptable living standard?

To avoid criticism the Henderson team chose a deliberately austere base level, equivalent to the male minimum wage. With this standard they concluded that 7.7 per cent of all family units in Melbourne lived on or below the poverty line and a further 5.2 per cent hovered dangerously close to the minimum level. If the Melbourne figures were typical then Australia-wide there were half a million Australians living in poverty, a figure closely approximating Stubbs' estimates.[39] It was no longer possible to deny the existence of poverty in Australia, or to conclude that it was confined to a few isolated pockets of society. This was hailed as the 'rediscovery of poverty' in Australia. More accurately it was the grudging acceptance of the argument that there was a dark underside to Australia's prosperity. It was apparent that governments had failed to address the problem of poverty and these arguments and the concept of the poverty line gave significant impetus to the poverty debate in Australia in the 1970s and 1980s.

8 A banana republic?

In 1972, in a volatile Federal election climate, the failure of the social security system to eradicate poverty became an important issue. The McMahon Coalition government appointed Professor Ronald Henderson to head an inquiry into the problem. McMahon lost the election but the incoming Labor administration of Gough Whitlam retained the Inquiry, expanding its resources and terms of reference. Over the next three years the Inquiry completed a series of detailed reports charting the dimensions of poverty in Australia. Using the 'austere' level of a male basic wage as a poverty line measure the Inquiry concluded that 6.9 per cent of all family units could be classified as very poor, living below the poverty line, and a further 7.7 per cent were poor, living on or just above the poverty line.[1] These figures confirmed that the Melbourne findings were national in scope. The Inquiry also found that three-quarters of those classified as very poor received social security benefits. Far from being a safety net, social security was a major signifier of poverty.

The Henderson Poverty Inquiry drew its conclusions at the high point of Australian prosperity. In 1973 the OPEC oil crisis signalled the beginnings of a downturn in the world economy, uniquely combined with rapid inflation. The Australian economy, as in previous world recessions, suffered badly. By 1975 inflation had risen to 17 per cent and by 1978 the unemployment rate reached 7.4 per cent or nearly half a million people. Governments adopted tough economic measures, reducing expenditure and tightening controls on the money market. By the mid-1980s inflation was below 10 per cent but unemployment at 6 to 7 per cent was still high.[2] Australia faced serious economic problems. A worsening balance of trade highlighted that Australian industry was uncompetitive. In 1987 Paul Keating, Treasurer in the Hawke Labor government, warned that unless Australians were prepared to restrain consumption, restrict wage demands, increase investment and restructure the economy, then we might become 'a banana republic'.

In these straitened economic times welfare groups struggled to maintain services for Australia's growing poor population. They noted disturbing trends in Australian society. By 1987 significant wealth was being created in Australia; there were 30 000 millionaires who owned 60 per cent of all Australia's wealth but poverty was also increasing. By conservative estimates 12.4 per cent of Australian households lived below the poverty line, almost double the figure for 1973. The proportion of the population dependent on social security rose from 9.3 per cent in the early 1970s to 18.2 per cent in 1981. The gap between rich and poor seemed to be widening and the ideal of an egalitarian society appeared increasingly difficult to sustain.[3]

Poverty and welfare

The Henderson poverty line provided a yardstick for the measurement of poverty, but it was not an entirely secure measure. Fixing a poverty line required some assessment of a minimum acceptable standard of living below which people should not live and Henderson recognised that such a level was as much a social and moral question as it was an economic one. Henderson was responding to the current debate about absolute and relative poverty. Most social welfare commentators drew a distinction between the absolute poor—eking out a bare subsistence living—and the relatively poor, whose standard of living was significantly below that of the majority of citizens. Australia, with by some estimates 40 000 destitute homeless people, had very little absolute poverty.[4] The poverty line was a device to measure relative poverty and its social incidence. Poor Australians were those who struggled to afford decent housing, sufficient food and clothing and did not have the same access to adequate education, health and aged care facilities as other Australians.

In hindsight what is most surprising is the general acceptance of the Henderson poverty line. Across the political spectrum the poverty line was accepted as an adequate measure of poverty in Australia. While this has ensured the legitimacy of the poverty line it obscures the fact that a significant number of Australians live in quite poor circumstances but just above the poverty line.

The Henderson Inquiry found that the Australians with the lowest incomes were the single aged; invalids; single, deserted or widowed mothers; large families; rural families; newly arrived migrants and most Aborigines. Over a third of low income households were the single aged. Most of these findings consolidated the conclusions drawn from earlier studies. A surprise was the high incidence of

The aged were still a large proportion of the poor. A Melbourne pensioner in 1970. (*Social Security*, Volume 1, 1973)

rural poverty. The Inquiry found that a sixth of all farms in Australia had incomes below the poverty line, although there were significant regional differences. Many of the poor rural families owned dairy farms in Queensland or apple orchards in the Huon Valley in Tasmania, ruined by the entry of Britain into the EEC.

The high incidence of rural poverty was partly due to the high proportion of large families, unemployed and aged people in country districts. The major reasons, however, were the lower wages for rural work and the few opportunities for country women to supplement an inadequate family income with part-time work. As a consequence many rural people lived in substandard housing and had inadequate diets. In North Queensland 10 per cent of the population lived in caravan parks. In Northern New South Wales the Henderson Inquiry found some farmers reduced to a diet of fried onions.[5]

Low income was not the only factor in poverty. The cost of housing was also important. Many single aged and rural families owned their own homes and were thus significantly better off than those forced to rent. When housing costs were also calculated, the Henderson Inquiry found that single, deserted and widowed mothers were the poorest Australians. Almost half of all fatherless families lived below the poverty line and many more lived just above that line. A third of all deserted mothers in Australia had debts of more than $500 and only 5 per cent of single mothers and 12 per cent of deserted mothers had more than $200 in savings; an inadequate buffer against unexpected bills or small emergencies such as sudden illness.[6]

The overwhelming conclusion of the researches of Stubbs, the Melbourne survey and the Poverty Inquiry was that social welfare benefits had failed to eradicate poverty. Pensions were meagre and child endowment insufficient to meet the needs of large families. The long period of Coalition government (1949–72) had seen little change in the social security system established by the Curtin and Chifley Labor governments. Successive Coalition administrations had increased the proportion of Gross National Product spent on social security from 4.7 per cent to 6.7 per cent, but these were modest gains by world standards. Between 1955 and 1970 Australia had the smallest growth in welfare expenditure of any OECD country and by 1966 had the fourth-lowest rate of expenditure on welfare of fourteen developed countries. Individuals also fared badly. Although residence and means tests for pensions were liberalised, increasing the number of aged pensioners, between 1967 and 1971 the pension as a proportion of average weekly earnings fell by 5 per cent.[7] In 1972 the Labor Party, led by Gough Whitlam, campaigned strongly on the issue of overcoming the welfare neglect of previous governments. But how was this to be done?

The Henderson Report recommended a new solution to the problem of inadequate incomes—a guaranteed minimum income scheme. This involved integrating the social security system within the general wage and taxation system. All Australians would be guaranteed a minimum income equivalent to or greater than the poverty line, paid either as a direct sum or a tax credit with payments according to position added to this minimum. This scheme had the advantage of ensuring that everyone received an income on or above the poverty line. It had the added objective of removing the need for special benefits and thus breaking down the supposed stigma of being a welfare recipient. Critics, however, argued that it involved no signficant redistribution of income from rich to poor, addressed only income poverty and not wider issues of inequality, was inflexible and, by absorbing welfare into the tax structure, undermined the capacity of the poor to lobby for policies to address their special needs.[8]

These were important criticisms but the wider social and political context provided little opportunity for considering whether the guaranteed minimum income scheme could accommodate these problems. The Whitlam Labor government was in a hurry to fulfil its welfare election promises and it was easier to do this by working within existing frameworks than contemplating more complex changes. Whether it would have put these larger changes on the political agenda in due time is another matter. A rapidly deteriorating economy, cabinet inexperience, and a Governor-General robbed it of the chance.

The pace of reform during the Whitlam years was rapid. New benefits were introduced—the supporting mother's benefit (1973), the double orphan's pension (1973) and the handicapped child's allowance (1974). The rates for unemployment and sickness benefits were increased significantly (1973) to bring them into line with other pension benefits and were later (1975) indexed to cost of living increases. The residence qualification for the invalid pension was removed (1974), and the means test was abolished for pensioners aged over 75 in 1973 and for those aged over 70 in 1975. In addition a national medical, hospital and health benefits scheme (Medibank) was introduced for all Australians in 1975—a scheme bitterly opposed by the medical profession, which argued that this was the first step towards nationalising medicine, undermining the fee-for-service and family doctor principles at the heart of traditional health services. The government also provided funding for an ambitious community health program throughout Australia. Another innovative scheme was the Australian Assistance Plan, designed to tailor social services to local needs. Local government in Australia, unlike Britain and North America, played little role in the funding, administration or delivery of social services to the poor; instead policy was developed in the capital cities and applied to all regardless of local conditions. The Assistance Plan was an attempt to encourage local communities to formulate their own policies.[9]

These schemes required considerable financial outlays and Commonwealth funding for social services doubled between 1972 and 1975. Nevertheless Australia still lagged behind provisions in other Western nations which were similarly expanding their welfare programs in this period. The Whitlam government, however, faced a dilemma that had afflicted social welfare provision since the turn of the century. Should limited funds be directed towards the 'genuinely' needy or towards benefits for everyone? Australian governments had generally opted for a policy where the wages system protected the standard of living of workers and their families and selective benefits were used to assist the needy. By introducing new benefits, increasing the rate of existing benefits and removing residence qualifications the Whitlam government was providing selective assistance for the poorest Australians but by removing the means test for pensions and implementing a national health scheme the government was introducing some universal welfare benefits. Critics argued that this diverted funds from the needy to those who didn't need assistance; it was middle-class welfare. This was best exemplified when ex-Prime Minister Robert Menzies declared his intention to take the new means-test-free pension.

Between 1965 and 1975 the proportion of aged people in receipt of a pension rose from 53 per cent to 80 per cent. Nor was a national health system of direct benefit to the poor who had generally received free medical care. Instead it helped the 16 per cent of Australians on low incomes who although not 'very poor' could not afford private health insurance. But in a worsening economic climate opponents of Labor were able to accuse the government of extravagance, facilitating the election of the Fraser government in 1975.[10]

From 1973 governments also had to face the problem of rising unemployment and this placed particular strains on the social welfare system. Unemployment benefits had been a central feature of Chifley's safety net, but since their introduction unemployment had been negligible and mostly temporary. In 1974 the unemployment rate rose from 2 per cent to 6 per cent, by 1978 it was 7.4 per cent and it continues in the 1980s to hover between 6 per cent and 7 per cent. More serious was the fact that for many unemployment was not temporary. By the late 1970s a third of all those on unemployment benefits had been unemployed for more than six months. The highest incidence of unemployment was amongst women, newly arrived migrants and teenagers. By 1978, 35 per cent of all registered unemployed were aged between 15 and 19 years, giving Australia one of the three highest youth unemployment rates amongst the developed nations.

Official unemployment rates are only part of the story. Some have calculated that there is a significant number of unemployed not recorded. They include people who have given up the search for work, the homeless who no longer care to apply, married women who want to work but are ineligible for benefits, and those struck off benefits because they changed their address or refused to do particular jobs. The number of hidden unemployed could be as high as 6 per cent of the adult population, making the total number of unemployed in the 1980s nearly one million.[11]

Unemployment is now the single largest cause of poverty. The social consequences are serious. Charities such as St Vincent de Paul and the Salvation Army have noted a sharp rise in the number of teenagers on skid row, doubling between 1974 and 1977, and by the mid-1980s 20 per cent of all people seeking refuge in night shelters were aged under 25 years. At the other end of the spectrum 10 per cent of the unemployed were aged over 45 years, usually unskilled married men with little prospect of gaining new employment.[12]

Governments proved inadequate to the task of dealing with the unemployment crisis. The Whitlam government raised unemployment benefits but also sought to offset the increase in the unemployed by developing training programs to return people to the workforce. In 1974 the Regional Employment Development Scheme (REDS) was introduced, allowing local governments to fund the unemployed to work on specific projects. Over 30 000 people were employed in eighteen months at a cost of $123 million. In practice the scheme provided little training for permanent employment and instead closely resembled the public relief schemes of the 19th and early 20th centuries when the unemployed were used as a cheap labour force for public works. But these schemes proved expensive, much more so than just providing a dole payment, and were quickly abandoned.[13]

In 1975 public sympathy for the unemployed appeared to be fast disappearing. Media reports of welfare cheats and dole bludgers who lounged around on beaches instead of looking for work precipitated headlines such as 'Weed Out Dole Cheats'. The leader of the Liberal Party, Malcolm Fraser, campaigned strongly around the theme of Labor allowing the unemployed 'to laze around at the expense of the taxpayer'. These claims ignored the fact that the number of unemployed greatly exceeded the number of positions vacant. The election of the Fraser government in 1975 signalled a hardening of attitudes to the unemployed and in the next few years the work test became stricter, benefits were no longer indexed and the waiting period to receive benefits was extended. All of these made it more difficult for the unemployed to survive, forcing them to seek charity assistance. The antagonistic climate of opinion also suggested that fears about the supposed undeserving poor were still deeply ingrained in Australian political culture.[14]

In contrast many analysts of poverty were convinced that the problem lay in society, not with the individual. Ronald Henderson opened his report with the argument that 'poverty is inseparable from inequalities entrenched within the social structure'. There were fundamental inequalities of wealth, education, health, housing and employment which were the root cause of poverty. It was 'not just a personal attribute' but arose 'out of the organisation of society'. The Australian Council of Social Service agreed; the poor were 'victims of policies and power relationships outside their control'.[15] These views influenced the work of some charities and church organisations long concerned with poverty as a moral problem. In the early 1970s the Church of England Brotherhood of St Laurence reassessed its procedures and decided that they were 'blaming the victim' rather than tackling the real issues of inequality.[16] But these groups formed only one constituency for Australian governments. The other was the 'ordinary taxpayer' of popular media myth, concerned about 'dole cheats' and the waste of taxpayers' money. Although the incidence of welfare fraud was low, with only 246 successful prosecutions for welfare fraud between 1974 and 1976,[17] the legitimacy of social security rested on the maintenance of punitive policies to ensure people did not exploit the system.

The principle of less eligibility was still an integral part of the welfare system in the 1970s and 1980s. The pension and benefit rates were continually set at low levels to ensure that people worked, contributed to superannuation schemes, sought help from relatives or used their own savings in preference to seeking welfare assistance. Welfare applicants had to pass various tests. Applicants for unemployment benefits were required to demonstrate that they were actively looking for work. Single mothers were not allowed to have men stay overnight without risking losing benefits. Deserted mothers had to prove that their husbands or de factos had really left them. To enforce these checks Commonwealth and State governments used officers to interview and inspect welfare recipients and people on the dole could lose their benefits if they were not at home when government welfare officers arrived.

Some local organisations fought back and distributed pamphlets with such titles as 'The Snoops are in your Area'. Welfare and self-help groups complained about the demeaning and punitive attitudes of some government welfare officers. The Council for the Single Mother and Child in Tasmania found applicants abused by officers, who declared 'you are the one who has done wrong, why should we be expected to help you'. Applicants complained about the 'sadistic pleasure' of the interrogators as they were forced to go from desk to desk answering the same questions time and time again before qualifying for benefits. The Tasmanian Parents Alone Association described one case of a deserted wife who had just given birth to her ninth child when her husband left. She collapsed with a nervous breakdown, and friends and family sought to obtain a pension for her. A government officer who came to the hospital, where she was under sedation, refused to provide assistance until she filed for maintenance.[18]

The aim of many government officers was to minimise the number of people on benefit, not to identify those in need and provide support. Interviews and inspections were measures to find cheats but they also discouraged the poor from seeking assistance to which they were entitled. Studies in the New England district of New South Wales found that nearly 80 per cent of the local unemployed never registered for unemployment benefits. Others just did not know they were entitled to receive benefits. In Fremantle, the working-class port area near Perth, 40 per cent of the residents surveyed in 1973 did not know that a Department of Social Security existed. In the Adelaide suburb of Hindmarsh only 15 per cent of the residents had a reasonable knowledge of available social services.[19]

Other Australians found the rules and procedures mysterious. Mrs B, a widow, lost her unemployment benefits because of a change of address after moving to a dark, sparsely furnished weatherboard cottage in the Melbourne suburb of Kensington. She applied for special benefits, unaware that she could immediately reapply for unemployment benefits. While she waited for a decision on her application for special benefits she ran down her savings, got behind in the rent and lived on a diet of Bonox and biscuits, supplemented by an occasional meal supplied by a pensioner neighbour.[20]

Charities, church organisations, welfare rights groups and self-help groups, now more often called voluntary agencies or non-government organisations, attempted to fill the social security gap. They provided emergency food and clothing, and sometimes accommodation, referred people to government agencies if they qualified for benefits and provided temporary assistance for those who had applied but not yet received their benefits. In the 1970s the Brotherhood of St Laurence found that half of its clients needed food, clothing or accommodation, a quarter needed cash to pay gas, electricity and other bills and a fifth needed guidance on how to fill out government forms, apply for benefits or be placed on public housing waiting lists.[21] These were vital referral and material assistance services, particularly at a time when waiting periods for benefits were lengthening and criteria for receiving benefits were harsher. The non-government organisation sector expanded dramatically. By the 1980s it was estimated that there were at least 60000 voluntary agencies and charities in Australia, almost half of them established in the 1970s. By the late 1970s governments were providing $14 million a year to subsidise non-government organisations.[22]

Welfare was a growth industry in the 1970s. By 1980 there were thousands of volunteers working for non-government agencies, 30 000 social and welfare workers employed by these agencies and many thousands more employed as social workers, welfare workers, doctors, nurses, clerks and attendants in government health, housing and welfare departments. In addition the poor, disadvantaged and disabled began to form their own societies. Over 400 self-help groups were established in the 1970s.[23] Every day welfare workers experienced the frustrations of trying to deal with increasing poverty with inadequate resources. Some churches and other non-government organisations became important lobby groups pushing for improved welfare funding and facilities. They highlighted the long waiting lists for public housing, inadequate domiciliary services and overcrowded welfare institutions. Some, notably the Brotherhood of St Laurence and the Australian and various State Councils of Social Service, invested in extensive research to document the plight of the poor.

Some also protested government decisions. In 1976 the Social Security Action Group took the case of Karen Green, a Tasmanian school leaver who under new government guidelines had to wait six weeks before she could apply for the dole, to the High Court. This action proved unsuccessful but publicised the harshness of these new waiting policies. In 1980 new guidelines on invalid pensions resulted in a number of severely disabled persons being taken off the pension. The Australian Council of Social Service fought a long campaign to force the government to restore those benefits. But many protesting organisations believed they were in a difficult position, fearing they might lose funding if they campaigned too strongly.[24]

Welfare organisations argued that the problem of poverty went well beyond inadequate income. Poverty was the breeding ground for family violence, child abuse, crime, illegitimacy, alcoholism and mental breakdown. Social workers began to talk about multi-problem families to describe the ever widening problems faced by

A BANANA REPUBLIC?

> J. Walter Thompson's award-winning advertisement. The full page was donated by The Australian newspaper.

How do you tell a child there's nothing to eat?

What happens to a family when Dad is out of work and there's no money in the house?
When even the cheapest food is too expensive, we're the ones they turn to.
Last year, unemployment was responsible for 23 in every 100 families asking us for help. We see thousands every month, one-parent families, the sick, deserted and the unemployed.
When we're called to give help, your cash will help see that we can. Be generous. Please.

The Smith Family

All cash donations go directly to welfare. Send yours to The Smith Family, GPO Box 4068, Sydney NSW 2001

Charities, concerned at escalating levels of poverty, used sophisticated campaigns to broaden public support for their efforts. An award winning advertisement for the Smith Family in 1976. (Photo courtesy Smith Family) the poor.[25] They documented numerous cases of the poverty cycle that locked different generations of the same family into despair. One will suffice. Joan was a fifteen-year-old Melbourne girl when she left home. Her father had deserted some years before and her mother had no interest in her. She became pregnant but the father refused to marry her. She met another boy and they married and had three more children in quick succession. A local infant welfare nurse discovered that Joan's first child was severely malnourished and that Joan had little knowledge of diet or child care. The child was removed and temporarily placed with the Children's Protection Society. Although the other children were not well nourished, only the eldest was in a serious condition, suggesting to welfare officers that this child, because of the circumstances of its brith, had become the object of domestic tensions and resentments.

After the removal of the child, Joan and her husband had a series of violent arguments. Eventually the husband left, leaving Joan and the children in severe financial difficulty.[26] How did one solve this situation? For liberal reformers such as Ronald Henderson, tackling the problem of inadequate income was the first priority. But others questioned whether measures which redistributed income but failed to tackle more fundamental inequalities were sufficient. In the 1960s and 1970s a number of new political movements emerged, concerned with analysing some of the dominant structures of power underpinning many forms of poverty and criticising forms of state assistance which controlled the lives of the poor and disadvantaged.

New movements

In the 1960s and 1970s Aborigines stepped up their opposition to the well intentioned but paternalist assimilation policies of Australian governments. They campaigned for the right to govern their own lives and for improved conditions for Aborigines in urban and rural areas. In 1960 Aboriginal activist Doug Nicholls led the fight for the return of reserve land at Cumeroogunga to Aborigines and three years later led a similar struggle for the Aborigines at Lake Tyers in Victoria. In 1966 the Gurindji people went on strike at Wave Hill pastoral station in support of equal wages for Aboriginal workers. Aborigines such as Charles Perkins, Chicka Dixon and Faith Bandler worked in organisations to assist the growing numbers of Aborigines (estimated at 20 000 to 30 000) living in the poorer inner city areas of Australian capital cities. In the 1960s unemployment amongst urban Aborigines was five times greater than the Australian average and a quarter of all male Aboriginal workers earned less than the basic wage. In 1965 Aborigines and concerned reformers in Sydney established a welfare centre to find Aborigines employment and put them in contact with social services, assisting over 2000 in the first two years.[27]

Aboriginal activists directly confronted the social Darwinist ideas that shaped the attitudes of many white Australians, justifying the low wages of Aboriginal Australians, their confinement on reserves and the removal of Aboriginal children from their parents. Inspired by the black rights movements in America, Aborigines argued that the problems they faced were the product of racism, not some failure on their part. In 1965 Charlies Perkins organised Aborigines, reformers and students to bus into country towns in New South Wales in 'freedom rides' to publicise the pervasiveness of racial prejudice in Australia. The violent response to these rides highlighted racial antagonism. In 1972 Aboriginal activists established a tent embassy outside Parliament House in Canberra. They asserted that Australia had been invaded by Europeans and that the Aborigines who resisted this invasion had been slaughtered, or confined on reserves to facilitate colonisation. Far from being a peaceful process of settlement, the establishment of white Australia had been a violent conquest and Aborigines demanded compensation for the unlawful taking of their land. In this light the misguided policy of assimilation was a further assault on Aboriginal culture, denying Aborigines the right to determine their own future. Land rights became the linchpin of the Aboriginal struggle for self-determination. As one Aborigine declared: 'We don't want money, we want our land'.[28]

The struggle for land rights faced fierce opposition from local white communities, mining companies and State governments, particularly in Western Australia and Queensland, and success has been limited. In the courts land rights have been blocked by the 1971 Blackburn ruling that Aborigines had no inherent right to the land. In South Australia, New South Wales and the Northern Territory governments have granted limited land rights and helped establish Aboriginal land councils to allow Aborigines to order their own affairs. In Queensland and Western Australia, where a significant number of Aborigines live, land rights have not been granted and moves towards Aboriginal self-management have been minimal. Governments instead have found it easier to fund welfare services, thus maintaining Aborigines as a dependent group.

Aborigines also campaigned for welfare services operated by Aborigines rather than white welfare officers, claiming that only Aborigines are sensitive enough to the specific cultural problems of the urban Aboriginal poor. But Aboriginal legal, health and welfare services remain starved of government funds and many Aborigines remain dependent on direct government services. These government services have improved the health standards and well-being of Australia's 200 000 Aborigines but despite special funding they have not eradicated Aboriginal poverty.

In 1987 Aborigines still earned, on average, half the income of white Australians and had higher levels of unemployment. They had a high incidence of serious diseases, particularly blindness, leprosy, tuberculosis, hepatitis, syphilis and diabetes. Aborigines had three times the rate of still births in the white population, three times the rate of infant mortality and nine times the rate of maternal mortality.[29] In addition continuing high rates of criminal prosecution, violence, deaths in custody, alcoholism and petrol sniffing demonstrate that Aborigines face special problems produced by dispossession and racism. This suggests that Aboriginal poverty will be ameliorated not just by more money but more importantly by measures to restore Aboriginal cultural confidence and give them control over their own lives.

In the 1960s and 1970s the women's movement highlighted other structures of power and discrimination in Australian society. Feminists argued that women of all classes were oppressed in male dominated cultures and this was reflected in sexual violence, restricted work opportunities and low wages. Feminists such as Bettina Cass, Lois Bryson and Jill Roe argued that these social disadvantages were responsible for the high incidence of poverty amongst Australian women.[30] By the mid-1980s greater female unemployment, increasing numbers of deserted, single and widowed mothers and the fact that the majority of the aged are women ensured that two-thirds of all social security payments (excluding child endowment) were made to women.[31]

These problems were reflected in the plight of fatherless families, one of the poorest groups in contemporary Australia. Social security payments for mothers with dependent children were inadequate and one of the few means of escaping the poverty trap was employment. But despite equal pay legislation since 1973, women remained confined to the poorly paid sections of the workforce and the average female wage was only 67 per cent of the male wage.[32] Mothers seeking paid employment required adequate child-care facilities but in the 1980s government child-care provisions in Australia fell short of those in many other developed nations. In Australia there were only places for 5 per cent of children aged under three years, in contrast to France where there were places for 31 per cent and the United States which provided for 11 per cent.[33]

Feminists argued that widespread beliefs that women's proper place was in the home meant inadequate provision of services to allow women to enter the workforce. These obstacles also prevented women from leaving violent relationships. An important feminist campaign saw the opening of refuges for abused women and children. The first, Elsie, was opened in Glebe, Sydney, in 1974. By 1980 there were 100 refuges in Australia providing temporary shelter, advice and assistance for women who sought to leave violent men. In addition feminists campaigned for greater levels of state intervention to combat rape, domestic violence, incest and child abuse.[34] The object of these feminist campaigns was to maximise women's options and provide the means for women to escape their dependent social role. But many government, church and social welfare groups also became involved in providing refuges, health services and family counselling services for women, with the aim of maintaining the family unit.[35] Despite the conflict of aims, feminist and family welfare groups shared a recognition that combating female poverty required special services for the specific needs of women and children.

In recent years the character of particular welfare services has come under increasing criticism. In the 1960s and 1970s the confident hope of psychiatrists that they held the key to curing a broad range of social problems was challenged by anti-psychiatrists, students, feminists and the gay liberation movement. These groups argued that psychiatry was a form of social control, defining a wide range of behaviours as deviant and using ECT, drugs, surgery and incarceration as the means for confining people who did not conform to narrowly defined social roles. In 1969 this message was brought forcefully home to Australian psychiatrists when an historic joint American and Australian psychiatric congress in San Francisco was picketed by demonstrators. Popular media, with films such as *One Flew Over the Cuckoo's Nest*, novels such as Peter Kocan's *The Treatment* and newspaper stories such as 'Surgery Used on Psychiatric Patients' mobilised widespread fears about mental illness and psychiatry.[36]

Similar concern was expressed about the treatment of the aged, mentally handicapped and delinquents in institutions. Critics argued that institutions punished people from poorer classes. While the better-off could afford private care, the poor were confined to overcrowded and inadequately maintained government institutions. They pointed to the high numbers of Aboriginal children in custody. Although Aborigines were only one per cent of Australia's population Aboriginal children were 14 per cent of all juveniles in welfare institutions in New South Wales and 50 per cent in Western Australia.[37] There were other problems. Some staff violently mistreated inmates of institutions and sexually abused children in their

> **If you've always thought of Serenace as a potent, low dose psychotropic, we'd like you to think again.**
>
> AUSTRALIAN AND NEW ZEALAND JOURNAL OF PSYCHIATRY
>
> **SERENACE dosage—a new profile.**
> For many years SERENACE has been recognized as an effective neuroleptic when used in relatively low doses. However, recent evidence suggests that when higher doses (30-200 mg or more daily) are employed, SERENACE can provide control in a greater number of patients. Patients refractory to lower doses, or 'failures' on other agents may especially benefit from re-evaluation on high dose SERENACE.
> **SERENACE may convert inpatients to outpatients.**
> Current medical opinion has endorsed the use of high dose antipsychotic therapy.
> "A sizeable number of chronic schizophrenics do not benefit substantially from usual doses of neuroleptics."[1]
> "Consequently, many therapists have begun to use high dose or meganeuroleptic therapy for chronic schizophrenics who without such treatment would be prisoners of psychosis indefinitely."[1]
> High dose SERENACE may play an important role in permitting outpatient management for previously hospitalized patients.
> **High dose SERENACE increases efficacy—not side-effects.**
> In contrast with many other major tranquillizers, high dosage SERENACE does not appear to cause a marked increase in side-effects, especially extrapyramidal reactions.
> "Those experienced with high dose haloperidol testify that it is remarkably safe and that it does not cause a significantly higher incidence of extrapyramidal reactions than low dose therapy."[1]
> [1]Ayd, F.J.Jr.:Dis. Nerv.Syst., 33:459, 1972.
> Further information is available from:
>
> **SEARLE**
> The Medical Department
> Searle Laboratories,
> Division of Searle Australia Pty. Ltd.,
> P.O. Box 473,
> North Sydney, N.S.W. 2060.
>
> SERENACE is Haloperidol.
>
> **High dose Serenace may be the way out for chronic psychotics.**

In the 1970s drug companies advertised their role in assisting the process of deinstitutionalisation. (*Australian and New Zealand Journal of Psychiatry*, April 1973) care. These revelations added to the serious disquiet amongst reformers about institutionalisation as a form of treatment for children, the handicapped and the mentally ill and led to measures to safeguard the legal rights of those committed to institutions and restrict the powers of welfare officers to place people in institutions. In 1979 South Australia took the lead and granted legal representation to all people brought to psychiatric hospital committal proceedings.[38]

In the 1970s and 1980s deinstitutionalisation, or decarceration, became the preferred solution of many doctors and welfare workers concerned with the problems of those in institutions. For doctors it offered a final opportunity to escape the custodial role that had made them so unpopular. The alternative was community care; returning the aged, handicapped, delinquent and ill to families to be assisted by community workers, or placing them in hostels, halfway houses, therapeutic communities and other residences where people could learn to become independent, self-reliant and reintegrate into the wider community. Overseas research suggested that those treated outside large institutions had the best prospects for rehabilitation. This was the solution embraced by the 1983 Richmond Inquiry in New South Wales, into the care of the mentally ill and handicapped. The Report recommended the closure of all the State's large mental hospitals and the creation of integrated community services for all patients except the small number who might require some specialised care.

The Report, however, met a hostile reception in many quarters. Representatives of the New South Wales Nurses Association and the Public Medical Officers Association argued that deinstitutionalisation was really a means of cutting costs rather than helping patients and cited overseas research to show that the policy had resulted in widespread homelessness amongst former inmates. Boarding-house ghettoes, where ex-patients were maintained on high drug doses and had little contact with relatives or friends, were common in America and Europe. Many families complained that they did not have the resources to care for relatives returned from institutions and critics argued that the ideal of community treatment was a metaphor for shifting the burden of care back onto wives and mothers.[39]

Early reports on community treatment have not been universally favourable. Many of the services have been found inadequate. They suffer from insufficient funds, poorly trained residential care assistants, high staff turnover and low morale. Staff in refuges for the homeless noted an alarming increase in the number of ex-institutional inmates amongst those seeking a bed for the night.[40] These problems prompted the Greiner Coalition government in

New South Wales to reconsider the policy of deinstitutionalisation.

But other problems have emerged with respect to child care. Justifiable concerns about the legal rights of children and families have meant greater restrictions on the capacity of child welfare officers to remove children. Now only in extreme cases are children placed in care.

This policy has endangered some children. In 1982 ten-year-old Paul Montcalm was burned to death by his mother. The family had been visited a number of times by child welfare officers after reports that Paul had been locked in cupboards, physically abused and given bleach baths.[41] This was one of a number of cases where the government had failed to remove children in danger, suggesting that the balance between protection of children and safeguarding the legal rights of families was not always achieved. In recent years the pendulum seems to have swung from excessive state intervention to devolving the responsibility for welfare to inadequately supported mothers, community services and non-government organisations and this has not always benefited individuals or families.

Retreat from the welfare state

In 1975 one of the promises of the newly elected Fraser Coalition government was to ensure that 'dole bludgers' did not waste the taxpayers' money. The government undertook to reduce welfare expenditure. In subsequent years criteria for eligibility for unemployment benefits were tightened, surveillance of welfare recipients increased and in 1978 indexation of unemployment benefits was removed. There were broader economic imperatives for these policies. The Fraser government, influenced by the monetarist theories of American economist Milton Friedman, advocated the virtues of smaller government, fiscal restraint, balanced budgets and individual initiative. These were seen as the best means of solving the pressing problem of economic recession and rampant inflation. The traditional Keynesian remedy of increased public expenditure and government controls on the economy was rejected in favour of the free market.

The rhetoric of the Fraser government, however, was not matched in practice. Although many services were cut or starved of funds, by 1983 government spending was as high as it had been in 1976. Increasing numbers of aged pensioners and pressures to bolster the family unit by increasing child endowment (after 1976 known as family allowances) meant that welfare spending remained a large area of government expenditure.[42] Nor had the economy shown significant signs of improvement.

The failure of the Fraser government to achieve its aims provided the context for the emergence of the 'new right' in Australia. In the late 1970s and early 1980s a group of influential academics, business leaders and political commentators, committed to the free market philosophy gaining credence in Britain and the United States, mounted a sustained campaign in favour of smaller government, privatisation, the family, and individual choice. A major target for criticism was the welfare state. As one 'new right' critic explained it: 'The Welfare State has run its course. It has ruined the finances of governments and nations, it has given a false dream of a life of ease for all but the rich, it has corrupted our youth and destroyed the zest of the aged.'[43]

The answer was to significantly cut back all welfare services, except for the 'genuinely needy', as a means of reviving the will to work. These arguments have a familiar ring, recalling some of the classic arguments of 19th century liberals and philanthropists. Nor has the 'new right' devoted much effort to defining the 'needy' and as any definition is a moral and political one, welfare groups, feminists, ethnic groups and supporters of Aboriginal rights feel apprehensive about the 'new right' agenda.[44]

In 1983 the immediate prospect of dismantling the welfare state was averted by the election of the Hawke Labor government. But improving welfare services has not been a major objective of the new government. The key strategy of Labor has been to seek cooperation between government, unions and business to revive the economy. Welfare groups have felt excluded from these larger decision-making processes that have a significant bearing on the poor and although welfare funding has risen slightly since 1983, it is still well short of levels attained in the mid-1970s—despite worsening poverty since then.

Important economic ministers in the government, notably Paul Keating and Peter Walsh, have argued that in difficult economic times it would be irresponsible to expand government welfare programs.[45] The Labor government instead revived the tradition of the earlier Curtin and Chifley administrations—full employment and the welfare safety net. They have devoted considerable energy to job creation and employment training in an effort to reduce the number of unemployed. On the other hand they have attempted to target welfare spending for the needy by reducing outlays in the area of 'middle-class' welfare.

In 1985 the government introduced an assets test on pensions, removed family allowances for student children aged over sixteen except in low income families, and abolished indexation for unemployment benefits paid to those aged under twenty. But pension benefits were increased, income tests for unemployment and sickness benefits liberalised, carer's pensions introduced and special family allowance payments for large families increased. In 1987 a comprehensive review of the social security system, headed by Bettina Cass, was announced. It has forecast wide-ranging reforms in the area of retirement policy aimed at encouraging superannuation and reducing pension outlays.[46] Regardless of the outcome of these deliberations the Hawke government has clearly indicated that it is withdrawing from universal welfare schemes to concentrate its limited resources on selective benefits for those most in need.

In the 1980s some cost-cutting measures have exacerbated the plight of the poor. In 1985 the Commonwealth withdrew from the States $15 million for emergency poor relief. This forced State governments to close their cash assistance programs, leaving many families unable to pay bills or buy food.[47] Only concerted campaigns by welfare groups forced governments to restore these programs. The increasing reliance on residual and selective welfare benefits has left recipients open to the stigma of being 'bludgers', a charge often used by new right critics. Since 1985, however, welfare groups such as the Australian Council of Social Service have gone on the attack and attempted to focus attention on the far more serious problem of tax cheats. This has proved remarkably successful and the Hawke government has made the eradication of tax rorts an important part of its platform. But it is likely that in the future the spectre of 'welfare cheats' will be used again to mobilise antagonism to the welfare state. While there are welfare cheats, their number is small and the government has systems to minimise the incidence of welfare fraud. The concern about fraud is understandable but the rhetoric of welfare cheats diverts attention from the cases of real need and the shortcomings of the welfare state in addressing the plight of the poor.

The continuing high incidence of poverty, however, has had an impact on the Hawke government. In 1987 the Prime Minister Bob Hawke announced a far-reaching campaign to eradicate child poverty by 1990.[48] Increasing family allowances will undoubtedly improve the circumstances of many poor parents and their dependent children. But focusing solely on income does not solve the more complex problems of violence and conflict within families, poor job opportunities for women and inadequate child care, which contribute significantly to child poverty and homelessness.

Despite improved economic conditions in the late 1980s, lower rates of unemployment and falling inflation, the number of Australians living below the poverty line has not substantially changed. Two million Australians live in difficult circumstances, largely dependent on inadequate welfare benefits and services. The 'new right' has pinpointed important weaknesses in the welfare state because, despite vast expenditure, poverty remains. This failure has led some to plead for a new social reform vision in Australia but the content of that vision remains the site of political contest.[49] The 'new right' may have diagnosed weaknesses in the welfare state but its remedy of winding down services ignores the history of poverty. Liberal reformers at the turn of the century introduced welfare state measures because it was apparent that private, charitable and selective systems had failed, leaving many Australians in chronic destitution. The welfare state may not have eradicated poverty but it has improved the living standards of some of the poorest Australians and we should not ignore these lessons.

An alternative is to redistribute more income to the poor. But this scheme faces serious obstacles. Although Australia is the fourth-lowest-taxed country of 22 OECD nations,[50] the high rate of home ownership and rising home prices and interest rates mean that many Australians have most of their savings tied up and understandably resist measures to expand the tax base or fund welfare services through insurance and contributory schemes. These facts place considerable restrictions on the capacity of governments to direct funds to assist the poor. Despite these limitations a number of important proposals have been canvassed in recent years. Apprehending tax cheats and closing tax loopholes is an important means of increasing available revenue. Increasing the number of Australians in superannuation schemes will save money on old age pensions, creating revenue for other welfare schemes. The government is also considering plans to ensure that deserting and divorced fathers do not escape family maintenance obligations. These policies, geared to increasing the availability of funds, are necessary for the development of improved welfare services.

But some problems cannot be solved by increased funding alone. The evidence of feminist, Aboriginal and other welfare groups suggests that the shape and character of welfare services is equally important. Services have to be sensitive to economic, race, sex and age inequalities and geared to ensuring self-sufficiency and local decision making. To achieve this aim Australians have to overcome the long tradition of less eligibility at the heart of the welfare system. Since the 18th century the poor have been treated with suspicion and seen as other to mainstream society. This suspicion has justified low payments, restricted service, demeaning interviews and surveillance of the poor. It is only when this legacy is overcome that welfare policies can achieve greater social justice.

Notes

Introduction
1 R. Twopeny *Town Life in Australia* Ringwood: Penguin, 1973 (first published 1883), p. 111
2 R.V. Jackson *Australian Economic Development in the Nineteenth Century* Canberra: Australian National University Press, 1977, p. 22
3 W.C. Wentworth 'Social Services and Poverty' in G.G. Masterman (ed) *Poverty in Australia* Sydney: Angus and Robertson, 1969, p. 17
4 Case from Colonial Secretary Special Bundle *Applications for Employment 1878–80* AONSW 4/821.2
5 Royal Commission into Public Charities *NSWLAV&P* vol. 3, 1898, Appendix, p. 97
6 J. Stubbs *The Hidden People: Poverty in Australia* Melbourne: Lansdowne, 1966, pp. 47–48
7 J. O'Neill and R. Nairn *The Have-Nots: A Study of 150 Low Income Families* Melbourne: Brotherhood of St Laurence, 1972, p. 75 (I have given a name to this anonymous case)
8 P. Browne '1981–1986: Poverty on the Rise' *Australian Society* 6, 4, April 1987, pp. 34–35
9 R.F. Henderson, A. Harcourt and R.J.A. Harper *People in Poverty: A Melbourne Survey* Melbourne: Cheshire, 1970, p. 32
10 J. Roe 'Social Policy and the Permanent Poor' in E.L. Wheelwright and K. Buckley (eds) *Essays in the Political Economy of Australian Capitalism* vol. 1, Sydney: Australia and New Zealand Publishing Co., 1975, pp. 130–34
11 These findings are summarised in D. Fraser *The Evolution of the British Welfare State* 2nd edition London: Macmillan, 1984, pp. 135–37
12 See C.T. Stannage 'Uncovering Poverty in Australian History' *Early Days* 7, 1976, pp. 90–106. Many of these new works are listed in the notes and bibliography.
13 The concept of 'sexual economics' is developed in L. Leghorn and K. Parker (eds) *Women's Worth: Sexual Economics and the World of Women* London: Macmillan, 1981
14 See M.D. Lambert *Franciscan Poverty* London: SPCK, 1961
15 See G. Himmelfarb *The Idea of Poverty* London: Faber and Faber, 1984, pp. 23–144

1 A poor colony
1 See J. Lindsay *The Monstrous City: Defoe's London 1688–1730* London: Granada, 1978, p. 8; A. Briggs *The Age of Improvement* London:

Longmans, 1959, p. 41; and M.D. George *London Life in the Eighteenth Century* London: Kent, Paul, Trench, Trubner, 1925, p. 111
2. George, *London Life in the Eighteenth Century*, p. 112
3. R.B. Schwartz *Daily Life in Johnson's London* Madison: Wisconsin University Press, 1983, p. 6
4. See E.P. Thompson 'The Moral Economy of the English Crowd in the Eighteenth Century' *Past and Present* 50, February 1971, pp. 76–136; and D. Hay 'Property Authority and Criminal Law' in D. Hay et al. *Albion's Fatal Tree* London: Allen Lane, 1975, p. 14
5. Quoted in M. Clark (ed) *Select Documents in Australian History* vol. 1, Sydney: Angus and Robertson, 1977, pp. 7–8
6. The following argument draws heavily from George *London Life*.
7. Discussion of poor relief draws heavily from Fraser *Evolution of the British Welfare State*, pp. 31–36; K. Williams *From Pauperism to Poverty* London: Routledge and Kegan Paul, 1981, pp. 21–58; and D. Owen *English Philanthropy 1660–1960* Cambridge: Harvard University Press, 1964
8. The poor law debate is analysed extensively in Himmelfarb *The Idea of Poverty*, pp. 32–146 and J.R. Poynter *Society and Pauperism: English Ideas on Poor Relief 1795–1834* Melbourne: Melbourne University Press, 1969, pp. 106–85
9. Cited in Himmelfarb *The Idea of Poverty*, p. 77
10. This argument is developed more fully in Himmelfarb *The Idea of Poverty*, pp. 288–304
11. Quoted in Fraser *Evolution of the British Welfare State*, p. 41
12. For analyses of these developments see Himmelfarb *The Idea of Poverty*, pp. 371–400; A. Digby and P. Searby *Children, School and Society in Nineteenth Century England* London: Macmillan, 1980, chs. 1–3
13. On the English fear of police see C. Emsley *Policing and its Context 1750–1870* London: Macmillan, 1983, ch. 2. For discussion of the prevailing fears which precipitated moves to improve policing in the late 18th and early 19th centuries see also C. Emsley *Crime and Society in England 1750–1900* London: Longmans, 1987, pp. 171–94; and J.J. Tobias *Crime and Industrial Society in the Nineteenth Century* London: B.T. Batsford, 1967, pp. 22–50
14. See Emsley *Crime and Society*, pp. 203–13 and Tobias *Crime and Industrial Society*, p. 38
15. Figures from D. Philips *Crime and Authority in Victorian England* London: Croom Helm, 1977, p. 15. Philips' judicious account also warns of the dangers of interpreting the statistics too literally. They tell us more about the administration of crime than its actual committal, see Philips *Crime and Authority in Victorian England*, pp. 41–87. On changing patterns of crime see also Emsley *Crime and Society,* pp. 18–47. Both these studies prove more satisfactory than Tobias' conclusion that the statistics cannot be used. See Tobias *Crime and Industrial Society*, pp. 14–21
16. M. Ignatieff *A Just Measure of Pain: The Penitentiary in the Industrial Revolution 1750–1850* London: Macmillan, 1978, pp. 44–79

17 See Himmelfarb *Idea of Poverty*, pp. 371–400, Emsley *Crime and Society*, pp. 48–72, Tobias *Crime and Industrial Society*, pp. 52–75
18 Quoted in Clark *Select Documents in Australian History* vol. 1, p. 53
19 For the early accounts see C.M.H. Clark 'The Origins of the Convicts Transported to Eastern Australia 1787–1852' *Historical Studies* 7, 1956, L.L. Robson *The Convict Settlers of Australia: An Enquiry into the Origin and Character of the Convicts Transported to New South Wales and Van Diemen's Land, 1787–1852* Melbourne: Melbourne University Press, 1965 and A.G.L. Shaw *Convicts and the Colonies: A Study of Penal Transportation from Great Britain and Ireland to Australia and Other Parts of the British Empire* London: Faber, 1966. The most recent and comprehensive revision of these arguments is S. Nicholas (ed) *Convict Workers: Reinterpreting Australia's Past* Melbourne: Cambridge University Press, 1988. They draw on the important revisionist histories of crime in Britain, notably Philips *Crime and Authority in Victorian England*.
20 Select Committee on Transportation, 1812, *BPP* (Irish University Press Series), 'Crime and Punishment' vol. 1, p. 1 and p. 84
21 A. Frost 'New South Wales as terra nullius: The British Denial of Aboriginal Land Rights' *Historical Studies* 19, 77, 1981, pp. 513–23
22 L. Davey et al. 'The Hungry Years: 1788–1792' *Historical Studies* 3, 1947, pp. 187–210
23 *HRA*, Series 1, vol. 2, p. 23
24 D.D. Mann *The Present Picture of New South Wales*, 2nd edition, Sydney: John Ferguson, 1979, p. 45
25 J.C. Foley *Droughts in Australia* Australian Bureau of Meteorology, Bulletin No. 43, 1957
26 *HRA*, Series 1, vol. 5, p. 649
27 *HRA*, Series 1, vol. 3, pp. 421–23
28 *Sydney Gazette* 1 January 1804
29 *Sydney Gazette* 27 April 1807
30 *Sydney Gazette* 15 September 1805
31 M. Roe 'Colonial Society in Embryo' *Historical Studies*, 7, 26, 1956, p. 151. Roe's arguments concerning the lack of recorded crime have been extended in P. Robinson *The Hatch and Brood of Time* Melbourne: Oxford University Press, 1985, pp. 60–61
32 *Sydney Gazette* 15 September 1805
33 For a survey of early developments see B. Dickey *No Charity There: A Short History of Social Welfare in Australia* 2nd edition, Sydney: Allen and Unwin, 1987, pp. 1–20
34 D. Collins *An Account of the English Colony in New South Wales* 2nd edition, Adelaide: Libraries Board of South Australia, 1971, p. 193
35 Quoted in Clark *Select Documents in Australian History* vol. 1, p. 53
36 Mann *The Present Picture of New South Wales*, p. 53
37 Discussion of orphans draws heavily on J. Ramsland *Children of the Backlanes: Destitute and Neglected Children in Colonial New South Wales* Kensington: New South Wales University Press, 1986, pp. 1–23. All quotations from this discussion, unless otherwise attributed, come from this work.

38 Mann *The Present Picture of New South Wales*, p. 35
39 *HRA* Series 1, vol. 10, p. 94
40 N. Butlin *Our Original Aggression: Aboriginal Populations of Southeastern Australia 1788–1850* Sydney: Allen and Unwin, 1983. A more recent assessment puts the original pre-contact population at 750 000. See D.J. Mulvaney and P. White (eds) *Australians to 1788* Sydney: Fairfax, Syme, Weldon, 1987, pp. 115–17
41 Quoted in W.C. Wentworth *A Statistical, Historical and Political Description of the Colony of New South Wales* London: Whittaker, 1819, pp. 20–22. For a comprehensive discussion of prevailing attitudes towards Aborigines see H. Reynolds *Frontier* Sydney: Allen and Unwin, 1987, pp. 83–130. On later missionary efforts see R. Broome *Aboriginal Australians* Sydney: Allen and Unwin, 1982, pp. 101–19
42 See Broome, pp. 48–49
43 Benevolent Society *Annual Report* 1820, p. 8. The early history of the Society is detailed in Dickey *No Charity There*, pp. 20–29
44 J.T. Bigge *Report on the State of Agriculture and Trade in the Colony of New South Wales* London: Government Printer, 1822, pp. 77–78
45 ibid. p. 77

2 Survival of the fittest

1 P. Cunningham *Two Years in New South Wales* vol. 1, London: Henry Colburn, 1827, p. 40 and vol. 2, p. 59
2 Select Committee on the Condition of the Working Classes in the Metropolis *NSWLAV&P* vol. 4, 1859–60, Report, p. 8
3 Population figures and patterns of immigration from G. Sherington *Australia's Immigrants 1788–1978* Sydney: Allen and Unwin, 1980, pp. 23–66
4 See J. Ritchie *Evidence of the Bigge Reports* vol. 1, Melbourne: Heinemann, 1971, p. 74, Cunningham *Two Years in New South Wales* vol. 1, pp. 226–34, James Macarthur *New South Wales* London: D. Walther, 1837, pp. 209–10 and J. Mudie *The Felonry of New South Wales* (1837) Melbourne: Lansdowne Press, 1964
5 Cases from R. Hughes *The Fatal Shore* London: Collins Harvill, 1987, p. 263 and p. 480
6 The best analysis of the task work system and its broader consequences is J. Hirst *Convict Society and its Enemies* Sydney: Allen and Unwin, 1983, pp. 28–77. Eyre quoted in L. Evans and P. Nicholls (eds) *Convicts and Colonial Society, 1788–1868* 2nd edition, Melbourne: Macmillan, 1984, pp. 168–70
7 S. Nicholas 'Introduction' in Nicholas (ed) *Convict Workers*, p. 11
8 Cases of ill-treatment from Hughes *Fatal Shore*, pp. 402–80. See also M. Hazzard *Punishment Short of Death: A History of the Penal Settlement of Norfolk Island* Melbourne: Hyland House, 1984
9 Figures from K. Alford *Production or Reproduction? An Economic History of Women in Australia 1788–1850* Melbourne: Oxford University Press, 1984, pp. 15–16
10 For an analysis of male sexual violence see A. Summers *Damned*

Whores and God's Police Ringwood: Penguin, 1975, pp. 267–90. For attitudes towards convict women see also M. Sturma 'Eye of the Beholder: The Stereotype of Women Convicts 1788–1852' *Labour History* 34, 1978

11 H. Weatherburn 'The Female Factory' in J. Mackinolty and H. Radi (eds) *In Pursuit of Justice: Australian Women and the Law 1788–1979* Sydney: Hale and Iremonger, 1979, p. 22
12 Details on factories from Weatherburn 'The Female Factory', pp. 18–30, Summers *Damned Whores and God's Police*, pp. 280–85 and A. Salt *These Outcast Women: The Parramatta Female Factory 1821–48* Sydney: Hale and Iremonger, 1984
13 Hughes *The Fatal Shore*, pp. 258–64
14 Alford *Production or Reproduction?*, pp. 24–28 and p. 162
15 For land grants and economic growth see M. Dunn *Australia and the Empire* Sydney: Fontana, 1984, pp. 28–29 and M. Roe '1930–50' in F. Crowley (ed) *A New History of Australia* Melbourne: Nelson, 1974, pp. 100–101
16 *HRA* Series 1, vol. 16, pp. 86–87, Series 1, vol. 14, p. 231, Series 3, vol. 5, p. 703
17 For these developments see Roe '1830–50', pp. 84–89 and W.A. Sinclair *The Process of Economic Development in Australia* Melbourne: Cheshire, 1976, p. 104 and p. 138
18 L. Frost *No Place for a Nervous Lady: Voices from the Australian Bush* Ringwood: McPhee Gribble/Penguin, 1984, pp. 87–101
19 T.A. Coghlan *Labour and Industry in Australia* vol. 1, Melbourne: Macmillan, 1969, pp. 200–12
20 Sherington *Australia's Immigrants*, pp. 36–55
21 *HRA* Series 1, vol. 17, p. 279 and *SMH* 27 September 1832
22 M. Kiddle *Caroline Chisholm* Melbourne: Melbourne University Press, 1950, ch. 5
23 Coghlan *Labour and Industry* vol. 1, pp. 202–5 and pp. 425–427
24 *HRA* Series 1, vol. 18, pp. 516–21
25 Quoted in B. Dickey *Rations, Residences, Resources* Cowandilla: Wakefield Press, 1986, p. 8. Wage rates from Coghlan *Labour and Industry* vol. 1, pp. 429–36
26 Quoted in M. Sullivan *Men and Women of Port Phillip* Sydney: Hale and Iremonger, 1985, p. 223
27 Coghlan *Labour and Industry* vol. 1, pp. 429–31 and pp. 440–42, and *HRA* Series 1, vol. 23, p. 95
28 Dickey *Rations, Residence, Resources*, pp. 8–12
29 Quoted in Kiddle *Caroline Chisholm*, p. 47
30 Quoted in Sullivan *Men and Women of Port Phillip*, p. 224
31 ibid, pp. 216–31, and Kiddle *Caroline Chisholm*, pp. 19–68
32 Coghlan *Labour and Industry* vol. 1, pp. 477–88, and D. Shineberg 'Richard Jones' *ADB* vol. 2, pp. 24–25
33 Details on unemployment from Coghlan *Labour and Industry* vol. 1, pp. 438–49
34 Quoted in Dickey *Rations, Residence, Resources*, p. 23

35 G. Serle *The Golden Age: A History of the Colony of Victoria 1851–61* Melbourne: Melbourne University Press, 1963, p. 85
36 Sinclair *The Process of Economic Development*, pp. 76–119 and H. Reynolds 'That Hated Stain: The Aftermath of Transportation in Tasmania' *Historical Studies* 53, 1969, p. 21
37 Dickey *Rations, Residence, Resources*, p. 33
38 Select Committee on the Unemployed *NSWLAV&P*, vol. 5, 1866, pp. 1–20. See also Sinclair *The Process of Economic Development*, pp. 88–89
39 See J. Lee and C. Fahey 'A boom for whom? Some developments in the Australian labour market 1870–1891' *Labour History* 50, 1986
40 Colonial Secretary Special Bundle *Applications for Employment*
41 A. Harris *Settlers and Convicts* Melbourne: Melbourne University Press, 1969, pp. 47–58. Fowler quoted in G. Davison and D. Dunstan 'This Moral Pandemonium: Images of Low Life' in G. Davison, D. Dunstan and C. McConville (eds) *The Outcasts of Melbourne: Essays in Social History* Sydney: Allen and Unwin, 1985, p. 30 and M. Dixson *The Real Matilda* 2nd edition, Ringwood: Penguin, 1985, p. 99
42 ibid. See also Cunningham *Two Years in New South Wales* vol. 1, p. 68
43 S. Grant and G. Serle (eds) *The Melbourne Scene 1803–1956* Melbourne: Melbourne University Press, 1957, p. 37
44 *The Australian* 18 November 1824 and *SMH* 14 November 1831
45 Cases collected in Royal Commission into Public Charities *NSWLAV&P* vol. 6, 1873–74, 2nd Report, Appendix 3
46 This concept is developed in J. McCarty 'Australian Capital Cities in the Nineteenth Century' *Australian Economic History Review* 10, 2, 1970, pp. 107–37. On population density see Jackson *Australian Economic Development in the Nineteenth Century*, pp. 100–104
47 Committee on Condition of the Working Classes, 1859–60, pp. 1–15
48 ibid. p. 9
49 Davison 'Introduction' in *Outcasts of Melbourne*, pp. 7–8
50 Select Committee on Common Lodging Houses *NSWLAV&P* vol. 6, 1875–76, Minutes of Evidence, pp. 2–18
51 Statistics from M. Lewis and R. MacLeod 'A Workingman's Paradise? Reflections on Urban Mortality in Colonial Australia 1860–1900' *Medical History* 31, 1987, pp. 387–402 and S. Fitzgerald *Rising Damp: Sydney 1870–90* Melbourne: Oxford University Press, 1987, pp. 97–100
52 See in particular Fitzgerald *Rising Damp*, pp. 69–100, J. Lack 'Worst Smelbourne: Melbourne's Noxious Trades' in Davison *Outcasts of Melbourne*, P.H. Curson *Times of Crisis: Epidemics in Sydney 1788–1900* Sydney: Sydney University Press, 1985, A.J.C. Mayne *Fever, Squalor and Vice: Sanitation and Social Policy in Victorian Sydney* St Lucia: University of Queensland Press, 1982

3 Colonial charity
1 *SMH* 14 February 1833

2 Royal Commission into Charitable Institutions *VV&P* vol. 2, 1871, Report, p. 12
3 *HRA* Series 1, vol. 14, p. 39
4 The following discussion of charity draws heavily on the pioneering work of Brian Dickey *No Charity There*, pp. 34–38
5 Ramsland *Children of the Backlanes*, pp. 52–53
6 This was the estimate of a survey undertaken in 1910. See Charity Organisation Society *A Guide to Charity and to the Philanthropic Work of Victoria* Melbourne, 1912, pp. 38–40
7 Select Committee into the Benevolent Asylum *NSWLAV&P* vol. 2, 1861–62, Minutes of Evidence, p. 2
8 For details on government responsibility see Dickey *No Charity There*, pp. 34–44
9 Dickey *Rations, Residence, Resources*, pp. 17–40
10 See Royal Commission into Charitable Institutions *Journals of Tasmanian Legislative Council*, no. 47, 1871, Report, pp. xvii–xviii, R. Evans 'Charitable Institutions of the Queensland Government to 1919' M.A. thesis, University of Queensland, 1969, and C.T. Stannage *The People of Perth* Perth: Perth City Council, 1979, pp. 259–60
11 See E. Windschuttle 'Feeding the Poor and Sapping their Strength: the Public Role of Ruling Class Women in Eastern Australia 1788–1850' in E. Windschuttle (ed) *Women, Class and History* Melbourne: Fontana, 1980, pp. 53–72, and J. Godden 'The Work for Them and the Glory for Us! Sydney Women's Philanthropy 1880–1900' in R. Kennedy (ed) *Australian Welfare History: Critical Essays* Melbourne: Macmillan, 1982
12 Benevolent Society of New South Wales *Annual Report* 1828, pp. 10–11 and 1838, p. 11
13 ibid, 1828, p. 10
14 Figures from Dickey *Rations, Residence, Resources*, pp. 22–24, New South Wales Benevolent Society *Annual Reports* 1850–60 and Commission of Inquiry into Municipalities and Charitable Institutions *VV&P* vol. 4, 1862–63, Minutes of Evidence, p. 53 and pp. 61–62
15 Victorian Commission into Municipalities and Charitable Institutions, Minutes of Evidence, p. 60
16 Public Charities Royal Commission, 1873–74, First Report, p. 74
17 See New South Wales Benevolent Society *Annual Reports* 1860–70, Melbourne Ladies Benevolent Society *Annual Reports* 1850–70, Victorian Commission into Municipalities and Charitable Institutions, 1862–63, Report, p. 51 and Select Committee on Hospitals in the Colony *QLAV&P* vol. 1, 1866, Minutes of Evidence, p. 1620
18 Melbourne Ladies Benevolent Society *Annual Reports* 1855, pp. 10–11 and 1857, p. 10
19 Sydney Strangers Friend Society *Annual Report* 1842, p. 5
20 Melbourne Ladies Benevolent Society *Annual Report* 1855, pp. 10–11
21 Tasmanian Commission into Charitable Institutions, 1871, Minutes of Evidence, p. 28

NOTES 179

22 Victorian Commission into Municipalities and Charitable Institutions, 1862–63, Report, p. 60
23 Victorian Royal Commission into Charitable Institutions, 1871, Minutes of Evidence, p. 2
24 Committee of the Ladies Melbourne and Suburban City Mission Society *Annual Report* 1858, p. 12
25 ibid, 1859, p. 9
26 Queensland Select Committee on Hospitals, 1866, Minutes of Evidence, p. 1629
27 Tasmanian Commission into Charitable Institutions, 1871, Minutes of Evidence, p. 60
28 ibid, p. 61
29 Tasmanian Commission into Charitable Institutions, 1871, Minutes of Evidence, p. 46
30 Victorian Commission into Municipalities and Charitable Institutions, 1862–63, Minutes of Evidence, p. 60
31 ibid. pp. 62–63
32 Public Charities Royal Commission, 1873–74, First Report, p. 97 and Minutes of Evidence, p. 125
33 Victorian Commission into Municipalities and Charitable Institutions, 1862–63, Minutes of Evidence, p. 62
34 New South Wales Committee into the Benevolent Asylum, 1861–62, Minutes of Evidence, p. 4
35 ibid. p. 14
36 Tasmanian Commission into Charitable Institutions, 1871, Report, p. xviii
37 Figures from the annual reports of these institutions and Dickey *Rations, Residence, Resources*, p. 29 and p. 123. Figures on ageing from colonial census and statistical registers compiled by Fran Boyle for the Griffith University Gender and Ageing Project.
38 Select Committee on the Management of the Dunwich Benevolent Asylum *QLAV&P* vol. 1, part 2, 1884, Minutes of Evidence, p. 3
39 Colonial Secretary's Department Special Bundle *Admissions to Government Asylums, 1878–79* AONSW 4/809.1
40 Victorian Commission into Charitable Institutions, 1871, Minutes of Evidence, p. 15
41 F. and R. Hill *What We Saw in Australia* London: Macmillan, 1875, p. 143
42 *Rules and Regulations of the Tasmanian Pauper Depot* Hobart, 1868
43 Colonial Secretary's Department Special Bundle *Report on Australian Hospitals 1878* AONSW 4/1086. For Friendly Societies see Royal Commission into Friendly Societies *NSWV&P* vol. 3, 1883
44 NSW Committee into the Benevolent Asylum, 1861–62, Report, pp. 5–6
45 NSW Public Charities Royal Commission, 1873–74, First Report, pp. 64–68
46 See S. Garton *Medicine and Madness: A Social History of Insanity in*

New South Wales 1880–1940 Kensington: New South Wales University Press, 1988, chs. 1 and 8
47 *HRA* Series 3, vol. 5, p. 471
48 Tasmanian Commission into Charitable Institutions, 1871, Report, p. xiii, and earlier cases cited in J.C. Brown *Poverty is Not a Crime: The Development of Social Services in Tasmania, 1803–1900* Hobart: Tasmanian Historical Research Association, 1972, pp. 27–28
49 Society for the Relief of Destitute Children *Annual Report* 1853, p. 8
50 Hobart Ragged School *Annual Report* 1870. The best coverage of these developments in child welfare (although it concentrates largely on NSW) is Ramsland *Children of the Backlanes*
51 For an examination of the work of Neitenstein and the industrial school system see S. Garton 'Frederick William Neitenstein: Juvenile Reformatory and Prison Reform in NSW, 1878–1909' *Journal of the Royal Australian Historical Society* 75, 1, 1989 and Ramsland *Children of the Backlanes*, pp. 111–56

4 Workers' welfare
1 Quoted in T.H. Irving '1850–70' in Crowley *A New History of Australia* p. 134
2 J.D. Langley 'The Unemployed' and B.R. Wise 'What Parliament can do for Labour' *Sydney Quarterly Magazine* September 1891
3 S. Macintyre *Winners and Losers* Sydney: Allen and Unwin, 1985, pp. 19–39
4 This is the argument of D.W.A. Baker 'The Origin of Robertson's Land Acts' *Historical Studies* 8, 30, 1958
5 See S. Roberts *History of Australian Land Settlement 1788–1920* Melbourne: Macmillan, 1968, pp. 236–306
6 Select Committee on Conditional Homestead Selectors *QLAV&P* vol. 2, 1879, Minutes of Evidence, pp. 7–9
7 Figures from Roberts *History of Australian Land Settlement*, pp. 236–306
8 Quoted in M. Lake 'Building Themselves up with Aspros: Pioneer Women Reassessed' *Hecate* vol. 7, no. 2, 1981. This important article examines many of these issues in greater detail.
9 ibid.
10 Figures from W. Vamplew (ed) *Australians: Historical Statistics* Sydney: Fairfax, Syme and Weldon, 1987, p. 41. For discussion of broader impact of urbanisation see S. Glynn *Urbanisation in Australian History 1788–1900* Melbourne: Nelson, 1970; J.W. McCarty and C.B. Schedvin (eds) *Urbanization in Australia: The Nineteenth Century* Sydney: Sydney University Press, 1974
11 Quoted in Fitzgerald *Rising Damp*, p. 3
12 Figures from Vamplew *Historical Statistics*, pp. 76–83, Sinclair *Process of Economic Development*, pp. 76–119, and G.J.R. Linge 'The Forging of an Industrial Nation: Manufacturing in Australia 1788–1913' in J.M. Powell and M. Williams (eds) *Australian Space, Australian Time:*

Geographical Perspectives Melbourne: Oxford University Press, 1975, pp. 157–63
13 Coghlan *Labour and Industry in Australia*, vol. 3, pp. 1425–1590
14 See C. Moore 'Used and Abused: The Melanesian labour trade' in V. Burgmann and J. Lee (eds) *A Most Valuable Acquisition* Ringwood: McPhee Gribble/Penguin, 1988, K. Saunders *Workers in Bondage: The Origins and Bases of Unfree Labour in Queensland* St. Lucia: University of Queensland Press, 1981, and Broome *Aboriginal Australians*, pp. 120–30
15 Linge 'Forging of an Industrial Nation', pp. 157–63, N.G. Butlin *Investment in Australian Economic Development 1861–1900* Canberra: Australian National University Press, 1976, pp. 201–14, R. Markey *The Making of the Labor Party in New South Wales 1880–1900* Kensington: New South Wales University Press, 1988, pp. 28–51, E.C. Fry 'The Condition of the Wage Earning Class in Australia in the 1880s' Ph.D. thesis, Australian National University, 1956, pp. 37–40
16 Markey *The Making of the Labor Party*, pp. 28–51, K . Buckley and T. Wheelwright *No Paradise for Workers: Capitalism and the Common People 1788–1914* Melbourne: Oxford University Press, 1988, pp. 140–63
17 Fitzgerald *Rising Damp*, pp. 103–37
18 Coghlan *Labour and Industry*, vol. 3, p. 1587
19 D. Deacon 'Political Arithmetic: The Nineteenth Century Australian Census and the Construction of the Dependent Woman' *Signs* vol. 11, no. 1, 1985, and W.A. Sinclair 'Women at work in Melbourne and Adelaide since 1871' *Economic Record* 57, 1981
20 Sinclair 'Women at work' and B. Kingston *My Wife, My Daughter and Poor Mary Ann* Melbourne: Nelson, 1975, pp. 56–73
21 These conditions are revealed in a series of inquires into factory and shop conditions. See Factories Act Inquiry Board *VV&P*, vol. 2, 1893, Royal Commission into Shops, Factories and Workshops in the Colony *QLAV&P*, vol. 2, 1891, Select Committee on the Alleged Sweating Evil, *SAPP*, vol. 2, 1904 and Royal Commission into Female and Juvenile Labour *NSWPP*, vol. 2, 1911–12
22 Queensland Royal Commission into Shops, Factories and Workshops, 1891, Minutes of Evidence. pp. 25–27 and pp. 40–41
23 See E. Fry 'Outwork in the Eighties: An examination of outwork in the infant industries of the Eastern Australian Colonies 1880–89' *University Studies in History and Economics* 2, 4, July 1956 and Select Committee on Alleged Sweating Evil, 1904
24 K. Wimshurst 'Child labour and school attendance in South Australia 1890–1915' *Historical Studies* 19, 76, 1981
25 Factories Act Inquiry Board Report *VV&P* vol. 2, 1893, pp. 8–23
26 Select Committee on the Employment of Children *NSWLAV&P* vol. 6, 1875–76, Minutes of Evidence, pp. 13–21
27 ibid. p. 34
28 See A. Lynzaat 'Respectability and the outworker: Victorian Factory

Acts 1885–1903' in Mackinolty and Radi *In Pursuit of Justice*, pp. 85–94 and J. Rickard 'The anti-sweating movement in Britain and Victoria: the politics of empire and social reform' *Historical Studies* 18, 73, 1979

29 Colonial Secretary's Department Special Bundle *Reports on Unemployment in Country Districts 1884–86* AONSW 4/863

30 Colonial Secretary's Department Special Bundle *Casual Labour Board 1887–89* AONSW 4/891 and Select Committee on the Unemployed Problem *SAPP* vol. 2, 1894, p. 25

31 P.G. Macarthy 'Wages in Australia 1891–1914' *Australian Economic History Review* 10, 1, 1970

32 See the important work of S. Swain 'The Victorian Charity Network' Ph.D. thesis, University of Melbourne, 1976, pp. 7–64 and p. 142. See also Melbourne Charity Organisation Society and New South Wales Benevolent Society *Annual Reports* 1890–1900 and Dickey *No Charity There*, pp. 72–83

33 J. Goldstein 'The Unemployed' *Australasian Conference on Charity* 1891, p. 98. See also B. Scates and C. Fox 'The Beat of Weary Feet' in V. Burgmann and J. Lee (eds) *Staining the Wattle* Ringwood: McPhee Gribble/Penguin, 1988

34 South Australian Select Committee on the Unemployed Problem, 1894, p. 5

35 ibid. p. 25

36 R. Kennedy 'The Leongatha Labour Colony: Founding an Anti-Utopia' *Labour History* 14, 1968, pp. 54–8 and Langley 'The Unemployed'

37 Government Labour Bureau *Annual Report* 1893, pp. 2–7. Details on other colonies South Australian Select Committee on Unemployed Problem, 1894, pp. 17–25

38 Select Committee on the Working of the Government Labour Bureau *NSWLAV&P*, vol. 8, 1892–93, Report, pp. 3–4

39 George's view quoted favourably in H.L. Jackson 'Pauperism—Its nature, causes and remedies' *Australasian Conference on Charity* 1890, p. 38. For a major analysis of William Lane on which I have drawn here see M. Lake 'Socialism and Manhood: The case of William Lane' *Labour History* 50, 1986

40 On development of colonial liberalism and the labour movement see Markey *The Making of the Labor Party in New South Wales*, pp. 260–83, Macintyre *Winners and Losers*, pp. 40–58, and R. Gollan *Radical and Working Class Politics: A Study of Eastern Australia 1850–1910* Melbourne: Melbourne University Press, 1960, pp. 110–50

41 Information on this legislation and accident statistics summarised in Australian Bureau of Census and Statistics *Labor Bulletins* 1913, pp. 49–59. A number of works discuss new welfare and social legislation, such as Asian immigration and protection. See J. Rickard *Class and Politics: New South Wales, Victoria and the Early Commonwealth, 1890–1910* Canberra: Australian National University Press, 1976, pp. 204–22, Gollan *Radical and Working Class Politics*, pp. 151–69 and R. Norris *The Emergent Commonwealth: Australian Federation, Expecta-*

tions and Fulfilment 1889–1910 Melbourne: Melbourne University Press, 1975, pp. 162–98
42 NSW Royal Commission on Female and Juvenile Labour, 1911–12, Report, pp. v–xli
43 Regulations from Bureau of Census and Statistics *Labor Bulletins* 1913, pp. 53–59
44 See Lynzaat 'Respectability and the outworker' and Kingston *My Wife, My Daughter and Poor Mary Ann*, pp. 56–73
45 NSW Royal Commission on Juvenile and Female Labour, 1911–12, p. lv
46 ibid. p. liii
47 South Australian Committee on Alleged Sweating Evil, 1904, Minutes of Evidence, p. 13 and pp. 17–22
48 Quoted in Macintyre *Winners and Losers*, p. 53 and *CPP*, vol. 15, 1903, p. 2862. The discussion of workers' welfare draws heavily on the ideas in the important work of F. Castles *The Working Class and Welfare* Sydney: Allen and Unwin, 1985
49 P. Macarthy 'Victorian Wages Boards: Their Origins and the Doctrine of the Living Wage' *Journal of Industrial Relations* 10, 2, 1968 and J. Lee 'A redivision of labour: Victoria's Wages Boards in action. 1896–1903' *Historical Studies* 22, 88, 1987
50 See P. Macarthy 'Justice Higgins and the Harvester Judgement' *Australian Economic History Review* xi, 1, 1969 and 'Labour and the Living Wage, 1890–1910' *Australian Journal of Politics and History* 13, 1967, J. Rickard *H.B. Higgins: The Rebel as Judge* Sydney: Allen and Unwin, 1984, pp. 170–204. Employer quotes from Alleged Sweating Evil Inquiry, 1904, Minutes of Evidence. p.125. Figures on wage rates from *NSW Statistical Registers*, 1900–1914
51 Royal Commission into the Basic Wage, *CPP*, vol. 4, 1920. G. Anderson, *Fixation of Wages in Australia* Melbourne: Melbourne University Press, 1929, pp. 222–68
52 See E. Ryan and A. Conlon *Gentle Invaders* Melbourne: Nelson, 1975, pp. 10–70, R. Francis 'No more amazons: Gender and work process in the Victorian clothing trades 1890–1939' *Labour History* 50, 1986, Lee 'A redivision of labour', L. Bennett 'Job classification and women workers: Institutional practices, technological change and the Conciliation and Arbitration System' *Labour History* 51, 1986

5 Pensions and pills
1 E.E. Morris *Newer Methods of Charity* Melbourne: Charity Organisation Society, 1895, p. 11
2 A. Macully 'The Unemployed' in *Conference on Charity* 1890, p. 114 and Royal Commission into the Aged Poor *SAPP* vol. 2, 1898–99, Minutes of Evidence, pp. 15–19
3 Quoted in T.H. Kewley *Social Security in Australia, 1901–72* Sydney: Sydney University Press, 1973, p. 61
4 Editorial 'Medical Men and Social Problems' *Australasian Medical Gazette* 30, 1911, p. 332

5   See R. Kennedy *Charity Warfare: The Charity Organisation Society in Colonial Melbourne* Melbourne: Hyland House, 1985, pp. 80–87
6   E.E. Morris 'Organised Charity' *Conference on Charity* 1890, p. 4
7   Morris *Newer Methods of Charity*, pp. 11–12
8   Col. Goldstein 'Charity Organisation: Its Principles and Methods' *Conference on Charity* 1890, p. 126
9   C.H. Spence 'Charity in South Australia' *Conference on Charity* 1890, pp. 16–17
10 On the growth of charity see the important arguments of A. O'Brien in *Poverty's Prison: The Poor in New South Wales 1880–1918* Melbourne: Melbourne University Press, 1988, pp. 200–24. On Western Australia see *Jubilee Survey of Social Welfare in Western Australia 1901–51* Canberra: Government Printer, 1951, pp. 1–5
11 See A. Hyslop 'Temperance, Christianity and Feminism: The Women's Christian Temperance Union of Victoria 1887–97' *Historical Studies* 17, 66, 1976, pp. 27–49, J.D. Bollen *Protestantism and Social Reform in New South Wales 1890–1910* Melbourne: Melbourne University Press, 1972, pp. 140–79
12 See the important arguments of M. Lake 'The Politics of Respectability: Identifying the Masculinist Context' *Historical Studies* 22, 86, 1986, J. Allen 'Our Deeply Degraded Sex and the Animal in Man: Rose Scott, Feminism and Sexuality 1890–1925' *Australian Feminist Studies* 7–8, 1988
13 Select Committee of the Legislative Council on the Destitute Poor *SAPP* vol. 3, 1867
14 Public Charities Royal Commission, 1873–74, Second Report. See also Ramsland *Children of the Backlanes*, pp. 159–89
15 Hobart Queen's Asylum *Annual Report* 1866, p. 6
16 Hill *What We Saw in Australia*, p. 308
17 Public Charities Royal Commission, 1873–74, 2nd Report, p. 40
18 Hill *What We Saw in Australia*, p. 283
19 J. Ramsland 'The development of boarding-out systems in Australia: A series of welfare experiments in child care 1860–1910' *Journal of the Royal Australian Historical Society* 60, 1974, pp. 186–98
20 Report of Superintendent of Public Charities *WAPIP* vol. 1, 1901–2, p. 19
21 Figures from *Commonwealth Year Book* 1901–1911, p. 931. On the closure of institutions see Ramsland 'The development of boarding-out systems'
22 NSW Royal Commission on Public Charities, 1898, Appendix, p. 98
23 Figures from State Childrens Relief Board *Annual Reports* 1900–14. For discussion of introduction of boarding-out allowance see Dickey *No Charity There*, pp. 97–102 and O'Brien *Poverty's Prison*, pp. 32–47
24 See Broome *Aboriginal Australians*, pp. 82–84 and P. Read *The Stolen Generations: The Removal of Aboriginal Children in NSW 1883–1969* Sydney: New South Wales Ministry of Aboriginal Affairs, 1985, pp. 2–9
25 See Royal Commission on Charitable Institutions *VV&P* vol. 6, 1891,

Report, pp. xii–xiii and Royal Commission into Public Charities, Third Report, *NSWLAV&P* vol. 1, 1899, p. xliv
26 Figures and evidence from O'Brien *Poverty's Prison* pp. 211–21
27 Select Committee on the Management of the Benevolent Asylum, Dunwich *QLAV&P* 1884, Minutes of Evidence, Interim Report, pp. 28–30 and Minutes of Evidence, Final Report, pp. 21–23
28 Board of Inquiry into Government Asylums, Newington and Parramatta *NSWLAV&P* vol. 12, 1887, Report, pp. 14–37
29 Select Committee on Old Age Pensions *NSWLAV&P* vol. 5, 1896, Minutes of Evidence, p. 20
30 NSW Royal Commission on Public Charities, 1898, Appendix, pp. 97–98
31 Figures from *Commonwealth Census* 1911 and Griffith University, Gender and Ageing Project, compiled by Fran Boyle
32 See Swain 'Victorian Charity Network', pp. 72–97 and O'Brien *Poverty's Prison*, pp. 51–61
33 South Australian Royal Commission on Aged Poor, 1898, Report, pp. v–vi and NSW Select Committee on Old Age Pensions, 1896, Minutes of Evidence, pp. 49–51
34 South Australian Royal Commission on Aged Poor, 1898, First Dissenting Report. For discussion of broader context for introduction of pensions see J. Roe 'Old Age, Young Country: The First Old Age Pensions and Pensioners in New South Wales' *Teaching History* July 1981 and Kewley *Social Security in Australia*, pp. 28–83
35 Kewley *Social Security in Australia*, p. 134
36 The argument that these measures were a form of state charity is forcefully presented in O'Brien *Poverty's Prison*, pp. 71–78. For an illuminating study of turn of the century social reform see J. Roe 'Leading the world 1901–14' in J. Roe (ed) *Social Policy in Australia: Some Perspectives 1901–75* Stanmore: Cassell, 1976
37 Commonwealth Royal Commission into Old Age Pensions *CPP* vol. 3, 1906, Minutes of Evidence, p. 43
38 O'Brien *Poverty's Prison*, pp. 60–61
39 Kewley *Social Security in Australia*, pp. 99–116 and N. Hicks *This Sin and Scandal: Australia's Population Debate 1891–1911* Canberra: Australian National University Press, 1978, pp. 7–17
40 See Garton *Medicine and Madness*, pp. 53–64, J. Docker 'Can the Centre Hold? Conceptions of the State 1890–1925' in *What Rough Beast?*, pp. 57–88 and M. Roe *Nine Australian Progressives: Vitalism and Bourgeois Social Thought 1890–1960* St Lucia: Queensland University Press, 1984, pp. 1–20
41 H.L. Jackson 'Pauperism: Its Nature, Causes and Remedies' *Conference on Charity* 1890, pp. 37–38
42 This argument is proposed and convincingly argued in Godden 'The work for us and the glory for them'
43 All quotes and evidence from S. Garton 'Once a drunkard always a drunkard: Social reform and the problem of habitual drunkenness in Australia, 1880–1914' *Labour History* 53, 1987

44 Garton *Medicine and Madness*, pp. 53–69
45 See Hicks *This Sin and Scandal*, pp. 79–102, Docker 'Can the Centre Hold?', Roe *Nine Australian Progressives*, pp. 1–20 and S. Garton 'Sir Charles Mackellar: Psychiatry, Eugenics and Child Welfare in New South Wales 1900–1914' *Historical Studies 22*, 86, 1986. Quote from Garton *Medicine and Madness*, p. 59
46 Garton *Medicine and Madness*, pp. 53–85 and quotes p. 59 and p. 187. See also A. Turtle 'Education, Social Science and the Commonweal' in R. MacLeod (ed) *The Commonwealth of Science* Melbourne: Oxford University Press, 1988
47 Garton 'Sir Charles Mackellar'
48 See Garton *Medicine and Madness*, pp. 53–85, K. Reiger *The Disenchantment of the Home: Modernising the Australian Family 1880–1940* Melbourne: Oxford University Press, 1985 and J.J. Matthews *Good and Mad Women: The Historical Construction of Femininity in Twentieth Century Australia* Sydney: Allen and Unwin, 1984, pp. 74–108

6 One long Depression

1 W. Lowenstein *Weevils in the Flour* Melbourne: Scribe, 1978, p. 47
2 See L. Soltow 'The Censuses of Wealth of Men in Australia in 1915 and the United States in 1860 and 1870' *Australian Economic History Review* 12, 2, 1972
3 For general economic figures see Vamplew *Historical Statistics*, p. 133. For Newcastle see S. Gray 'An evil long endured: Newcastle's Depression' in J. Mackinolty (ed) *The Wasted Years: Australia's Great Depression* Sydney: Allen and Unwin, 1981 and for Western Australia G. Bolton *A Fine Country to Starve In* Nedlands: University of Western Australia Press, 1972, pp. 32–58
4 F.B. Boyce *A Campaign for the Abolition of Slums in Sydney* Sydney: William Andrews, 1913, pp. 7–8
5 Select Committee on the Housing of the People in the Metropolis *VPP* vol. 1, 1913–14, Minutes of Evidence, pp. 18–20 and p. 104; Royal Commission on the Housing of the People in the Metropolis *VPP* vol. 2, 1915, First Report, pp. 6–9 and vol. 2, 1917, Second Report, pp. 13–17, Minutes of Evidence, pp. 3–5
6 Commission of Inquiry into the Housing of Workmen in Europe and America *NSWPP* vol. 1, 1913, Report, pp. 2–23. For Melbourne see Royal Commission on Housing in the Metropolis, 1915, First Report, p. 9
7 On war-time economic conditions see E. Scott *Australia During the War* Sydney: Angus and Robertson, 1936, pp. 495–99 and 633–65
8 S. Macintyre *The Oxford History of Australia*, vol. 4, Melbourne: Oxford University Press, 1986, pp. 168–97 and J. Smart 'Feminists and Food: The Cost of Living Demonstrations in Melbourne, August–September 1917' *Labour History* 50, 1986
9 A.G. Butler *Official History of the Australian Army Medical Services in the 1914–18 War*, vol. 3, Canberra: Australian War Memorial, 1943, pp. 50–187 and pp. 769–963

NOTES

10 ibid. pp. 152–87. H. McQueen 'The Spanish Influenza Pandemic in Australia, 1918–19' in Roe *Social Policy in Australia*, pp. 131–47
11 Butler *History of the Australian Army Medical Services*, p. 842
12 On charitable endeavours see D.I. McDonald 'The Australian Soldiers' Repatriation Fund, An Experiment in Social Legislation' in Roe *Social Policy in Australia*, pp. 113–30, M. Lyons, *Legacy: The First Fifty Years* Melbourne: Lothian, 1978. On crime and returned soldiers see J. Allen *Sex and Secrets: Crimes Involving Australian Women Since 1880* Melbourne: Oxford University Press, 1990, ch. 6
13 L. Hills and A. Dene *The Returned Sailors and Soldiers Imperial League of Australia* Melbourne: RSSILA, 1938, pp. xxci–xxxv, and RSSILA, *Year Book* 1938, pp. 296–99
14 Butler *History of the Australian Army Medical Services*, pp. 958–71
15 Much of the following discussion draws on the pathbreaking study of Marilyn Lake *Limits of Hope: soldier settlement in Victoria, 1915–38* Melbourne: Oxford University Press, 1987
16 Report by Mr Justice Pike on Losses Due to Soldier Settlement *CPP* vol. 2, 1929, Report, pp. 6–24
17 These cases and conclusions are drawn from Lake *Limits of Hope*, esp. pp. 101–74, Lester case pp. 190–91
18 On general economic developments see H. Radi '1920–29' in Crowley *New History of Australia*. For the Western Australia scheme see Bolton *A Fine Country to Starve In*, pp. 35–55
19 From R. Wilson (ed) *Good Talk* Ringwood: Penguin, 1984, pp. 1–26
20 Interview with M. McBride 20 May 1986
21 R. Cilento *The White Man in the Tropics* Melbourne: Government Printer, 1925, pp. 5–93
22 Report by J.W. Bleakley on the Aboriginals and Half Castes of Central Australia and Northern Australia *CPP* vol. 2, 1929, Report, pp. 6–10. For a detailed study of conditions in Northern Australia see A. McGrath *Born in the Cattle* Sydney: Allen and Unwin, 1987
23 See Broome *Aboriginal Australians*, pp. 160–70, C.D. Rowley *The Destruction of Aboriginal Society* Ringwood: Penguin, 1972, pp. 305–40 and J. Horner *Vote Ferguson for Aboriginal Freedom* Sydney: Australia and New Zealand Publishing Co., 1974
24 Kewley *Social Security in Australia*, pp. 132–35
25 S. Tiffin 'In pursuit of reluctant parents: Desertion and non-support legislation in Australia and the United States 1890–1920' in *What Rought Beast?*, pp. 130–50
26 All the above cases are from NSW Premiers Department Special Bundle *Requests for Food Relief* AONSW, 7/5970
27 Statistics from Charity Organisation Society (Sydney Branch) *Annual Reports* 1921–29; St Vincent de Paul Society *Annual Reports* 1920–28; Benevolent Society *Annual Reports* 1920–29; Dickey *Rations, Residence, Resources*, p. 123; *War Cry* 1920–39; Smith Family *Bringers of Cheer* Sydney: Smith Family, 1924. Cases from NSW Colonial Secretary Special Bundle *Benevolent Society Unemployment Relief 1920–21* AONSW, 5/5345.1

28 A.E. Pratt *Letting in the Light* Melbourne: Presbyterian Bookroom, 1933, pp. 49–56
29 ibid. pp. 18–30
30 Victorian Select Committee on Housing of People in the Metropolis, 1913–14, Minutes of Evidence, p. 12
31 On Daceyville see P. Spearritt *Sydney Since the Twenties* Sydney: Hale and Iremonger, 1978, pp. 10–12. For Queensland see R. Hollander 'The Workers Dwellings Act' unpub. M.A. qual. thesis, Griffith University, 1987
32 F.B. Boyce *Four Score Years and Seven* Sydney: Angus and Robertson, 1934, pp. 93–95 and Victorian Royal Commission into Housing in the Metropolis, 1917, Minutes of Evidence, p. 4
33 Material on Fair Rents and the sharp practices of landlords and agents in NSW Attorney-General and Justice Department Special Bundle *Fair Rents Act* AONSW 5/7776
34 These developments are discussed in a number of works. See J. Roe 'Left Behind' in Roe *Social Policy in Australia*; Dickey *No Charity There* pp. 109–30; Macintyre *Winners and Losers*, pp. 59–78; Kewley *Social Security in Australia*, pp. 117–69; F. Jelly 'Child Endowment' in H. Radi and P. Spearritt (eds) *Jack Lang* Sydney: Hale and Iremonger, 1977. For national insurance see Royal Commission on National Insurance *CPP* vol. 2, 1925, First Report and vol. 4, 1926–28, Second Report
35 The general economic and political developments of the Depression are extensively discussed in C.B. Schedvin *Australia and the Great Depression* Sydney: Sydney University Press, 1970, esp. pp. 169–282
36 See S. Macintyre 'Australian responses to unemployment in the last Depression' in J. Roe (ed) *Unemployment: Are There Lessons from History?* Sydney: Hale and Iremonger, 1985; C. Forster 'Australian unemployment 1900–40' *Economic Record* 41, 1965; B. Costar 'The Great Depression: Was Queensland Different?' *Labour History* 26, 1974
37 *Commonwealth Census* 1933. See also Forster 'Australian unemployment'
38 St Vincent de Paul Society *Annual Reports* 1930–35; *War Cry* December 1930 and 1931; Sydney Benevolent Society *Annual Report* 1930; Dickey *Rations, Residence, Resources*, p. 181
39 Macintyre 'Australian Responses to unemployment' and F.A. Bland, 'Unemployment Relief in Australia' in Roe *Social Policy in Australia*, Bolton *A Fine Country to Starve In*, pp. 97–98 and R. Broomhill *Unemployed Workers: A Social History of the Great Depression in Adelaide* St. Lucia: University of Queensland Press, 1978, pp. 30–51
40 Cases from NSW Premiers Department *Requests for Food Relief*
41 Lowenstein *Weevils in the Flour*, pp. 142–44
42 See Bolton *A Fine Country to Starve In*, pp. 149–52, Costar 'The Great Depression', L. Richardson 'Political Protest in Wollongong' in Mackinolty *The Wasted Year?* and Attorney-General and Justice Department Special Bundle *Protests by Various Organisations at the Treatment of Demonstrations by the Unemployed* AONSW 5/7787.1

43 See Broomhill *Unemployed Workers*, pp. 166–80 and N. Wheatley 'The disinherited of the earth' in Mackinolty *The Wasted Year?* and 'NSW Relief Workers' Struggles 1933–36' in Roe *Social Policy in Australia*
44 Macintyre 'Australian responses to unemployment' and F.A. Bland 'Unemployment Relief in Australia'
45 These efforts to survive are graphically recalled in Lowenstein *Weevils in the Flour*
46 Wheatley 'The disinherited of the earth'
47 Figures on decline from United Nations *Population of Australia* Country Monograph Series No. 9, New York, 1982, p. 202. For expert investigations focusing on the role of abortion see Report of Dame Janet Campbell on Maternal and Child Welfare in Australia *CPP* vol. 2, 1929–31, pp. 4–19
48 Quotes from National Health and Medical Research Council *Interim Report on the Decline in the Birth Rate* Canberra: Government Printer, 1944, pp. 70–81

7 A welfare state?

1 F.A. Bland 'An Appraisal of Results' and G.V. Portus 'The Nature and Purpose of Social Services' in W.G.K. Duncan (ed) *Social Services in Australia* Sydney: Angus and Robertson, 1939, p. 160 and p. 2
2 For the best general coverage of Labor's program see Dickey *No Charity There* ch. 6 and R. Watts *The Foundations of the National Welfare State* Sydney: Allen and Unwin, 1987. My discussion of these developments draws heavily on these works.
3 R. Maddock and F. Stilwell 'Boom and Recession' in A. Curthoys, T. Rowse and A.W. Martin (eds) *Australians From 1939* Sydney: Fairfax, Syme, Weldon, 1987
4 W. Kinnear, Report on Health and Pensions Insurance *CPP* vol. 5, 1937, p. 7. See also G. Ince, Report on Unemployment Insurance in Australia *CPP* vol. 5, 1937
5 *CPD* vol. 155, 1938, p. 1354, Figures on pension costs from Kewley *Social Security in Australia*, p. 134
6 See the debates on national insurance in *CPD* vols. 155–56, 1938
7 Kinnear 'Report on Health and Pensions', p. 7. Similar ideals were present in the First Report of the 1925 Royal Commission on National Insurance, p. 7
8 See Watts *Foundations of the National Welfare State*, pp. 1–24
9 See G. Davison and J. Lack 'Planning the New Social Order: The Melbourne University Social Survey, 1941–43' *Australian and New Zealand Journal of Sociology* 17, 1, March 1981; W.G. Shearer *Report June 1942 on Research in Redfern* Sydney, 1942 quoted n D. Cottle 'A New Order for the Old Disorder: The State, Class Struggle and Social Order, 1941–45' in Kennedy *Australian Welfare History*, p. 262. Menzies quoted in Watts *Foundations of the National Welfare State*, p. 45
10 See J. Roe 'Never Again 1939–49' in Roe *Social Policy in Australia*, pp. 217–25, Watts *Foundations of the National Welfare State*, pp. 25–27, Dickey *No Charity There*, pp. 131–32. For a recent contribution to

this debate which aruges that war was a crucial context see W. De Maria 'From Battlefield to Breadline: The State of Charity 1938–45' Ph.D. thesis, University of Queensland, 1988

11 Joint Committee on Social Security, First Interim Report, *CPP* vol. 2, 1940–43, p. 5. The first six reports are in *CPP* vol. 2, 1940–43, the seventh vol. 2, 1944–45 and the final two in vol. 3, 1945–48. For a detailed analysis of the Committee see S. Shaver 'Design for a welfare state: The Joint Parliamentary Committee on Social Security' *Historical Studies* 22, 88, 1987

12 See M.A. Jones *The Australian Welfare State* Sydney: Allen and Unwin, 1983, p. 48 and De Maria 'Battlefield to Breadline' p. 396. Watts and Shaver point to the important ideological role of the Committee, a view shared here.

13 Joint Committee on Social Security, First Report, p. 6

14 The following discussion draws heavily on the work of Watts *Foundations of the National Welfare State*, passim and S. Macintyre *Winners and Losers*, ch. 5

15 De Maria 'Battlefield to Breadline', p. 482

16 A comprehensive summary of the medical profession's views is in Joint Committee on Social Security, Sixth Report, pp. 8–40

17 For GNP figures see Watts *Foundations of the National Welfare State*, p. 117. Rejection rates are from De Maria 'From Battlefield to Breadline', p. 173. Other figures from *Commonwealth Year Book* 1947

18 Figures from M. McKernan *All In! Australia During the Second World War* Melbourne: Nelson, 1983, p. 138. On post war housing crisis see R.T. Appleyard *Low Cost Housing and the Migrant Population* Melbourne: Committee for Economic Development of Australia, 1963, pp. 7–29

19 The following discussion is a summary of some of the findings from M. Ravenscroft *Planning Social Services to Eliminate Slums* Sydney, 1946. Drew Cottle's assiduous research uncovered this valuable source and he quotes from it in 'A New Order from the Old Disorder', p. 265. For a detailed study of working-class community networks and conflict see Janet McCalman's brilliant *Struggletown* Melbourne: Melbourne University Press, 1984

20 Figures from *Commonwealth Year Book* 1947 and 1966. For inner city population changes see P. Spearritt *Sydney Since the Twenties*, p. 252

21 Figures from *Commonwealth Year Book* 1946–70; St Vincent de Paul Society *Annual Report* 1965; R. Mendelsohn *Condition of the People: Social welfare in Australia 1900–1975* Sydney: Allen and Unwin, 1979, pp. 125–134. Figures on charitable societies quoted in C. Baldock 'Volunteer Work as Work: Some theoretical considerations' in C. Baldock and B. Cass (eds) *Women Social Welfare and the State* Sydney: Allen and Unwin, 1983, p. 280

22 The classic account of this transformation is K. Woodroofe *From Charity to Social Work in England and the United States* London: RKP, 1962. Discussion of Australian developments draws heavily on R.J. Lawrence *Professional Social Work in Australia* Canberra: Australian

National University Press, 1965 and E. Martin 'Social Work and Services 1935–65' in Dickey *Rations, Residence, Resources*, pp. 226–68. Jill Roe has argued that the transition from charity to casework was more complex in Australia in 'The end is where we start from: Women and welfare since 1901' in Baldock and Cass *Women, Social Welfare and the State*, p. 15.
23 Royal Commision into Operation of the Housing Acts of Victoria, *VPP*, vol. 2, 1955–56, p. 78
24 R.G. Ellery 'A Psychiatric Programme for Peace' *MJA* 1, 1946, p. 464
25 See A. Stoller 'Social Health and Psychiatric Service' *MJA* 2, 1948, p. 35 and Editorial 'Neurosis and Industry' *MJA* 2, 1947 pp. 753–54. See also Editorial 'The Future of Psychiatry in Australia' *MJA* 2, 1945, pp. 185–86 and W.S. Dawson 'Medical Education in Psychiatry in Australia' *MJA* 2, 1946, pp. 721–30
26 These developments are discussed in greater detail in S. Garton 'Changing Minds' in Curthoys *Australians From 1939*.
27 ibid. For criticisms see A. Stoller and K.W. Arscott *Mental Health Facilities and Needs in Australia* Canberra: Government Printer, 1955
28 For postwar social and economic developments see Connell and Irving *Class Structure in Australian History*, pp. 292–97; Sherington *Australia's Immigrants*, pp. 127–50; W. Hudson '1951–72' in Crowley *New History of Australia*; R. Ward *Australia Since the Coming of Man* Melbourne: Nelson, 1982, pp. 196–203; and Vamplew *Historical Statistics*, pp. 155–57
29 B. Hutchinson *Old People in a Modern Australian Community* Melbourne: Melbourne University Press, 1954
30 Kewley *Social Security in Australia*, pp. 320–21
31 J. Aitken-Swan *Widows in Australia* Sydney: NSW Council of Social Service, 1962. See also Report of Advisory Committee on Juvenile Delinquency *VPP* vol. 2, 1955–56, pp. 21–52
32 Brotherhood of St. Laurence *On Benefit: A Study of Unemployment and Unemployment Benefits in Australia* Fitzroy: Brotherhood of St Laurence, 1961, p. 13
33 These issues are discussed in Brotherhood of St Laurence *Memorandum on the Eviction of Families from Housing Commission Homes* Melbourne: Brotherhood of St Laurence, 1958, pp. 1–5, and E. Martin *High Rents and Low Incomes: Housing Problems of Low Income Families* Melbourne: Brotherhood of St Laurence, 1964. For further evidence and case studies such as the Piper family see Victorian Council of Social Service *How 56 Low Income Families Live* Melbourne: VCOSS, 1961
34 For figures on migration and problems faced by migrants see Sherington *Australia's Immigrants*, pp. 127–50 and J. Collins *Migrant Hands in a Distant Land: Australia's Post-War Immigration* Sydney: Pluto, 1988, pp. 156–75. For a discussion of mental health problems of migrants see Australian Council of Social Service *Immigrants and Mental Health* Sydney: ACOSS, 1976, pp. 2–12. Case study from R. Turner 'The Smith Family' in Masterman *Poverty in Australia*, p. 32

35   R. Brown 'Poverty in Australia' *Australian Quarterly* 35, 2, June 1963
36   D. Scott 'Poverty in Australia' *Dissent* 15, Spring 1965
37   Discussion of overseas work and the quote from Holt are from Stubbs *The Hidden People*, pp. 1–32
38   ibid.
39   Henderson et al. *People in Poverty*

8   A banana republic?

1   R.F. Henderson *Poverty in Australia* Commission of Inquiry into Poverty, First Main Report, Canberra: Australian Government Publishing Service, 1975. The Commission also produced a number of other reports and special papers dealing with specific aspects of poverty
2   See Macintyre *Winners and Losers*, pp. 89–91 and B. Cass and P. Garde 'Unemployment and family support' in A. Graycar (ed) *Retreat from the Welfare State* Sydney: Allen and Unwin, 1983, pp. 89–100
3   Browne 'Poverty on the rise', P. Raskall 'Wealth' *Australian Society* 6, 5, May 1987, pp. 21–24, Jones *The Australian Welfare State*, p. 106
4   G. Wettenhall 'Housing: What has happened to the great Australian dream?' *Australian Society* 6, 7, August 1987, pp. 26–27
5   Henderson *Poverty in Australia*, pp. 163–81
6   ibid. pp. 199–201
7   Jones *Australian Welfare State*, pp. 60–61, pp. 102–113
8   Henderson *Poverty in Australia*, pp. 3–4. For criticisms see P. Saunders 'A Guaranteed Minimum Income Scheme for Australia? Some Problems' and M. Edwards 'A Guaranteed Income Scheme: Implications for Women' in A. Graycar (ed) *Perspectives in Australian Social Policy* Melbourne: Macmillan, 1978
9   These changes are comprehensively summarised in Dickey *No Charity There*, pp. 168–77. See also *Commonwealth Year Book* 1988, pp. 381–83 and Department of Social Security *People Power: Australian Assistance Plan* Canberra: Australian Government Publishing Service, 1975
10   Figures from Jones *Australian Welfare State*, p. 115 and p. 243. For an analysis of middle-class welfare, which began with earlier attempts by Menzies to liberalise the means test, see Dickey *No Charity There*, pp. 145–57. For criticisms of these directions in Labor's policy see Australian Council of Social Service *Who Wins, Who Loses* Sydney: ACOSS, 1979, p. 21
11   K. Windschuttle *Unemployment: A Social and Political Analysis of the Economic Crisis in Australia* Ringwood: Penguin, 1979, pp. 11–48. For hidden unemployment see also Cass and Garde 'Unemployment and family support'
12   Windschuttle *Unemployment*, pp. 64–68, Jones *Australian Welfare State*, pp. 200–206
13   Jones *Australian Welfare State*, pp. 213–14
14   This discussion draws heavily on Windschuttle *Unemployment*, pp. 155–220. See also Macintyre *Winners and Losers*, pp. 89–96
15   Henderson *Poverty in Australia*, p. viii and p. 1; Australian Council of Social Service *Who Wins, Who Loses*, p. 10

NOTES

16 D. Scott *Don't Mourn for Me—Organise: Social and Political Uses of Voluntary Organisations* Sydney: Allen and Unwin, 1981, p. 89
17 Windschuttle *Unemployment*, p. 213
18 For neighbourhood organisation see G. Brewer *Rough Justice: A Study of the Causes and Effects of the Termination of Unemployment Benefit* Fitzroy: Brotherhood of St Laurence, 1978, pp. 17–18. Cases from Australian Council of Social Service *Are We Second Class Citizens?* Sydney: ACOSS, 1974
19 Henderson *Poverty in Australia*, pp. 95–97 and pp. 138–39
20 Brewer *Rough Justice*, p. 74
21 O'Neill and Nairn *The Have Nots*, pp. 45–46
22 See Scott *Don't Mourn for Me*, pp. 15–24; I. Yates and A. Graycar 'Non-government Welfare: Issues and Perspectives' in Graycar *Retreat from the Welfare State*, pp. 157–58; C. Baldock 'Volunteer work as work; some theoretical considerations' in Baldock and Cass *Women, Social Welfare and the State*, pp. 282–94
23 H. Raysmith 'How Welfare has Changed' *Australian Society* 4, 6, June 1985, pp. 8–10
24 For ACOSS and Karen Green cases see Scott *Don't Mourn for Me*, pp. 25–27. See also Anglican Diocese of Sydney *Poverty: Is Money the Answer?* Sydney, 1977, Australian Council of Social Service *Real Reform or Sideways Shuffle?* Sydney: ACOSS, 1977
25 O'Neill and Nairn *The Have-Nots*, pp. 2–5
26 Case from P. Hollingworth *Australians in Poverty* Melbourne: Nelson, 1979, p. 31
27 See C. Rowley *Outcasts in White Australia* Ringwood: Penguin, 1972, pp. 305–415, and Broome *Aboriginal Australians*, pp. 170–201
28 Quoted in Broome *Aboriginal Australians*, p. 196
29 R. Haupt 'The Facts that Shame Australia' *SMH* 7 November 1987
30 See B. Cass 'Wages, women and children' in R.F. Henderson (ed) *The Welfare Stakes: Strategies for Australian Social Policy* Parkville: University of Melbourne, 1981, J. Roe 'The end is where we start from: Women and welfare since 1901' and L. Bryson 'Women as welfare recipients: women, poverty and the state' in Baldock and Cass *Women, Social Welfare and the State*
31 S. Shaver 'Sex and money in the welfare state' in Baldock and Cass *Women, Social Welfare and the State*, p. 151
32 Bryson 'Women as welfare recipients', pp. 131–41
33 C. O'Donnell and D. Brennan *Caring for Australia's Children* Sydney: Allen and Unwin, 1986, p. 113
34 H. Saville 'Refuges: a new beginning to the struggle' in C. O'Donnell and J. Craney (eds) *Family Violence in Australia* Melbourne: Longmans, 1982
35 ibid.
36 This discussion is based on arguments and evidence developed in Garton, 'Changing Minds'
37 T. Sweeny 'Child welfare and child care policies' in Graycar *Retreat from the Welfare State*, pp. 41–44
38 Garton 'Changing Minds'

39 ibid.
40 See F. Ainsworth and P. Hansen 'After the Institutions' *Australian Society* 4, 2, February 1985, pp. 23–25
41 A. Gorman 'Finding out why a boy died' *Australian Society* 2, 8, September 1983, pp. 9–11
42 Jones *Australian Welfare State*, pp. 64–67
43 M. Newton 'Slash Welfare State' *Australian* 25–26 May 1980. For an analysis of the emergence of the new right see R. Poole 'Markets and motherhood: the advent of the new right' in A. Burns et al. (eds) *The Family in the Modern World* Sydney: Allen and Unwin, 1983
44 For discussion of the literature on the 'retreat' see A. Graycar 'Retreat from the Welfare State' in Graycar *Retreat from the Welfare State*
45 P. Browne 'Outside the Trilogy' *Australian Society* 5, 5, May 1986, pp. 16–19.
46 A. Farrar 'Labor gets back to basics' *Australian Society* 7, March 1988, pp. 39–40. Policy changes from *Commonwealth Year Book* 1988, pp. 381–83
47 S. Prasser 'Welfare Bandaids coming unstuck' *Australian Society* 4, 2, December 1985, pp. 23–24
48 See P. Saunders and P. Whiteford 'Pricing the Poverty Pledge' *Australian Society* 6, 8, September 1987, pp. 22–24 and L. Fell 'Tax Reform: ACOSS takes the running' *Australian Society* 7, 2, February 1988, pp. 20–21
49 R. Mendelsohn 'The Dream that Died' *Australian Society* 4, 10, October 1985
50 Jones *Australian Welfare State*, p. 158

Select bibliography

There are many themes relevant to a history of poverty. They include work, health, education, inequality, poverty, social policy and welfare, and the literature on each is now very extensive. This bibliography is restricted (with a few exceptions) to a selection of some important works on the history of social policy and welfare in Australia. The references in each of these works provide a guide for further reading. Readers interested in current social policy debates will find much of interest in journals such as *Australian Society* and the *Australian Journal of Social Issues* and the numerous publications of the University of New South Wales *Social Welfare Research Centre*.

General Works
Castles. F.G. *The Working Class and Welfare: Reflections on the Political Development of the Welfare State in Australia and New Zealand 1890–1980* Sydney: Allen and Unwin, 1985
Dickey, B. *No Charity There: A Short History of Social Welfare in Australia* 2nd edn, Sydney: Allen and Unwin, 1987
—— 'Problems in Writing Welfare History' *Journal of Australian Studies* 21, 1987
—— *Rations, Residence, Resources: A History of Social Welfare in South Australia since 1836* Cowandilla: Wakefield Press, 1986
Gandevia, B. *Tears Often Shed: Child Health and Welfare in Australia from 1788* Sydney: Pergamon Press, 1978
Graycar, A. *Social Policy: An Australian Introduction* Melbourne: Macmillan, 1977
—— (ed) *Perspectives in Australian Social Policy: A Book of Readings* Melbourne: Macmillan, 1978
Jones, M.A. *The Australian Welfare State: Growth, Crisis and Change* 2nd edn, Sydney: Allen and Unwin, 1983
Kennedy, R. (ed) *Australian Welfare History: Critical Essays* Melbourne: Macmillan, 1982
Kewley, T.H. *Social Security in Australia 1901–72* 2nd edn, Sydney: Sydney University Press, 1973
Macintyre, S. *Winners and Losers: The Pursuit of Social Justice in Australian History* Sydney: Allen and Unwin, 1985
Mendelsohn, R. *The Condition of the People: Social Welfare in Australia 1900–75* Sydney: Allen and Unwin, 1979

Roe, J. 'Social Policy and the Permanent Poor' in E.L. Wheelwright and K. Buckley (eds) *Essays in the Political Economy of Australian Capitalism* vol. 1, Sydney: Australia and New Zealand Publishing Co., 1975

—— (ed.) *Social Policy in Australia: Some Perspectives 1901–75* Stanmore: Cassell, 1976

Stannage, C.T. 'Uncovering Poverty in Australian History' *Early Days* 7, 1976

Western, J. *Social Inequality in Australian Society* Melbourne: Macmillan, 1983

Before 1914

Brown, J.C. *Poverty is Not a Crime: The Development of Social Services in Tasmania 1803–1900* Hobart: Tasmanian Historical Research Association, 1972

Buckley K. and Wheelwright, T. *No Paradise for Workers: Capitalism and the Common People 1788–1914* Melbourne: Oxford University Press, 1988

Cage, R. 'The origins of poor relief in New South Wales: an account of the Benevolent Society 1809–1862' *Australian Economic History Review* 20, 2, 1980

Cummins, C.J. *The Development of the Benevolent Asylum 1788–1855* Sydney: Department of Health, 1971

Davison, G., Dunstan, D. and McConville, C. (eds) *The Outcasts of Melbourne: Essays in Social History* Sydney: Allen and Unwin, 1985

Dickey, B. 'Evolution of care for destitute children in New South Wales 1875–1901' *Journal of Australian Studies* 4, 1979

—— 'The Sick Poor in New South Wales 1840–1880: Colonial Practice in an Amateur Age' *Journal of the Royal Australian Historical Society* 59, 1, 1973

—— 'Hospital Services in New South Wales 1875–1900: Questions of Provision, Entitlement and Responsibility' *Journal of the Royal Australian Historical Society* 62, 1, 1976

—— 'Charity in New South Wales 1850–1914: Out-door relief to the Aged and Destitute' *Journal of the Royal Australian Historical Society* 52, 1, 1966

Dunning, B. 'Being poor and female in colonial Western Australia' *Hecate* 3, 2, 1977

Fitzgerald, S. *Rising Damp: Sydney 1870–90* Melbourne: Oxford University Press, 1987

Fry, E.C. 'Out-work in the Eighties: An Examination of Out-Work in the Infant Industries of the Eastern Australian Colonies 1880–1890' *University Studies in History and Economics* 2, 4, 1956

Garton, S. *Medicine and Madness: A Social History of Insanity in New South Wales 1880–1940* Kensington: University of New South Wales Press, 1988

—— 'Sir Charles Mackellar: Psychiatry eugenics and child welfare in New South Wales 1900–1914' *Historical Studies* 22, 86, 1986

SELECT BIBLIOGRAPHY

Godden, J. 'A New Look at Pioneer Women' *Hecate* 5, 2, 1979
Horsburgh, M. 'Child Care in New South Wales in 1870' *Australian Social Work* 29, 1976
—— 'Government Policy and the Benevolent Society' *Journal of the Royal Australian Historical Society* 63, 2, 1977
—— 'Child Care in New South Wales in 1890' *Australian Social Work* 30, 1977
Inglis, K. *Hospital and Community: A History of the Royal Melbourne Hospital* Melbourne: Melbourne University Press, 1988
Kelly, M. (ed) *Nineteenth Century Sydney: Essays in Urban History* Sydney: Sydney University Press, 1978
Kennedy, R. *Charity Warfare: The Charity Organisation Society in Colonial Melbourne* Melbourne: Hyland House, 1985
—— 'Poor relief in Melbourne: The Benevolent Society's Contribution' *Journal of the Royal Australian Historical Society* 60, 4, 1974
—— 'The Leongatha Labour Colony: Founding an Anti-Utopia' *Labour History* 14, 1968
Kyle, N. 'Agnes King inter alios: Reformatory school administrators in New South Wales 1869–1904' *Journal of Australian Studies* 15, 1984
Lake, M. 'Building themselves up with aspros: Pioneer Women Reassessed' *Hecate* 7, 2, 1981
Lee, J. and Fahey, C. 'A Boom for Whom? Some Developments in the Australian Labour Market 1870–1891' *Labour History* 50, 1986
Lewis, M. and MacLeod, R. 'A workingman's paradise? Reflections on urban mortality in colonial Australia 1860–1900' *Medical History* 31, 1987
Macarthy, P.G. 'Labour and the Living Wage 1890–1910' *Australian Journal of Politics and History* 13, 1, 1967
—— 'Wages in Australia 1891–1914' *Australian Economic History Review* 10, 1, 1970
McDonald, D. 'Child and female labour in Sydney 1876–1898' *Australian National University Historical Journal* 10–11, 1973–74
Markey, R. *The Making of the Labor Party in New South Wales 1880–1900* Kensington: New South Wales University Press, 1988
Mayne, A. 'The question of the poor in the nineteenth century city' *Historical Studies* 20, 81, 1983
—— 'City back-slums in the land of promise: Some aspects of the 1876 Report on overcrowding in Sydney' *Labour History* 38, 1980
—— *Fever, Squalor, Vice: Sanitation and Social Policy in Victorian Sydney* St Lucia: University of Queensland Press, 1982
Mitchell, A. *The Hospital South of the Yarra: A History of the Alfred Hospital* Melbourne: Alfred Hospital, 1977
O'Brien, A. *Poverty's Prison: The Poor in New South Wales, 1880–1918* Melbourne: Melbourne University Press, 1988
Ramsland, J. *Children of the Backlanes: Destitute and Neglected Children in Colonial New South Wales* Kensington: New South Wales University Press, 1986

—— 'An Anatomy of a Nineteenth Century Child Saving Institution: The Randwick Asylum for Destitute Children' *Journal of the Royal Australian Historical Society* 70, 3, 1984

—— 'The Development of Boarding-Out Systems in Australia: A Series of Welfare Experiments in Child Care 1860–1910' *Journal of the Royal Australian Historical Society* 60, 3, 1974

Reynolds, H. 'That Hated Stain: The Aftermath of Transportation in Tasmania' *Historical Studies* 14, 53, 1969

Ritter, L. 'Boarding-Out in New South Wales and South Australia: Adoption, Adaptation or Innovation' *Journal of the Royal Australian Historical Society* 64, 2, 1978

Sinclair, W.A. 'Women at work in Melbourne and Adelaide since 1871' *Economic Record* 57, 3, 1981

Swain, S. 'Destitute and Dependent: Case Studies of Poverty in Melbourne 1890–1900' *Historical Studies* 19, 74, 1980

Templeton, J. *Prince Henry's: The Evolution of a Melbourne Hospital 1869–1969* Melbourne: Robertson and Mullens, 1969

Van Krieken, R. 'Children and the State: Child Welfare in New South Wales 1890–1915' *Labour History* 51, 1986

Windshuttle, E. 'Women, Class and Temperance: Moral Reform in Eastern Australia 1832–57' *Push from the Bush* 3, May 1979

—— 'Feeding the Poor and Sapping their Strength: The Public Role of Ruling Class Women in Eastern Australia 1788–1850' in E. Windshuttle (ed) *Women and Class and History: Feminist Perspectives on Australia 1788–1978* Melbourne: Fontana, 1980

After 1914

Appleyard, R.T. *Low Cost Housing and the Migrant Population* Melbourne: Committee for Economic Development of Australia, 1963

Australian Council of Social Service *Who Wins, Who Loses?* Sydney: ACOSS, 1979

—— *Real Reform or Sideways Shuffle?* Sydney: ACOSS, 1977

Baldock, C.V. and Cass, B. (eds) *Women, Social Welfare and the State* Sydney: Allen and Unwin, 1983

Barbalet, M. *Adelaide Children's Hospital, 1876–1976* Adelaide: Children's Hospital, 1975

—— *Far From a Low Gutter Girl: The Forgotten World of State Wards, South Australia 1887–1940* Melbourne: Oxford University Press, 1983

Bolton, G. *A Fine Country to Starve In* Nedlands: University of Western Australia Press, 1972

Brennan, D. and O'Donnell, C. *Caring for Australia's Children: Political and Industrial Issues in Child Care* Sydney: Allen and Unwin, 1986

Brewer, G. *On the Breadline: Oral Records of Poverty* Melbourne: Hyland House, 1980

—— *Rough Justice: A Study of the Causes and Effects of the Termination of Unemployment Benefit* Fitzroy: Brotherhood of St Laurence, 1978

Broomhill, R. *Unemployed Workers: A Social History of the Great Depression in Adelaide* St Lucia: University of Queensland Press, 1978

SELECT BIBLIOGRAPHY

Brotherhood of St Laurence *On Benefit: A Study of Unemployment and Unemployment Benefits in Australia* Fitzroy: Brotherhood of St Laurence, 1961

Brown, R. 'Poverty in Australia' *Australian Quarterly* 35, 2, June 1963

Duncan, W.G.K. (ed) *Social Services in Australia* Sydney: Angus and Robertson, 1939

Forster, C. 'Australian Unemployment 1900–40' *Economic Record* 41, 1965

Francis, R. 'No More Amazons: Gender and Work Process in the Victorian Clothing Trades 1890–1939' *Labour History* 50, 1986

Graycar, A. *Welfare Politics in Australia: A Study in Policy Analysis* Melbourne: Macmillan, 1979

—— (ed) *Retreat from the Welfare State: Australian Social Policy in the 1980s* Sydney: Allen and Unwin, 1983

Henderson, R.F. (ed) *The Welfare Stakes: Strategies for Australian Social Policy* Melbourne: IAESR, 1981

Henderson, R.F., Harcourt, A., and Harper, R.J.A. *People in Poverty: A Melbourne Survey* Melbourne: Cheshire, 1970

Henderson, R.F. *Poverty in Australia: Commission of Inquiry into Poverty, First Main Report* Canberra: AGPS, 1975

Hollingworth, P. *The Powerless Poor: A Comprehensive Guide to Poverty in Australia* Melbourne: Stockland, 1972

—— *Australians in Poverty* Melbourne: Nelson, 1979

Hutchinson, B. *Old People in a Modern Australian Community* Melbourne: Melbourne University Press, 1954

Jelly, F. 'Child endowment' in Radi, H. and Spearritt, P. (eds) *Jack Lang* Sydney: Hale and Iremonger, 1977

Lawrence, R.J. *Professional Social Work in Australia* Canberra: Australian National University Press, 1965

Lowenstein, W. *Weevils in the Flour: An Oral Record of the 1930s Depression in Australia* Melbourne: Hyland House, 1978

Macintyre, S. 'Australian Responses to Unemployment in the Last Depression' in J. Roe (ed) *Unemployment: Are There Lessons from History?* Sydney: Hale and Iremonger, 1985

Mackinolty, J. (ed) *The Wasted Years?: Australia's Great Depression* Sydney: Allen and Unwin, 1981

Martin, E. *High Rents and Low Incomes: Housing Problems of Low Income Families* Melbourne: Brotherhood of St Laurence, 1964

Masterman, G. (ed) *Poverty in Australia* Sydney: Angus and Robertson, 1969

Mendelsohn, R. *Fair Go: Welfare Issues in Australia* Ringwood: Penguin, 1982

O'Neill, J. and Nairn, R. *The Have Nots: A Study of 150 Low Income Families* Melbourne: Brotherhood of St Laurence, 1972

Rodd, L. *A Gentle Shipwreck* Melbourne: Nelson, 1975

Roe, J. 'Chivalry and Social Policy in the Antipodes' *Historical Studies* 22, 88, 1987

—— 'Old Age, Young Country: The First Old Age Pensions and Pensioners in New South Wales' *Teaching History* 15, July 1981

Rowley, C.D. *Outcasts in White Australia* Ringwood: Penguin, 1972

Scott, D. *Don't Mourn for Me — Organise: Social and Political Uses of Voluntary Organisations* Sydney: Allen and Unwin, 1981

—— 'Poverty in Australia' *Dissent* 15, Spring 1965

Shaver, S. 'Design for a Welfare State: The Joint Parliamentary Committee on Social Security' *Historical Studies* 22, 88, 1987

Stoller, A. and Arscott, K.W. *Mental Health Facilities and Needs in Australia* Canberra: Government Printer, 1955

Swan, J. Aitken- *Widows in Australia* Sydney: New South Wales Council of Social Service, 1962

Tulloch, P. *Poor Policies: Australian Income Security 1972–77* London: Croom Helm, 1979

Watts, R. *The Foundations of the National Welfare State* Sydney: Allen and Unwin, 1987

Windschuttle, K. *Unemployment: A Social and Political Analysis of the Economic Crisis in Australia* Ringwood: Penguin, 1979

Index

Aborigines, 6, 15, 19–20, 37, 66, 94, 99, 117–18, 141, 162–5, 169, 171; protection of, 118; land rights for, 162–4; health of, 164
abortion, 89, 130, 139
accommodation, 25, 29, 39, 48, 54, 56, 66, 78, 117, 159
Act of Settlement, 9–10
Adelaide, 31, 39, 56–7, 60, 85, 90, 127, 129, 131, 142, 149, 159
Adelaide Benevolent Asylum, 56–7
agriculture, 6, 15–16, 22, 27–8, 33, 39, 64–6, 114–15, 132
Allen, George, 46, 54
alms, 11; *see also* poor relief
America, 23, 33, 43, 87, 105, 108, 113, 142, 149, 155, 164, 169; War of Indepedence, 14
anthropometrics, 105
arbitration, 81–3
Ardill, George, 95
Arthur, George, 45, 59
Arthur, Richard, 105
aristocracy, 8
Asia, 78, 99, 101, 105
assignment, 16–17, 24
asylums, 9, 12, 19, 45–6, 48, 51, 54–61, 84, 98–9, 103–4, 106; benevolent, 44, 56, 58; conditions in, 58, 90, 96
Australasian Medical Gazette, 85
Australian Agricultural Company, 27
Australian Assistance Plan, 155–6
Australian Council of Social Service, 142, 158, 160, 170

Baby Health Centres, 107, 140
banana republic, 151
Bandler, Faith, 162
bankruptcy, 32, 78
banks, 32, 74
Barnet, James, 58
Barrett, J.B., 121
Basic Wage Royal Commission, 82
Baxter, Annie, 29
Baynton, Barbara, 65
begging, 8, 37–8, 48, 60
Bellamy, Edward, 77
benevolence, 4, 20–2, 44, 47, 85, 94, 99, 142
Benevolent societies, 45–6, 86; Ladies, 54; Launceston, 45, 52–3; Melbourne Ladies, 51–1, 74–5, 88; Hobart, 45
Benevolent Society of New South Wales, 2, 21, 44, 46, 48–50, 54, 75, 87, 92, 96–8, 120, 126
Bentham, Jeremy, 13–14
Berry, Alexander, 24–5, 27
Berry, R.J.A., 105
Beveridge Report, 135
Bible Society, 21, 45
Bigge, J.T., 21, 25–5
Biloela Girls Reformatory, 90
birth rate, decline in, 80, 99, 105, 130, 132
Bland, F.A., 131
Bleakley, J.W., 117
blind institutions, 54, 57
boarding houses, 39–40, 138, 140, 149, 167
boarding-out, 91–5, 106; allowance

for, 92, 94–5
Booth, Charles, 3
Bourke, Richard, 30, 45
Boyce, F.B., 98, 109, 122
Brighton Reformatory School, 90
Britain, 6, 18, 23, 27–8, 33, 37, 42–5, 50, 68, 77–8, 87, 90, 105, 110, 113, 121, 123–4, 132, 134–5, 142, 149, 155, 169
British Medical Association, 136
Brisbane, 41, 50, 52, 66, 69, 75, 120, 126
Brisbane Hospital, 50, 52
Broken Hill, 76
Brotherhood of St Laurence, 2, 141, 143, 146, 148–9, 158–60
Brown, Ray, 149
Bruce, Stanley Melbourne, 115, 124; government of, 115, 124
Bryson, Lois, 164
building societies, 74
Bulletin, the, 89

Campbell, Francis, 101, 103–4
Canada, 113
capital, 30, 63–4, 77, 114
capitalism, 4, 6, 77, 135
Casey, R.G., 132–3
Cass, Bettina, 164, 170
Castle Hill, 17
Casual Labour Board, 72, 74, 76; Sydney, 72, 74; Brisbane, 74
Central Methodist Mission, 87, 95, 141
charity, 4, 8, 11–12, 21, 43–62, 74–6, 85–9, 94–5, 108, 112, 119–21, 126–7, 140–2, 146–8, 157–9; crisis in, 84; inspectors of, 95; new and scientific, 85–9, 103; resentment of, 121; state, 99; stigma of, 99, 133; *see also* non-government organisations and welfare rights groups
Charity Organisation Society, 75–6, 84–7, 142; conferences of, 84–9, 103
Charleston, D.M., 75
chartism, 63

Chifley, Ben, 131, 154, 157; governement of, 131, 154, 169
child abuse, 160, 165, 168; sexual, 165
child care facilities, 164, 168, 170
child endowment, 123, 131, 134, 137, 139, 154, 164
child welfare, 90–5, 105–7, 141, 162, 165, 167–8; Department of, 119
children, 9, 12, 19, 40, 47–8, 50, 52–4, 59–61, 69–70, 80–1, 85, 87, 89–95, 105–7, 112, 115, 130, 137–8, 141, 147, 165, 168; Aboriginal, 94; court for, 106; health of, 106–7; neglected, 19, 47, 54, 59–60, 85, 91–2, 94–5, 141
Childrens Protection Society, 162
China, 33, 40–1
Chisholm, Caroline, 30
christianity, 4, 8, 11, 20, 45, 52, 54, 95
churches, 45–6, 59, 71, 87–9, 94–5, 99, 141–2, 158–9; Anglican, 95; Catholic, 45, 87, 95; Presbyterian, 95, 120–1
city missionary societies, 52, 85, 98
civilisation, 20, 94, 101
Clark, Emily, 91
Clark, Manning, 14
clergy, 21, 27, 37, 53, 84, 97, 103
Coghlan, T.A., 68, 99
Coleridge, Samuel Taylor, 10
Collins, David, 18
colonial secretary, 47, 53, 56, 72
colonisation, 4, 6, 15, 30, 45
colonists, 16–17, 20, 23–4, 45–6, 63
Colquhoun, Patrick, 7, 14–15
Commonwealth, 81, 99, 101, 108, 114, 123, 131–2, 136–7, 141
community care, 167–8
Conolly, John, 58
convicts, 6, 14–19, 21–4, 26, 32, 34, 43, 55; resistance of, 25, 27
Cook, James, 19
Coombs, H.C., 135
Cooper, William, 118

INDEX

Cootamundra Girls Home, 94
Coranderrk, 118
cottage homes, 91–3, 105–6
Council for Single Mother and Child, 159
Cowper, Charles, 62
Cowper, William 24
Creed, J.M., 104
crime, 7, 12–17, 37, 39, 59, 84, 87, 90, 101, 103, 112, 144, 160, 164; intra-class, 17; rates of, 13, 17
criminal class, 12, 14–15, 23, 37, 105
Crook, W.P., 19
Cumeroogunga, 118
Cunningham, Peter, 23, 36
Curtin, John, 131–3, 135, 154; government of, 131–3, 135, 154, 169

Daceyville, 121
Darling, Ralph, 28, 44–5
Darling Downs, 63–4
Darwinism, social, 78, 101, 163
deaf and blind institutions, 54
Deakin, Alfred, 62, 77, 81, 124,
death, 4, 67, 78–9, 116, 132; in custody, 164
debt, 17, 28, 65, 114, 123, 148
deinstitutionalisation, 165–8
delinquency, 54, 59, 60, 90–1, 94, 101, 103, 106, 141, 146–7, 167
Depression; 1840s, 30–3, 84, 134–5; 1890s, 1–2, 62, 68, 74–7, 108; 1930s, 2, 108, 124–31
deserted mothers, 2–3, 9, 50, 86, 92, 119, 131, 135, 138–9, 147, 149, 152, 158–9, 164
desertion, 4, 9, 12, 33, 39–40, 48, 50, 60, 65, 89, 171
Destitute Board of South Australia, 33–4, 47–8, 87, 91, 98, 120; *see also* Public Relief Department
destitution, 2, 17, 22, 36–7, 39, 59, 98, 140, 171
disability, 112–3; *see also* handicapped
diseases, 8, 16, 41–2, 80, 90, 101, 103–4, 111, 164; crop, 16;
venereal, 112; *see also* illness
dispensaries, 58
divorce, 114
Dixon, Chicka, 162
doctors, 41–2, 56–7, 80, 85, 98, 101, 103–7, 111, 116, 121, 133, 136–7, 144, 155, 160, 167; *see also* medicine
dole, 10, 127–9, 158, 170; sustenance, 127–9
domestic service, 7, 27, 37, 61, 68–9, 116
Downing, Richard, 135
Dr Barnardo's Homes, 141
drink, 8, 36, 48, 57, 88–9, 103–4, 115, 121, 144, 146, 160, 164; *see also* drunkenness
drought, 16–17, 28, 66, 108–19
drugs, 104, 144–5, 165–7; addiction to, 112; tranquilliser, 145
drunkenness, 8, 15, 37, 41, 60, 76, 84, 99, 101, 103–4, 119
Duncan, Annie, 80–1
Dunwich Asylum, 56–7, 96, 98

economy, 24, 30, 66, 77, 108, 124, 132, 136, 151, 169; expansion of, 27, 33–4, 66,108, 146; dependent, 30, 68; recovery of, 115
Eden Frederick, 10, 20
education, 12, 19–20, 40, 59–60, 70, 95, 106–7, 112, 142, 152, 158; moral, 60–1, 107; physical, 107; psychological, 107
Ellery, Reg, 144
Elsie Women's Refuge, 165
emancipists, 17, 29, 32, 55
Emigration Agent, 31–2, 47
employers, 4, 29, 68, 70, 72, 74, 77–8, 80, 133
employment, 23, 27, 57, 65–6, 143; full, 131, 135
enclosures, 6–7
environmentalism, 60–1, 91–2, 103, 113, 135
epidemics, 19, 41–2
equal pay, 83, 164
Eucalyptus Town, 110

evangelicals, 4, 8, 12, 14, 19, 21, 46, 48, 53–4, 84, 88
eviction, 130, 139
Eyre, Edward John, 25

factories, 7, 65, 67, 69–70, 79, 146; see also manufacturing
Factory and Shop Acts, 72, 78–9, 80–1; inspectors of, 80–1
families, 16, 24, 30, 33, 39–40, 48, 50, 56, 60, 70, 75, 83, 91–2, 97, 110–11, 114, 116, 126, 130, 134, 137–9, 143, 145, 147–9, 152, 154, 156, 167–8; multi-problem, 145, 160, 162
Famity Loan Colonization Society, 30
farm colonies, 92
farmers, 16–17, 24, 28–9, 63–5, 113–14, 133; see also agriculture
Father and Son Movement, 107
female factories, 26–7
Female Orphans Asylum, 19, 21, 45
feminism, 81, 89, 164–5, 169, 171
Ferguson, William, 118
Fielding, Henry, 8
Fitzgerald, Shirley, 67–8
Flinders Island, 20
flogging, 24–5
fostering, 91–2
Fowler, Frank, 37
Franciscans, 4
France, 113, 164
Fraser, Malcolm, 157; government of, 156–7, 168–9
Friedman, Milton, 168
Friendly societies, 57–8, 79, 98, 101 112, 124, 133
funeral benefits, 57, 120, 131

gambling, 8, 37, 41
George, Henry, 77
Gipps, George, 31
Godfrey, C.G., 104
gold, 24, 33–4, 45–6, 48, 60, 74
Goldstein, Jacob, 75, 86–7
Goldstein, Vida, 89
Gorton, government of John, 1

government, 75–7; local, 155–7; state, 85, 88, 94, 99, 112, 114–15, 127, 129, 134, 136, 141–2, 156, 158; Federal, 123, 134, 136, 141, 156, 158; see also Commonwealth
government order, 47, 56, 58
government stores, 16, 17, 20, 22, 24, 45
government subsidy, 43–7, 95, 142
governors, 15, 17, 20–2, 24, 27, 31, 45, 47
Goyder Line, 29
Graham, Henry, 23
Green, T.H., 78
Grey, George, 31
Griener, government of Nick, 167–8

handicapped, 167–8
Harris, Alexander, 36–7
Harvester judgment, 82
Hawke, Robert, 2, 151, 170
health, 17, 23, 41–2, 79–80, 107, 111, 113, 135–4, 137, 142, 144, 152, 155–6, 158, 163; officers of, 110; see also medicine, hospitals
Henderson, Ronald, 150–5, 162; Report of, 151–5, 158
heredity, 101, 104–7
Hetherington, John, 146
Higgins, H.B., 82
Higinbotham, George, 62
Hill, Florence and Rosamund, 57, 91
Hobart, 17, 30, 33, 55, 59–60
Hobart Queens Asylum, 55, 91
Holt, Harold, 149
homeless, 9, 37, 39, 54, 87, 141, 149, 152, 157, 167, 170
Horne, Donald, 1
hospitals, 9, 17, 20, 44–6, 49, 51, 54, 56–8, 75, 95, 104–5, 131, 134, 137, 139, 141–2, 155; admissions to, 145; conditions in, 58; district, 58; foundling, 9; mental, 141; repatriation, 112, see also individual hospitals
hostels, 141, 167
housing, 39–41, 116, 134, 137–8,

INDEX

141, 147, 149–50, 154, 158
Housing Crusade Committee, 109, 121
housing reform, 109–11, 121; resistence to, 122
Howard, John, 14
Hughes, William Morris, 85; government of, 82
Hunter Valley, 24, 108
hygiene, 107, 144; *see also* medicine, health

idleness and indolence, 10–12, 44, 48, 61–2, 84
illegitimacy, 89, 160
illness, 3–4, 9, 12, 22, 29, 47, 51–2, 54, 56–7, 80, 85, 87, 95, 116, 121, 124, 131–2, 137, 143, 148, 154; benefits for, 155
immigrants, 16, 23–4, 29–31, 33, 36, 39, 50, 54–5, 63, 115–16, 132, 138, 148, 152, 156
Immigrants Aid Society, 50
imposture, 44–5, 48, 51–4, 86; *see also* idleness
Ince, Godfrey, 132
income, 152–7, 160, 162, 164, 170
indigence allowance, 98
industrial schools, 54, 60–1, 90, 92; *see also* reformatories
industrialisation, 10, 14, 63
inebriate asylums, 54, 103–4; *see also* drunkenness
inequality, 155, 158, 162, 171
infant mortality, 41, 99, 101, 164
influenza, 111–12
insanity, 43, 47, 101, 103–4, 145; *see also* mental illness
insurance, 101, 132–3, 156; national, 124, 132–7
intelligence tasts (IQ), 105–6
International Workers of the World (IWW), 111
invalids, 34, 97–9, 119, 124, 135, 152; *see also* pensions
investigation, 45, 51–3, 75–6, 143, 159
Irvine, R.F., 110

Jackson, H.L., 87, 103
Jackson, R.V., 1
Johnson, Lyndon, 149
Johnson, Richard, 19
Jones, Richard, 32

Kalgoorlie, 108
Kanakas, 66–7
Keating, Paul, 2, 151, 169
Keynes, John Maynard, 135, 168
Kidston, William, 121
Kinchela Boys Home, 94
King, Anna, 19, 21
King, Phillip Gidley, 16–17, 19, 21, 45
King, Whitely, 77
King's Orphans Asylums, 45, 49
Kingston, C.C., 77
Kinnear, Walter, 132–3

La Trobe, Charles, 32
Labor Party, 124, 126, 131–3, 135–7, 140, 151, 154–7, 169
labour bureaus, 76–7
labour colonies, 76
labour market, 36, 66–8, 72
labour movement, 62, 76–7, 81, 84, 99, 111; *see also* Labor Party, trade unions
labourers, 6–8, 10, 17, 24, 32–4, 63, 65–6, 114; casual, 37, 68, 123, 138; forced, 25; juvenile and female, 68–72, 79; seasonal, 6, 29, 36, 65, 68; skilled, 6, 11, 15, 29, 66, 72; *see also* work, workers
Ladies Melbourne and Suburban Mission, 52
Lamb, John, 62
land, 6, 16–17, 24, 27, 29, 46, 63–5, 113–15; grants of, 16, 21–2, 27–8; taxation of, 62; *see also* selection, farmers, agriculture
landlords, 110, 122, 137; resentment of, 123; *see also* rent
Lane, William, 77, 89
Lang, J.D., 29, 62
Lang, J.T., 126
Langley, J.D., 62

Launceston, 17, 52–3
laundresses, 27, 70
Lawson, Henry, 65
Legacy, 112
Leongatha Labour Colony, 76
liberals, 4, 62–3, 71, 77–8, 84, 90, 99, 121, 162, 169, 171; new, 77–8,
Lindsay, Alf, 77
Liverpool Asylum, 56
living wage, 82–3, 123; *see also* wages
local and neighbourhood support, 98, 119–21, 128, 130, 138–40, 141
Loch, C.S., 86
lodgers, 138
lodging houses, 8, 23, 39–41
Logan, Patrick, 25
London, 1, 7–8, 30, 37, 41, 110
lunatic asylums, 9, 17, 20, 58–9, 101, 104; Tarban Creek, 59, 101; *see also* mental hospitals,
lying-in homes, 47, 54
Lyons, J.A., 125, 132

Macarthur, James, 24
McGowen, government of James, 121
Mackellar, Charles, 105–6
McMahon, government of William, 151
Macquarie, Lachlan, 17, 19, 21, 43, 45
Macully, A., 84
machinery, 65, 67, 72, 79–80; *see also* manufacturing
magistrates, 7–8, 13, 24, 51, 99
maintenance, 2, 50, 56, 119, 171; *see also* desertion
Male Orphans Asylum, 19, 45
Malthus, T.R., 10
Mann, D.D., 18–19
Manning, Frederick Norton, 59
Mansfield, Samuel, 54
manufacturing, 33–4, 42, 67–9, 115, 132, 146; *see also* machinery
Marist Brothers, 95
marriage, 27, 29
Marsden, Samuel, 19

Maternal and Dorcas Society, 45
maternity allowance, 101, 123, 131, 137
Mayhew, Henry, 3, 11
means test, 119, 136, 154–6
Medibank, 155
medical benefits, 155
Medical Journal of Australia, 106, 144
medicine, 85, 99, 101–7, 155; preventive, 107; *see also* doctors health
Melbourne, 31, 34, 37–42, 49, 52–3, 55, 57–8, 60, 66, 75, 84–6, 104, 109–10, 115, 120–2, 126–7, 142, 146, 148, 150–1, 159; social survey of, 133–4
Melbourne Benevolent Asylum, 55, 57
Melbourne Herald, 146
Melbourne Hospital, 49, 51, 53
Melbourne University Institute of Applied Economic Research, 3, 150, 154
Melville, Ninian, 34
mental illness, 141, 144–5, 148, 160, 165, 167–8; *see also* insanity
Menzies, R.G., 134, 156
middle classes, 6, 8, 14, 62, 105; better-off, 8, 18, 44, 84, 86; welfare for, 156, 169
milk services, 107
miners, 33, 108
Ministering Childrens League, 88
missionaries, 20, 37, 45; city, 52, 85, 98
Montcalm, Paul, 168
moral corruption, 14, 18–19, 24, 26, 36–7, 41, 48, 52–3, 59, 91, 101
moral reform, 4, 12, 14, 19, 21, 51–4, 59–62, 84, 88, 95, 101, 103, 106
moral therapy, 58–9, 89
Moreton Bay, 25
Morris, Edward Ellis, 84–7, 90, 103
mothers, 29, 48, 54, 60, 79, 92, 94, 107, 134, 167
Mudie, James, 24

INDEX

Muller, Leopold, 1
Murray River, 37

national efficiency, 105–7
national fitness, 134
National Health and Medical Research Council, 137
National Welfare Fund, 136
natives institution, 20
nautical training ships, 60–1, 92; Vernon, 60–1, 70; Nelson, 60; Fitzjames, 60; Sobraon, 60
Neitenstein, Frederick William, 60–1
New England, 159
new right, 169–71
New South Wales, 14, 21, 23–4, 28, 30, 33–4, 47, 49, 55, 64–5, 67, 72, 78, 81, 92, 94, 98–9, 112, 118–19, 122–3, 126–7, 142, 154, 163, 165
New South Wales Council of Social Service, 142, 147
New Zealand, 99, 132
Newington Asylum, 96
Newtown, 138–41
Nicholls, Doug, 162
Nicholls, George, 12
Niemeyer, Otto, 124
Norfolk Island, 15, 25
Northern Territory, 118, 163
noxious trades, 42
Nurses Association, 167

old age, 3, 9, 12, 17, 22, 47, 51, 54–6, 85, 95–101, 124, 132, 135, 141, 146, 148, 152, 154, 164, 168–9; *see also* pensions
Old Age Pensions League, 98
orphanages and orphans asylums, 9, 19, 21, 45–6, 54, 59, 90–2, 116; *see also* reformatories
orphans, 19, 20, 22, 45, 59, 124, 141
outwork, 69–70, 80–1
overcrowding, 58, 116, 138
Oxley, John, 24

Page, Earle, 115, 123
Palmer, James, 49, 53
Panopticon, 14
Parents Alone Association, 159
parishes, 4, 8–10, 12, 21–2, 43
Parkes, Henry, 62
Parramatta, 16, 17, 21, 55
Parramatta, Benevolent Aylum, 55–6, 96
pastoralism, 6, 27–8, 39, 66, 132
Pastoralists Union, 77
paternalism, 11, 137, 162
Paton, R.T., 99
pauperism, 10–12, 30–1, 34, 45, 48–9, 56, 59, 62, 85–7, 118, 120
Paving and Improvement Acts, 8
Pearson, Charles, 62
pensions, 9, 11, 43, 90, 95–101, 118–19, 123–4, 137–8, 140, 146–7, 153–6, 168, 170; deserted mothers, 131; invalid, 95–101, 118–19, 132, 137–8, 149, 155; old age, 85, 95–101, 118–19, 132, 137–8, 149, 155, 171; orphans, 155; restrictions on, 119, 136, 154–6; war, 113; widows, 123, 131, 137–8, 147
Perkins, Charles, 162–3
Perth, 128–9, 159
pharmaceutical benefits, 131, 136
philanthropy, 37, 39, 41, 43–62, 71, 75–6, 81, 84–90, 92, 95–6, 98–9, 101, 103, 107, 121, 133, 135, 169; women and, 47–8, 86, 89, 142
Philip, Arthur, 16, 17, 18
police, 7–8, 13, 26, 41, 56, 59–60, 76–7, 89, 92, 106, 109, 111, 127, 129, 142; poor relief and, 47, 118
political economy, 4, 10
poor, the, 7–8, 11, 12, 18, 21, 37, 43, 45–6, 48–9, 52, 50–6, 75, 85–6, 96, 142, 149; able-bodied, 9–10, 12, 14, 43, 72; impotent, 9–10; antagonism to, 158; resistence of, 121
Poor Law, 4, 9, 10–12, 20–1, 43, 47; new, 43
poor relief, 9–10, 20–2, 31–2, 43–8, 51, 72–7, 85, 87, 120, 142, 170; criticism of, 75; unemployed, 72,

126–30; out-door, 44, 48–54, 86; asylum, 54–61
population, 15, 23, 39, 66, 88, 98, 105, 146
Port Arthur, 25–6
Port Macquarie, 25
Port Phillip, 32, 37
Port Phillip Gazette, 31–2
Portus, G.V., 131
post-war reconstruction, 135, 138
poverty, 1–4, 30, 34, 61–2, 77, 80, 84, 87, 94, 108, 114, 121, 132, 135, 139–41, 143, 148–62, 169–71; types of, 3, 152; child, 170; women's, 149–50; Inquiry into, 151–5; moralisation of, 12, 142; permanent, 3, 149; increase in, 152; rediscovery of, 146–50; see also pauperism, the poor, poor relief
poverty line, 2, 150–2, 154–5, 170–1
Premier's Plan, 126
prices, 29–30, 33, 82, 110, 115, 117, 124, 146
prison, 57, 87
profit, 6, 7, 27, 29, 33, 78
pro-natalism, 105
prostitution, 8, 15, 19, 37, 52, 54, 89, 101, 110, 139
psychiatry, 59, 104–5, 112, 144–5, 148, 165
psychology, 104–7, 142–6
Public Charities Royal Commissions, 49–50, 53, 58, 90–1, 94–5
Public Medical Officers Association, 167
Public Relief Department of South Australia, 127; see also Destitute Board
punishment, 12–14, 25; secondary, 25–6

Queen's Jubilee Fund, 87
Queensland, 34, 47, 56, 63–4, 66–7, 78, 81, 96, 98, 112, 116–19, 121–3, 126–8, 137, 153–4, 163

Queensland Unemployment Relief Act, 123

race, 78, 80, 107, 144, 164, 171; decline of the, 78, 80, 107
radicals, 28, 62–3, 77, 84
Randwick Destitute Childrens Asylum, 60, 91–2
ragged schools, 54, 60; Hobart, 60
railway passes, 76, 128
Ravenscroft Mona, 138–40
recession, 34, 55, 72, 108, 151; see also Depressions
recommendations, 44, 47, 51, 53, 56, 58; failure of, 53–4
Redfern survey, 134
reformatories, 54, 59–61, 90–2; see also orphanages
refuges, 47, 141, 157, 167; women's, 165
Regional Employment Development Scheme (REDS), 187
registry offices, 34, 77
relief work, 9–10, 31–2, 128–30, 157
rent, 30, 39–40, 50, 52, 64, 97, 110, 119, 122, 137, 139, 148, 154, 159; Fair, 122–3
Renwick, Arthur, 92
repatriation, 112–13; see also returned soldiers
returned soldiers, 111–14, 123, 137, 144
Richmond Report, 167–8
Riley, William, 25
riots, 7, 27, 34, 90–1, 111; food, 7
Ripon regulations, 28
Robertson, John, 62
Robinson, George Augustus, 20
Robson, Lloyd, 14
Rocks, The, 23, 36–7, 40
Rodd, Lewis, 121
Roe, Jill, 3, 164
rookeries, 8, 14, 18; see also slums
Rowntree, Seebohm, 3
rural areas, 57, 65, 76; poverty in,

INDEX

152–4; *see also* selection, agriculture, farmers
Royal Prince Alfred Hospital, 140
Rum Hospital, 17–18

safety-net, 131–2, 135, 151, 156
Salvation Army, 87, 95, 120, 126, 141, 157
sanitation, 40, 42, 110
schools, 70, 105–6; *see also* education
science, 85–7, 103, 142
Scott, David, 149
Scott, Rose, 89
self-help, 12, 50, 84–5, 87, 99, 138; *see also* local and neighbourhood support
selection, 63–6, 113–14; *see also* agriculture, farmers
selectivity, 99, 101, 118–19, 156, 170
separate spheres, 68, 83, 164
Serle, Geoffrey, 33
sewerage, 42; *see also* sanitation
sexual economics, 4
Shaw, A.G.L., 14
single mothers, 152, 154, 158, 164
skid row, 149, 157; *see also* homeless
slums, 3, 36–42, 59, 91, 108–10, 120–2, 141, 149; reform of, 109–110, 121; *see also* rookeries, tenements
Smith, Adam, 10
Smith Ramsey, 103
Smith, W. Beattie-, 104
Smith Family, 119, 141, 161
social justice, 78, 135, 171
social laboratory, 5, 78, 101, 123, 131
social mobility, 67–8
social policy, 5, 123–4, 140
social security, 2, 123–4, 131–8, 140–1, 149–51, 154–51, 154–5, 158–9, 164, 170
Social Security Action Group, 160
social services, 142–4, 146, 155, 168–71

social work, 142–3, 145, 160, 167; training for, 143
socialism, 84, 87
Society for Bettering the Condition of the Poor, 9
Society for the Relief of Destitute Children, 60
sociology, 86–7, 138, 143
soldier settlement, 113–14; *see also* returned soldiers
soup kitchens, 46, 87, 141
South Australia, 28, 31, 33–4, 43, 47, 58, 64, 70, 75, 78, 80–2, 87, 98, 103, 106, 112, 118, 126, 163, 167
Speenhamland, 10
Spence, Catherine Helen, 87, 91
Springthorpe, J.W., 121
squatters, 27–9, 63
St Giles, 1, 8, 23, 37
St Kilda Industrial School, 90
St Vincent de Paul Society, 87, 95, 120, 126, 141–2, 157
St Vincents Boys Home, 95
standard of living, 2, 111, 135, 149–50, 152, 156, 171
state, the, 85, 89–90, 92, 94, 135, 162; intervention of, 78, 135, 165, 168
State Childrens Relief Board, 92–4, 106
starvation, 3, 7, 10, 45, 52, 117, 147
stealing 8, 15, 17, 37, 39, 60
Stephen, Alfred, 103
Stephens, A.G., 105
Stewart, Frederick, 132–3
Stoller, Alan, 144
Strangers Friend Society, 45, 50–1
strikes, 32, 74, 111, 133, 144; *see also* trade unionism
Stubbs, John, 149–50, 154
subscriptions, 21, 44–6, 48, 53, 126
sundowners, 37
superannuation, 158, 170–1
surgery, 104, 165; *see also* medicine
Sutherland, Selina, 88
sweating, 71, 81

Sydney Benevolent Asylum, 54–5, 58
Sydney Gazette, 20
Sydney Government Asylums, 57
Sydney Home Mission Society, 121
Sydney Morning Herald, 30, 36, 43
Sydney Quarterly magazine, 62

tariffs, 77–8
Tasmania, 23–4, 32–4, 47, 51, 54–5 59, 106, 153, 158, 160; *see also* Van Diemen's Land
Tasmanian Pauper Depot, 57
taxes, 129, 136, 155, 170–1
teachers, 59, 61, 107; *see also* schools
temperance, 88–9; *see also* drink
Tench, Watkin, 18
tenements, 8, 109, 149; *see also* slums
terra nullius, 15
Theodore, E.G., 123, 126
Threkeld, L.E., 20
thrift, 12, 28
toxins, 103–4
trade, 22, 24, 30, 32, 65–7, 72, 146
trade unionism, 62, 71, 74, 81, 111, 126; *see also* labour movement
transportation, 14, 18, 24–5, 34, 62
Trollope, Anthony, 66
tropics, 116; diseases in, 116
truck system, 29, 78
Tuke, Samuel, 58
Twopeny, Richard, 1

Ullathorne, W.B., 103
underemployment, 30, 36, 108, 126
unemployed, the, 123–32, 146–9, 154, 156–8, 162; protests by, 31–2, 34, 73, 75, 84, 129; resentment towards, 31, 73, 75, 128–9, 157–8
Unemployed Workers Movement, 129
unemployment, 1, 3, 10–11, 30–1, 34, 36–7, 39–40, 62, 66, 72–7, 84, 95, 109–10, 115–16, 123–32, 137, 140, 143, 146–9, 151, 154, 156–8, 162; benefits for, 131, 155–9, 168–9; hidden, 157; relief for, 72–3, 128–30, 157; rates of, 126, 156–7; youth, 156–7
universities, 90, 131, 134, 138, 142, 149
urbanisation, 39, 66, 115
universalism, 99, 101, 133, 137, 156, 170
utilitarians, 4, 13–14, 54

Victoria, 28, 33, 46–7, 58, 63, 65, 67, 70, 72, 81, 87, 98, 106, 118, 126, 146
villages, 7, 9, 11
villains, 19, 21
violence, 8, 146, 164; sexual, 26; family, 103, 114, 146, 160, 165, 170
visitors, 51, 86, 142
volunteers, 49–52, 142, 159–60; *see also* charity, non-government organisations

wages, 10, 15, 25, 29–34, 36, 63, 66–8, 70–1, 74, 77–8, 81, 85, 108, 124, 126, 129, 146, 154, 156, 162; basic, 62, 82–3, 126, 134, 150–1; children's, 70–1; women's, 69–71, 83, 164; relief, 76
Wages Boards, 82; *see also* arbitration, living wage
waifs, 39, 91
Wakefield, Edward Gibbon, 28
war, 108, 110, 116, 123, 132–7, 144; First World, 109, 133, 144; Second World, 131
War Service Homes, 113, 141
warders, 57, 96
Watson, J.C., 76
wealth, 6, 36, 45–6, 108, 152, 158
welfare benefits, 154–5, 158–60, 169–71
welfare expenditure, 129, 132, 137, 141, 154, 156, 168–71
welfare fraud, 157–8, 170; *see also* dole cheats
welfare officers, 159–60, 163

welfare rights groups, 151, 158–9, 60, 169, 171; protests by, 160
welfare state, 4–5, 78, 101, 124, 131–7, 140, 149, 168–71; stigma of, 136, 155, 170; retreat from, 168–71
Wentworth, W.C., 1
Western Australia, 24, 33–4, 47, 74, 78, 88, 92, 112, 115, 118, 127, 163, 165
whaling and sealing, 34
White Australia policy, 78
Whitechapel, 1, 37
Whitlam Gough, 151; government of, 154–7
widowed mothers, 9, 50, 92, 138–9, 147, 149, 152, 154, 164
widows, 9, 50–2, 96, 123–4, 135, 137–8, 147–8; war, 113
Wilson, Roland, 135
Windeyer, William Charles, 90–1
Windsor, 21
Wise, B.R., 62, 77
Wollongong, 129
women, 4, 26–7, 29, 31, 47, 54, 68–9, 77, 81, 83, 89, 111, 130, 133, 139, 145–6, 154, 156, 164–5; philanthropy and, 47–8; fallen, 47, 54, 89

Womens Christian Temperance Union, 89
Women's Co-operative Factory and Women's Mending Bureau, 81
wool, 27, 30, 32, 66, 146
work, 4, 6, 24, 27, 29–30, 36, 39, 55, 61, 66–70, 77–9, 85, 87, 111; bush, 36, 57, 108; casual and seasonal, 6, 36, 68, 108, 147; children's, 70–1; unskilled, 66–7, 138; skilled, 66–7; task, 25; women's, 68–9, 89, 154, 164; relief, 75–7; *see also* labourers
work test, 10, 12, 32, 62, 158
worker's compensation, 78–9
worker's co-operatives, 62
Workers Dwelling Act, 121
workhouse, 9, 12, 30, 57
working class, 11, 15, 23, 39, 49, 51, 62–3, 87, 116, 133–4, 138, 159; *see also* work, labourers
Working Women's Trade Union, 81
Workingman's paradise, 1, 2, 23, 36, 38, 162

yeoman, 28, 63–5, 113–14
Young, Arthur, 11

Zox, Ephraim, 57

THE AUSTRALIAN EXPERIENCE

ALSO IN THE SERIES
Geoffrey Sherington   *Australia's Immigrants*
Geoffrey Bolton   *Spoils and Spoilers*
Richard White   *Inventing Australia*
Richard Broome   *Aboriginal Australians*
Henry Reynolds   *Dispossession*